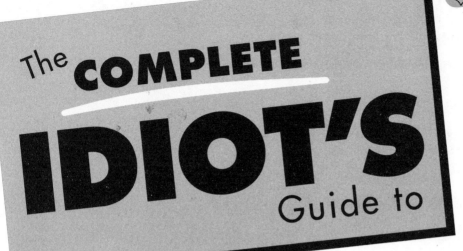

The **COMPLETE** **IDIOT'S** Guide to

Wills and Estates for Canadians ❦

- ♦ **Quick and easy strategies** for preparing a will
- ♦ **Idiot-proof steps** for creating an estate plan
- ♦ **Valuable tips** on legal and tax matters

**Steve Maple &
Edward Olkovich**

An Alpha Books/Prentice Hall Canada
Copublication

Prentice Hall Canada Inc.,
Scarborough, Ontario

Canadian Cataloguing in Publication Data

Maple, Steve

The complete idiot's guide to wills and estate for Canadians

ISBN 0–13–080124–0

1. Wills - Canada. 2. Estate planning — Canada. I. Olkovich, Edward, 1951- . II. Title.

KE808.M36 1998   346.7105'4   C97-932776-8
KF755.M36 1998

 ©1998 Prentice-Hall Canada Inc., Scarborough, Ontario

Prentice-Hall, Inc., Upper Saddle River, New Jersey
Prentice-Hall International (UK) Limited, London
Prentice-Hall of Australia, Pty. Limited, New Delhi
Prentice-Hall of Japan, Inc., Tokyo
Simon & Schuster Southeast Asia Private Limited, Singapore
Editora Prentice-Hall do Brasil, Ltda., Rio de Janeiro

ISBN 0–13–080124–0

Managing Editor: Robert Harris
Production Editor: Andrew Winton
Copy Editor: Kelli Howey
Editorial Assistant: Joan Whitman
Production Coordinator: Julie Preston
Cover Design: Kyle Gell
Page Layout: Gail Ferreira Ng-A-Kien

1 2 3 4 5   RRD   02 01 00 99 98

Printed and bound in the United States of America.

Visit the Prentice Hall Canada Web site! Send us your comments, browse our catalogues, and more. www.phcanada.com.

To Krystyna, my wife, and sons, Nick and Adam,
with all my love.

Contents at a Glance

Contents

Contents

Introduction

Welcome to the world of estate planning.

You'll notice I didn't say the "wonderful" world or the "fascinating" world. I don't want you rolling your eyes and muttering "Come on." But I *do* want you to continue reading this book.

Okay, making your way through a guide about putting together an estate plan will probably not be as lighthearted as reading about how to select wines or start a rock garden. Still, I honestly believe you will find this book not only informative but also engrossing.

Why? Because it's very relevant to *you* and your life, and perhaps there are some important parts of estate planning that you haven't given much thought to before. Learning something new, especially when it's about ourselves, is *always* interesting.

I think you'll soon be absorbed in exploring just how you want to lay out an estate plan, which includes a basic will and a few other documents. You'll set planning goals for yourself, now and at different stages of your life ahead. You'll learn about professionals who can help you along the way. You'll read stories about others and their experiences, too—tales that will be informative, puzzling, amusing and sometimes even touching. You'll learn from the mistakes some of those folks made—and from reading about the right steps others took at particular times in their lives.

So this book is about people as well as legal documents and tax talk. It's about how we *use* those papers, those directives and even those taxes, to put ourselves in control of our financial destiny.

If you have an estate plan—and you will when you finish this book, or will at least have started the ball rolling—then obviously you have an estate. Trust me. No matter how small you may think your assets are, you do have an estate. You'll want to protect it, watch it grow, and even see it spent in exactly the ways you choose.

Having an estate plan will make you feel like a million dollars—no matter that your net worth may be missing a few of those zeros.

How This Book Is Organized

The chapters that follow are laid out to guide you through the estate planning process as it is likely to occur in your life, no matter what your age right now. Let me introduce you to the book's five parts.

Part 1 Assets, Assets, Assets introduces you to what an estate is and will acquaint you with the planning process. It will help you sort out your own assets, so that you know what you own and, in particular, *how* you own it.

Part 2 About Wills, Trusts... and Probate will take you into the heart of the book: preparing a will, and perhaps a trust if that can be useful to you. There are some cautions, too, about what happens when you *don't* have a will.

Part 3 All in the Family—and Just a Little Beyond talks about your nearest and dearest and how you will probably want to provide for them in some specific estate-planning situations. I'll tell you how to head off potential arguments and misunderstandings, too.

Part 4 Taxes You Must Pay, and Those Maybe You Don't will introduce you to the sometimes complex world of income taxes and probate fees. I'll help you with terrific strategies for paying as little as possible on your estate, your income and when making gifts.

Part 5 Retirement, Elder Issues and the Broad Planning Picture eases you into planning for your retirement, no matter when that is coming up in your life. Along with other information, I'll tell you what you can expect from the government then—and what you'll have to put together on your own now.

Extras

To help you even further, and just for fun, you'll find small boxes with special items of interest in every chapter. You'll immediately see a clue to the subject matter of each box by the little cartoon at the top. Here's what you'll find:

Briefs

Intriguing stories about people in specific estate-planning situations.

Quote...Unquote

The words of the famous, from early history to the present day, speaking with humour or wisdom (and sometimes even both).

Tip

How to find more information or learn a different way of doing things.

Watch Out

Steps to avoid, products to skip, when to be careful, and when to seek help.

Words, Words, Words

Definitions of legal terms and other words that may be unfamiliar to you.

Acknowledgments

Catherine Bennett, Reg Bradburn, Darlene Jukes and J. Howard Lane helped with portions of the manuscript. I am indebted to them for their time and comments.

PART 1
Assets, Assets, Assets

We're going to talk first about your estate and what it comprises. Makes you feel rather prosperous, doesn't it, to hear the words "your" and "estate" in the same context? You should feel that way. Your assets—all of your possessions acquired through the years—are valuable to you now for your own satisfaction and enjoyment and will matter one day to your heirs.

What exactly are those assets? I'll help you sort them out. You might find you have more than you think you do—always a pleasant discovery.

Chapter 1

You've Got to Have a Plan, Whether Simple or Deluxe

In This Chapter

➤ "Later," "Someday," "When I hit 40," etc.

➤ What an estate comprises

➤ The perils of having no plan

➤ Setting goals

➤ Your estate planning team

I don't believe in dying. It's been done. I'm working on a new exit. Besides, I can't die now. I'm booked. — George Burns, 1987

As you probably know, the much-loved comedian finally "exited" in 1996, at the age of 100. Burns also played God in two hit motion pictures. Neither of those accomplishments, of course, prevented him from eventually having to go on to meet his Maker (did He critique the actor who played Him?)—and having to leave behind a well-planned estate for his heirs. Did George Burns have a proper estate plan? I was not one of his lawyers, but I'd bet the farm he left an estate in A-1 condition, spelling out his wishes clearly and taking advantage of every legitimate tax break.

Sure, George Burns had a larger estate—a *lot* larger—than you or I are likely to leave, and so he should have worked hard on its intricacies. However, whether we are young or old, employed or not working, wealthy or just getting by, single, married, or in a long-term relationship with a "significant other," we need to plan for when we are not here or, because of illness, are unable to speak for ourselves. Why on earth would anyone want someone else—perhaps, *Oh, God!*, the *state*—to make important, and very personal, decisions for him or her and the family left behind?

What IS an Estate?

"All right," you say, "I understand your point. But before you go any further would you tell me, please, what exactly *is* an estate? And what's an estate *plan*? Of course I know what a will is, but what specifically goes into that document?"

Good questions. The area of wills and estates is likely to seem hazy if you have not given that subject area much thought. You certainly need to understand the terminology used in this book, so let's start with a few explanations right now.

Your Assets

The dictionary defines *estate* as the assets and liabilities left by a person at death. Well, that's true, but I'd extend that definition a little. If you are able to leave an estate at death, its ingredients are carried along by you through much of your life, too.

Those ingredients are assets—everything you own by yourself or jointly with someone else. If you're 18 years old you probably don't own very much. But as you grow older you begin to acquire possessions—a home, a car, a pension plan, perhaps some stocks and the like. All of that is valuable, first, because all of it becomes your assets (which are good for anyone to have) and second, because you can will those assets (according to various ownership styles that we'll get into in the next couple of chapters) to anyone you choose.

As you get older, your responsibilities increase, along with your assets. You will want to see that your spouse and children, especially young children, are taken care of if you die. You will want your debts to be paid, too. You might have elderly parents or an ailing sibling you're looking out for. Your wishes for after your death can be carried out with a proper estate plan. Which brings me to your next question.

Your Estate Plan

What is an estate plan? Well, that's an arrangement for the conservation and transfer of your wealth after your death. It's seeing that you keep the most money and other property for your heirs at the least cost to you during your lifetime, and to them when they inherit.

The minimum any estate plan should contain is a will. I'll touch on the contents of that document soon.

A good estate plan could include a trust, if that is an additional choice for you. A trust is a written agreement that allows you to hold property and manage it for your beneficiaries in accordance with whatever instructions are in that trust agreement. It's a little like a will, but with a difference. We'll get to a fuller explanation of a trust later in the book, too.

Other documents you might want to add to an estate plan as you get older are a *power of attorney for property*, which legally gives someone you designate the right to make decisions for you even if you are incapacitated and cannot act on your own. You might eventually want a *power of attorney for health*, which gives the person of your choice the right to make decisions for you about your health care if you cannot make them yourself.

There are some other papers you may elect for your estate plan that I'll mention later in the book, but the most important component of an estate plan—the cornerstone—is the will.

> **Watch Out!**
>
> If you move to another province during your lifetime, you will have to review your estate documents. Most provinces have their own requirements for those papers, and you might well need to have some of them drawn up again.

Your Will

Finally, to answer your last question, a *will* is a legal document setting forth your wishes for the disposition of your estate after your death. Yes, it's that "I, John A. Macdonald, of Ottawa, Canada, being of sound

Tip

An estate plan is not carved in stone. Unfortunately, you can't complete your work and then forget what you've accomplished. You should review your papers every couple of years, certainly when there are major changes in your life such as a marriage or divorce, the birth of a child, or a lottery win.

mind..." document you've heard and read about over the years. It can be as long or as short as you like. You can briefly leave every last thing you own to your spouse or someone else, and that's that. Or—and there is more than one eccentric person who has done this—bequeath every piece of property, including individual jewellery items and various collections, to different people. And you can revise that will periodically, as relatives and friends rise and fall in your favour.

As you can now see, you may leave anything and everything that is yours in your will, including your pets and requests for their future care.

A will might also include guardianship wishes for minor children. Keep in mind what you are doing is essentially *nominating* the person or persons you choose. The appropriate court will ultimately decide who the guardian will be.

What makes your will legal? Signing it in the presence of two witnesses who are not (and whose spouses are not) beneficiaries in the will makes it valid. But what makes it *effective* is its being filed in the appropriate estate court after your death, and being recognized by the court as your valid will, revoking all previous wills and trusts.

Naturally, we'll talk more about wills later in the book. A lot more.

That's it. Do you feel a little more comfortable now about the terminology I'll be using? Then let's move further into these and other topics in more detail.

Why Many of Us Don't Plan

Here's a statement that may ring a bell with you: "I think I'll see my lawyer next week, or certainly sometime this month, about drawing up a will. I'll *definitely* do it before the end of the summer (fall, winter, spring)."

Many of us who do not put off tasks in other important areas of our lives drag our feet when it comes to estate planning. Why is that?

Kim, a 26-year-old marketing assistant, says "What do *I* have to make a will for? I share a rented apartment, I don't have a car, and I have $2,000 in the bank. Where's *my* estate?"

Quote...Unquote

He is a fool that makes his doctor his heir.

—*Benjamin Franklin*

Ah, but who would she like to inherit that $2,000? Instead of having the money turned over to her parents, which would probably happen if she dies *intestate* (or without a will, versus *testate*, which is having a valid will), she might prefer that it go to her younger brother. Kim could also have funds invested in a retirement fund. Has she already designated a beneficiary for them?

And what about that brooch of her great Aunt Mary's, the one she clips onto her lucky suit when she's preparing to make a major presentation at the office? If you asked her right now, she would say she'd like her godchild, her best friend's daughter, to have that favourite piece of jewellery.

But no one is going to know, or carry out, Kim's wishes if those wishes are not set down in black and white in a will.

Then there is Frank, a 50-year-old telecommunications employee who shrugs off making a will, saying he wants his wife, Amy, to inherit everything of his and theirs. He says that's what will happen, even without such a document. It makes Frank uneasy to talk about a will, let alone take the first steps to having one drawn for him. Why? Amy says she thinks it's because Frank's father died at the age of 47. Any mention of death or age or wills has spooked Frank since he himself passed that age.

Frank might not know that if he dies intestate the state will probably charge his wife a fee of a few hundred dollars, money that would not be levied against his estate if he had an estate plan and a valid will. Does Frank want her to pay that extra money? It's not likely. Besides a fee, property may go to their children, or Frank's parents, not just to Amy. With some advance planning, Frank could see to it that his estate is as large as it can be, with the least amount of taxes paid, through some clever investment and tax strategies.

Finally, there is Hélène. She is 61 years old, manages a boutique and, aside from a few minor ailments, is in good health. Hélène and her

friends talk a good deal about a living will and a health care power of attorney. Hélène has been quite vocal about not wanting to be kept alive "by extraordinary means" if she should fall seriously ill, a directive that is a major component of a living will. But she has not taken care of that aspect of estate planning. She keeps putting off the paperwork. If some day it does come to those extraordinary measures, Hélène might not be able to communicate her wishes about medical treatment.

Kim, Frank and Hélène are drifting along with what could be called a head-in-the-sand approach, in this instance, to estate planning. They know what they should be doing, they read articles about wills and other components of a long-range plan but, for their own reasons, they refuse to take action.

The Importance of Looking Ahead

If you see yourself in any of the above scenarios you are not alone. As many as 50 to 70 percent of the population die without having made a will (and we won't even get into the number of people who do not have other important estate documents). For some, death is the only tragedy, but for others, the failure to plan an estate has catastrophic consequences for loved ones.

The law makes a will for you if you do not have one, and the heirs it decides upon might not be the ones you would have chosen.

Our trio above could have rather simple estates, at least monetarily, but many other people have more complicated situations. There might

be quite sizable sums of money involved. Or there could be second marriages where there are children from that union, as well as from a previous marriage, to be considered. Or guardianship issues for minor children must be decided. Or perhaps there is a business that is part of an estate, and one with a partner or two at that.

Lack of planning by the deceased can keep the disposition of an estate on hold, sometimes for years. Then it could still not be disbursed the way that individual would have liked.

And let's not forget how poor planning—or no planning at all—can result in heirs being hit with higher taxes, and court and legal costs for processing the will, that they would otherwise not need to pay.

The advice columns in newspapers and magazines are full of letters from frustrated readers whose parents didn't make a will or take the time to plan properly. As a result, the heirs were left with a financial mess, not to mention the stress of coping with sometimes incomprehensible paperwork and demands at a time of mourning and change in their lives.

Putting It All Together Can Be Enjoyable—Really

I can hear you saying "Good grief, what do you mean enjoyable? We're talking about my *death*." No, we aren't. How and when you leave this vale is, of course, beyond the control of either of us. However, seeing the pieces of your estate plan fall into place, knowing how well organized you are now and that your wishes will be carried out later, will bring you peace of mind and, yes, some pleasurable sense of accomplishment.

It might also give you the additional pleasure of knowing you're one up on many folks by being so farsighted.

(And, hey, come on, you did buy this book, so deep down, perhaps *way* down, you know you should be tackling at least some of these issues and are prepared to do so now, no matter how jolly or dreary the idea seems. Am I right?)

As I said earlier in this chapter, planning ahead also means preparing for tomorrow, not just l0, 20, 30, or more years down the road. Judicious care of your current savings, and plans for anticipated income, can help your estate grow and bring you the comfort of knowing your money is working for you, working to make you even more comfortable in retirement. We're talking about a *life* plan here, with the opportunity to make wise choices and take advantage of perhaps unique opportunities from now on. Your aim should also be to build your assets and pay down your debts now so that you can retire to a pleasant, worry-free life later.

Look how many upbeat subjects we will touch on in this book that have to do with financial and lifestyle situations that could affect you in the years from now until ... well, may you, too, live to be l00!

➤ An inheritance

➤ A salary increase, and/or a special bonus

➤ A marriage or remarriage

➤ A new job, perhaps your own business

➤ Real estate purchases

➤ Your pension

So you see, an estate plan doesn't talk only about wills and other mechanisms that swing into effect when you are no longer here.

What Should Your Goals Be?

Everyone will have his or her own priorities, of course, based on age range and individual family and financial responsibilities and interests. As you read on, you will learn more about the various topics that fall under estate planning, and what you should strive for. However, generally speaking, after reading this book and implementing its suggestions, you will have achieved these specific goals:

➤ You will have a will

➤ You will know how a trust works

➤ You will have important auxiliary documents, such as powers of attorney

➤ You will know how to start saving money *now*

➤ You will be able to protect the assets you now have

➤ You can reduce your taxes

➤ You will be able to plan for retirement, securing the lifestyle you want in those years ahead

Watch Out

Unmarried same sex, or opposite sex, couples in long-standing relationships especially need careful estate planning. That should include pre-arranged funeral preferences: a dispute can arise if family steps in to carry out plans the deceased would not have wanted. Your will specifies who is responsible for your funeral.

You don't have to do *everything* covered in this book. No doubt some suggestions will not even apply to you, at least not at this point in your life. You may not be divorced, for example, or even married, so advice in those areas will not be relevant. You may not have your own business. Your parents might be in their early 50s, quite hale and hearty, with no need for you to concern yourself as a caregiver quite yet.

Still, whether you are 25 or 65, the information you need today to set up a solid estate plan can be found within these pages.

Starting Now

"What are your investments?" the broker asked.

I answered, "My sons, Nicholas and Adam."

That wasn't the reply the broker was looking for, of course, but he knew what I meant. You do, too. Still, while I am taking care of my children as they grow up, I must also, as mentioned above, tend to what is usually meant by the word "investments"—my home, my savings, a plan for retirement, and the like.

Are *you* as prepared as you think you are? Maybe yes, maybe no. To help you assess your particular situation right now, I've created a planning quiz. After you've answered the questions, mark or fold over the corner of the page so that you can come back and refer to it again. By the time you finish reading this book, you'll know what you need to do to be able to answer yes to every question on that list (see page 12).

Putting Together Your Estate Planning Team

Who can help define your needs, and then set you on the path toward setting up a valuable plan?

First, of course, *I* can. I won't hog the spotlight, though. There are other professionals you may want to consult, either on a one-time or a fairly steady basis.

Your team will be made up of men and women with expertise in different

> **Tip**
>
> Try to attend a few free estate-planning seminars in your community. They are usually held in the evening and sponsored by brokerage offices and banks. You can learn about saving taxes and other estate matters as they apply specifically to your province, and you can probably ask questions of the speaker. Check your daily newspaper for news briefs or advertisements about upcoming seminars.

ESTATE PLANNING CHECKLIST

Yes No

❑ ❑ 1. Do you and your spouse have current, signed wills?

❑ ❑ 2. Have you discussed your estate plans with your family?

❑ ❑ 3. Have you consulted an estate-planning professional?

❑ ❑ 4. Have you reviewed the ownership of your assets to determine which are solely-owned and which are co-owned?

❑ ❑ 5. Have you reviewed your life insurance needs?

❑ ❑ 6. Do you have a retirement plan?

❑ ❑ 7. Will your estate have enough cash to pay the bills, and enough left over to provide adequately for your family?

❑ ❑ 8. Do you know approximately how much you will receive in Canada Pension benefits upon retirement?

❑ ❑ 9. Have you designated anyone to handle your affairs if you are no longer capable of doing so?

❑ ❑ 10. Have you made arrangements for your long-term care, or that of your elderly dependants?

❑ ❑ 11. Have you taken any steps to reduce income taxes now, and probate fees on your estate?

❑ ❑ 12. If you own a business, have you consulted a professional to plan for its future?

If you have checked a number of "No" answers, then this book is definitely for you.

aspects of estate planning. Their knowledge and guidance can be invaluable. However, do not forget for one moment that *you* are in charge. No one on your team should tell you what to do. He or she can offer options and discuss consequences, but only you can determine what your best estate plan is. So you will have to do some homework here, to be as competent as possible when taking charge.

You may not need every member of this team, or at least not all of them at the same time in your life. The more complex your estate, however, the more likely you will be to call on a range of professional services.

Here's a list of some of the people you should consider.

➤ **Life Insurance Underwriter**
Most of us are underinsured. Life insurance should be an integral part of most estate plans. Young families need term insurance to provide support for the family if a parent dies. You may need life insurance to make an estate more liquid—to pay the taxes without being forced to sell assets.

Quote...Unquote

I don't mind dying, I just don't want to be there when it happens.

—*Woody Allen*

The life insurance underwriter can determine your needs and the amount and type of insurance that best meets those needs.

➤ **Trust Officer** You may need a retirement trust to help manage your assets. Your children could require a trust to avoid wasting their inherited assets because of their immaturity.

The trust officer at your trust company or other financial institution can discuss his or her services and fees. It is time well spent.

➤ **Accountant** No one is likely to be more familiar with your financial situation than your accountant. Few details in life are more intimate than one's tax returns. If you have a business, this is the individual who knows the balance sheet. Use your accountant to help gather the information necessary to focus on your financial picture, so that you can prepare a good estate plan.

➤ **Financial Planner** Your money can *always* be more productive. The financial planner's role is to advise you about appropriate investments that will meet your estate-planning goals.

"A financial planner," you say. "What exactly is that?" The profession of financial planner is rather new to the average consumer, and it is an unregulated pursuit. Do you want to be a planner? Hang out a shingle and *voilà!* you're in business.

For some protection when shopping for this assistance, try to engage a financial planner who belongs to a national professional group. Those groups can define their specific membership (they differ in requirements for joining and certification offered) and can send you free printed material about choosing a planner and a list of financial planners in your area who are members of their association.

➤ **Lawyer** The lawyer drafts your will and prepares a trust, which you may also require. He or she also prepares all estate documents. If you fill out your own documents from a form book or computer program, you do so at your own risk.

Where to Find Team Members

"Psst, know a good doctor?"

Most of us pick physicians, dentists—and estate-planning professionals—rather haphazardly. Consulting the telephone directory or asking your brother-in-law or next-door-neighbour, both who seem to know everything, is not the best way to proceed here.

A much better strategy is to talk with a number of friends and relatives whose opinions you value. Find out whom they have worked with and whether they would engage the same professionals again. Interview prospective team members. Discuss fees. Do they seem more interested in your money than your estate-planning goals? Do they appear to be in a hurry, too busy to talk with you, or do they take the time to answer your questions thoughtfully and completely?

Tip

Call your provincial Insurance Commission, or Consumer Relations or Consumer Affairs Office, to see if they offer free printed material on estate planning. Many government agencies have a number of brochures they can send you about various planning topics. And sometimes these include things to watch out for, like scams to avoid.

Check with the licensing or professional association for those you are considering engaging. That might be a provincial office regulating that profession, located in the provincial capital, or the group's national association, comprising members throughout the country. Regional chapters of these groups are usually located in provincial capitals or large cities. Ask whether there have been any complaints lodged against that individual or firm.

You are doing the hiring here, and it's certainly a buyer's market. Take the time to assemble the best team at an affordable price.

Okay. You have some idea what you will accomplish by reading this book and then taking steps to implement good suggestions. You know that planning is an ongoing process, to be revisited time and time again as situations change in your life. You have your planning team in place.

Let's proceed to succeed!

The Least You Need to Know

➤ Everyone needs a will, at the very least, in estate planning.

➤ If you do not have a will, the state will decide your heirs for you.

➤ Planning needs differ; determine your own personal goals.

➤ There are professionals who can form your planning team, helping you achieve those goals.

Chapter 2

What You've Got and How You've Got It

In This Chapter

➤ A close-up look at your assets
➤ Common ownership styles
➤ How property is classified
➤ Where to keep all your "papers"

Just what *do* you own? You boast of having the patent for a gizmo that's going to revolutionize life as we know it? Good for you. That's certainly a rare asset. You have a teeny island in the Caribbean? Again, congratulations, especially in January and February. That, too, is not on everyone's list of "haves." Most of us count the standard possessions, such as a home, a car, some savings, perhaps some art work and jewellery, maybe family heirlooms. Does that sound more like you?

Before we go on to consider your assets as part of your estate plan, you must know what those assets are. It's important to know, too, *how* you own them. Different ownership styles can be easier or more difficult to leave as part of an estate, as you will see throughout this book.

Taking Inventory

You might have—you *should* have—a household inventory you put together in case of a fire or a robbery at your residence. That listing, which you could do as a video recording rather than a written list, describes items of value and lists their serial numbers or other identifying marks. Your written list or videotape should be kept in a fireproof box at home, or perhaps with a relative or friend, or at your office. It will be helpful to the police and your insurance company in the unfortunate event your home is robbed or catches fire. In the former instance, serial numbers, and perhaps even better, photographs of special possessions along with a written inventory or that video can help the police reclaim your property.

It's reassuring to know you have such an inventory and, after you have put it together, perhaps surprising and nice to know, too, that you have so much. All those acquisitions over the years do add up, don't they?

In estate planning, a listing of your assets is also important. But here we are looking at a far broader picture than just household furnishings. Here we examine items like your home, automobile, retirement plan, and the like. It's just as important to have all of that itemized. Even more so, actually, since those belongings often have a higher monetary value.

What will be included in *your* estate? Here is a form that will help you determine your assets. Take a few minutes now to fill it in, then keep it handy for easy reference as you read this book. (*Note:* Jot down everything. We'll be talking about insurance, pensions, and owning your own business in the next few chapters, and about your other assets later in this one.)

Tip

Since household possessions are a part of your total assets picture, by all means put together an inventory like the one described here if you haven't already done so. You can purchase inventory forms at a stationery or office supply store. Also, many police departments around the country lend residents etching tools for engraving names or numbers on bicycles and other possessions for identification.

ESTATE PLANNING INFORMATION SHEET

Name _____ Birthdate _____ SIN _____

Name of Spouse _____ Birthdate _____ SIN _____

Residence Address _____

Age _____ Marital status _____ Number of children _____

Names of Children _____

ASSETS

Real Estate (residence and other land)

Description	Present value	Purchase price	Mortgage	How owned
_____	_____	_____	_____	_____
_____	_____	_____	_____	_____
_____	_____	_____	_____	_____

Business Interests (sole proprietor, partnership, corporation)

Form of business	Value of interest	Who owns
_____	_____	_____
_____	_____	_____

Accounts (bank, brokerage, certificates of deposit)

Type of account	Account name	Value	Who owns
_____	_____	_____	_____
_____	_____	_____	_____
_____	_____	_____	_____

Stocks and Bonds

Stocks/bond company	Market value	Cost	Who owns
_____	_____	_____	_____
_____	_____	_____	_____

Motor Vehicles

Make	Model	Year	Value	Who owns
_____	_____	_____	_____	_____
_____	_____	_____	_____	_____

Miscellaneous Personal Property (household goods, sporting equipment, jewellery, art, etc.)

Type of property	Value	Who owns
_____	_____	_____
_____	_____	_____

Life Insurance

Insurance company	Face value	Cash value	Insured	Owner	Beneficiary
_____	_____	_____	_____	_____	_____
_____	_____	_____	_____	_____	_____
_____	_____	_____	_____	_____	_____

Retirement Benefits (RRSPs, pension/profit sharing)

Type of Plan	Owner	Beneficiary	Value to date
_____	_____	_____	_____
_____	_____	_____	_____
_____	_____	_____	_____

Other Assets (including possible inheritances)

Type of Asset	Owner	Value
_____	_____	_____
_____	_____	_____
_____	_____	_____

Total Assets $ _____

LIABILITIES

Type of liability	Amount	Who owes
_____	_____	_____
_____	_____	_____
_____	_____	_____

Total Liabilities $ _____

Total Assets minus Total Liabilities equals Net Worth: $ _____

One Man's Story—Something Like Yours?

Okay, you have finished your Information Sheet. Let's suppose that one John Fisher also filled out the form, and, in an abbreviated style, it looked something like this:

Property	Value	Ownership
Residence	$100,000	With wife, Ellen
Household goods	$20,000	With wife
Savings/chequing account	$10,000	With wife
Automobile	$15,000	With wife
Corporate stock	$20,000	Solely
Family farm (inherited)	$125,000	With brother, George

I chose John because his estate shows the three most common ownership styles:

> ➤ **Solely** John's corporate stock is in his name only. It's his to do with as he will. He can sell it or give it away. At his death it becomes part of his estate and passes to the beneficiary of his will, or to his heirs if he has no will.

Let's say at some point after filling out this form John decides to invest in Canada Savings Bonds. If his name alone is on the bonds, they become part of his estate, too. But he may register a beneficiary designation on the bonds. For example, they might read "pay on death to Jenny Fisher" (John's 22-year-old daughter). Jenny would then inherit the bonds.

Words, Words, Words

Tenants, as used in the ownership styles discussed in this chapter, means owning and not renting. Of course, "tenant" more commonly refers to an individual or company that is leasing real property.

> ➤ **As "joint tenants with right of survivorship"** If John dies tomorrow, his wife will own everything outright that was in both their names because they have those items as "joint owners with right of survivorship." That's an ownership style that is… well, pretty much just what it says. The property, usually a home, is in both their names. When one party dies, the other automatically takes

over that co-owner's share, without the need for any mention of it in a will.

You do not have to be married to be a joint tenant. However, that is the most common ownership style among married couples. The next chapter talks more about joint ownership, in the context of spousal property. However, there is an important point to keep in mind here: Right of survivorship takes precedence over property bequeathed in a will. In other words, John can't leave his sister anything that is already jointly owned by him and Ellen—or him and anyone else, for that matter.

➤ **As "tenants in common"** This is how the farm, which had belonged to John and George's parents, was deeded to the brothers. That means they equally co-own the property, but each can leave his share to anyone he chooses. Both chose their wives. They could, however, have owned it as "joint tenants with right of survivorship."

Unrelated home buyers usually buy as tenants in common. For example, if the Fishers and their friends the Blacks bought a ski chalet in Banff together, that's how they would likely take ownership.

Your Life Estate Lasts As Long As You Do

Here is another ownership style, although one not nearly as common as the three previously discussed.

Sarah owned her home and everything in it. She lived on Canada Pension benefits and the small amounts of money her two sons gave her. One son, Herb, was concerned that Mom's small estate would be tied up in *probate court.* That is a special provincial office that handles the management of wills, of estates of those who have died without a will, and other, similar estate situations such as guardianships. Herb felt that once Mom's estate landed there, its monetary worth would go mostly to lawyers.

Herb read in a legal column of his daily newspaper that one could avoid probate by having an elderly homeowner deed over his or her property to a relative (or whomever else they wished to be the inheritor), but retain a *life estate* in it. That meant they could stay in it as long as they lived. The homeowner would continue paying expenses involved in maintaining that property, unless otherwise specified in writing.

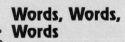

Words, Words, Words

A **life estate** can be created with any form of property, but usually it is in real estate. Ownership is divided into two parts: the *life estate*, which is the length of that homeowner's life, and the *remainder interest*, which is willed to the heir and becomes his or her absolute ownership when the property owner dies.

Tip

You won't want to donate your home to charity when you are too young—there are too many changes life can bring you, in finances and housing. This is usually a practice for those in their sixties, seventies, and beyond.

Herb called his brother, Fred, and both suggested this to Mom. Sarah, trusting her boys, executed a deed that gave her the right to live on the property the rest of her days. At her death the title automatically would go to her sons as tenants in common.

The sons' goal of avoiding probate was accomplished. But was this best solution for Sarah?

Well, if Sarah needed, or wanted, to sell her home and use the proceeds to move into a retirement community, she would have to get her sons' consent, since they have an ownership interest in the property. If a son dies, leaving his interest to his wife, Sarah would need to get her daughter-in-law to agree to her plan. Relatives, and particularly in-laws, sometimes do not act kindly when someone wants to spend their "inheritance."

Homeowners with no mortgage and no children, or perhaps children they have provided for in other ways, might want to leave their home to a favourite charity, retaining a life interest in it. You do not have to own a mansion for a charity to accept your place. There are some tax benefits to this gesture as well. The home's value is determined by a formula that includes your life expectancy and that of anyone else on the deed, using an approved mortality table and the appraised value of the residence.

Talk with your tax adviser, and keep in mind that an agreement between you and the charity can contain whatever specific arrangements you choose—the possibility you might want to move to a retirement community, for example. You could also agree that the charity will maintain the property, or maintain it *and* pay the property taxes. In a few cases it may be possible to secure a small income from the charity.

Is It Tangible, Intangible or Real Property?

Lawyers are experts on classifying things. Take property, for example: You might own *real property*, *tangible personal property*, and *intangible personal property*.

John and Ellen Fisher's home is *real property*, or, more commonly, real estate. Real property is land, buildings, and things permanently attached to the land, such as trees. In some provinces there are special inheritance and probate rights attached to real estate.

The couple's jointly-owned household goods and automobile are examples of *tangible personal property*. Other items under this heading include machinery, jewellery, sporting goods and art works. These are possessions we can see and touch.

The stock certificates owned by John, and the savings account jointly owned with his wife, are examples of *intangible personal property*. You can see it, but it's just paper, denoting ownership in something that is represented by a piece of paper, like shares in a corporation. Other intangible personal property includes bank certificates of deposit, corporate bonds, patents and copyrights. (The patent for that revolutionary gadget mentioned at the beginning of this chapter is intangible personal property, too.)

Inheritance laws, wills and gifts distinguish between the different types of property. That's why you need to know *how you own* what your estate comprises, not just what's in it.

Okay, now it's time to attack those desk drawers, rifle through cardboard files, and check anywhere else you keep valuable papers. Look to see how you own property. Check your deed(s), bank accounts, certificates of deposit, stock and bond certificates, title to your car—all should indicate which form of ownership you hold.

Tip

By all means, get duplicates of missing documents you need for your estate file. Contact your local government office (perhaps the Land Titles Registry Office, or a similarly named office) for help with a lost house deed. Insurance and brokerage houses can supply you with copies of those mislaid documents, too.

A Few Words About Condominiums, Cooperatives and Timeshares

A home isn't always a single-family house on a half-acre lot, of course. Many millions of Canadians live in condominiums and in cooperatives, or will be buying one in the years ahead. Does this apply to you? Then you might have special questions about estate issues and your home.

I've included timeshares in this section because owners of these vacation apartments also are frequently confused about just what they own, how they own it, and how they will pass it on to their heirs.

The Condo's Real

A condominium is real property, or real estate. Your community might consist of one-storey attached apartments, three-storey townhouses or even detached single-family houses. It's not the architectural style that determines a condo, but rather the joint ownership style. Each "unit" is owned separately. The rest of the property, known as the undivided common area, is owned jointly by all individual unit owners. That area consists of grounds, parking spaces, walkways and the like.

How does condo ownership affect your estate? Well, since you own your condo outright, you are free to leave it to whomever you choose, depending on the individual ownership style you have selected (solely, joint tenants, etc.). You do not need anyone's "permission" to sell your condo, and prospective buyers do not have to be approved by the condo association.

Keep in mind, however, that if you bequeath your condo to your son, Franco, and his wife, Julia, knowing as you do that they would love to live there, the couple will have to join the condo association and abide by its rules. Those regulations might say, for instance, no children are allowed—a problem if Franco and Julia have two pre-teens. Or the condo association could have a clause prohibiting pets, putting little Fluffy's future on the line. Or the rules and regulations might have other clauses that make it difficult, if not impossible, for Franco and Julia to live there. They might have to sell or rent out the property instead.

The Co-op's a Different Story

If you own, or plan to buy, a cooperative apartment, or co-op, you will, as you probably know, purchase shares of stock in the corporation that owns your building or complex. In your monthly maintenance fee, you pay for your share of the cost of running the building—like utilities, mortgages, and taxes, etc. A co-op is intangible because ownership is your stock certificates, and not tangible property just because you can see the apartment.

A cooperative may be co-owned or solely owned. If the latter, then the stock becomes part of a probate estate.

Watch Out!

Cooperatives often have important restrictions upon transfer, with the corporation retaining the right to veto a sale or, more accurately, veto the prospective buyer. You will want to check how your corporation handles inherited apartments. More of them these days are requiring heirs to qualify for entry as if they were new prospective buyers. That means conforming to the board's financial and other criteria.

What Timeshares Are—and Are Not

Anyone who hasn't been living under a rock for the last decade or so now knows what a timeshare is. It is, of course, a week (or two or more) that you buy and then own in a resort complex. You purchase the same week of each year for a specified period of time. That might be 25 or 40 years, or for as long as the complex is standing.

What you pay for your furnished timeshare apartment depends on its location, size, and, most especially, the time of the year you choose to buy. "High season" in that resort will, naturally, cost you more than an off-season week.

The timeshare can be co-owned or solely owned, the same as all of the other assets mentioned in this chapter.

There are a couple of things to keep in mind about timeshare purchases, as they apply to you and your heirs.

First, there are two styles of timeshares:

➤ A Fee-Simple Ownership

If you buy under this type of ownership, you own your apartment as you would real estate. Your ownership is a percentage of that apartment's use. If you have one week, you own 1/50th of the year in Unit 240 (complexes usually keep two weeks open annually for cleaning and repairs). You also own an undivided share in the common areas.

You can leave your one-week real estate property in your will to anyone you choose, considering, of course, the ownership style you have adopted—joint tenants, etc.

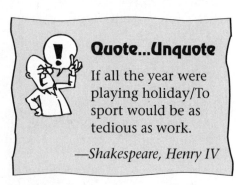

Quote...Unquote

If all the year were playing holiday/To sport would be as tedious as work.

—*Shakespeare, Henry IV*

Words, Words, Words

Illiquid means something not easily convertible to cash. A house, for example, is considered illiquid because even if you sold it the first day it was on the market you would not have cash in hand from that sale for several weeks or more. Your timeshare apartment is likely to be illiquid, too.

➤ A Long-Term Lease

Also known as *"right to use,"* this type of ownership means that you have personal property, not real estate. You can, however, leave this style of timeshare apartment to anyone you select, again depending on how you hold title to that unit.

Also, it's important to keep in mind that timeshares can be difficult to sell, unless your week is in the most glamorous of resorts in the most exciting geographic community in the high season. The reason: There are always new resorts opening up, not to mention resales in existing complexes, causing a flood of timeshare units on the market. "Right to use" apartments can be particularly difficult because you are selling less than the top number of years on your lease; for example, if you bought it with a 25-year lease, and held the timeshare for 10 years, you now have only 15 years to sell.

Your heirs, should they want to sell your timeshare, no matter what its style, may have trouble doing so, or might have to wait a longer time than they would like for a buyer. They may also have to sell at a price lower, sometimes a good deal lower, than what you paid for it.

But you can certainly adjust your view

of a timeshare and your expectations from it. You might want to tell your heirs not to expect a windfall profit here. But, hey, they may not *want* to sell their week in paradise, so the potential problem of unloading a timeshare may never come up.

Papers Galore—Where Do You Keep Them?

Where are you storing your deeds and other important papers in your life, no matter what ownership style you have chosen for your properties? Is there room for the several more documents you will add to that file when you have finished this book and implemented many of its suggestions?

Some folks purchase a fireproof and waterproof box to keep valuable papers at home. Others turn to a bank's safe deposit box. I know someone who put all his treasures in a safe deposit box, including his baby's first tooth, which, as the tooth fairy, he purchased for 25 cents. His daughter's first report card is in there, too.

Watch Out!

Did you know that if a bank robber steals the contents of your safe deposit box, you may not be insured by the bank for that loss? True! The bank guarantees the box is fireproof, but not theft-proof. Theft of safe deposit boxes isn't a frequent, or even occasional, occurrence, so you're probably quite safe leaving your belongings there. But do keep that point in mind when storing some items in a bank. You might want to see if your homeowner's insurance can pick up that coverage.

A safe deposit box is honoured by Revenue Canada, which may allow a tax deduction for its rental fee if you store investments, like stock certificates, there.

Besides the deed to your home, you might indeed want to keep investment certificates in the box, as well as papers like powers of attorney, and your birth certificate and passport. Expensive, rarely worn jewellery, rare coins and other valuable collectibles, and mementoes like that baby tooth could go into the box. One test of what to put there is gauging whether that item would be difficult, if not impossible, to replace and if it has considerable value. If the answer is yes to those questions you ask yourself, pop it in the safe deposit box.

Your Safe Deposit Box

Your will can be stored here, especially if your spouse is a co-owner of the box (keep a copy of your will at home so you can easily review it). But it is more practical to keep your will and funeral instructions more accessible to your next of kin, or whoever will be handling your affairs. A home safe or fireproof box will do just fine for those papers. Or you might want to leave your original will with the lawyer who drew it up. Make certain his or her name is in your estate file. Losing the original document can cancel your will and cause significant delay—and increase the costs of probate.

Here's a story that shows how well-meaning people can use a safe deposit box, which is good, but then put something in it that turns out to be, well, not exactly *bad*, but not a smart move either.

James died, leaving a will naming his wife, Mary, as beneficiary, so she received his probate estate. They had two daughters, Karen and Elaine. James had rented a safe deposit box in his own name at Trustworthy Bank. Among other items, he had placed two envelopes in the box, each containing $10,000, and each bearing a daughter's name. Mother and daughters were not on particularly good terms, and so they asked the estate lawyer to advise them about ownership of the cash.

The lawyer, after due deliberation and research, responded that since there was no actual delivery of the cash to the daughters, there could be no gift to them. Therefore, the cash became part of the probate estate.

This story does have a happy ending for the daughters, though. Mom gave them the cash anyway.

Dad had tried to leave his girls something special, but he almost failed. He should have given them the money outright, or established a joint bank account with each daughter, or left them the money in his will.

Keep in mind that a gift of property requires (1) intent to make a gift, (2) delivery to the recipient, and (3) acceptance of the gift by the recipient.

The Least You Need to Know

➤ You need to get together an inventory of all your assets before you proceed with effective estate planning.

➤ There are several styles of ownership you can select. The form of ownership determines whether the property may be distributed through your will or go to the surviving co-owner.

➤ Your estate is divided into real, tangible personal and intangible personal property.

➤ Be careful to store important papers where they are safe as well as reasonably accessible.

Chapter 3

Yours, Mine, and Ours: Marrieds and Property

In This Chapter

➤ Styles of buying together
➤ The famous "family property"
➤ Switching from one spousal style to another
➤ The prenuptial agreement

Marriage is a partnership, and like many partnerships, the marital couple owns property together and jointly manages it. This can be done in several legal ownership styles. If you are married, you are certain to recognize yourself and your spouse in one of these examples.

As I've pointed out throughout these pages, you need to know how you hold title to property in order to plan properly for its management in your lifetime, and its disbursal in a manner you choose through your estate. Maybe you want it to go directly to your spouse... or maybe not.

Jointly Speaking

You read briefly about buying property as *joint owners with right of survivorship* in the previous chapter. I said that anyone, single or married, could use that ownership style. Now I'll tell you about it in more detail, as it applies specifically to married couples.

If you are married and you own real estate, such as a principal and/or a vacation home, you probably do have it as joint owners. That applies to your personal property as well—household goods, bank accounts, automobiles, and the like.

What I mean here is that if one party dies, the other automatically inherits that co-owner's share, without it having to be mentioned in a will. It's quick, no questions asked. That's why it is so popular.

As an example, let's take Hal and Wendy. Like many couples across this broad land, they have been married several years and have two careers and two children.

> ### Quote...Unquote
>
> The truth is, I do indulge myself a little the more in pleasure, knowing that this is the proper age of my life to do it; and, out of my observation that most men that do thrive in the world do forget to take pleasure during the time that they are getting their estate, but reserve that till they have got one, and then it is too late for them to enjoy it.
>
> —Samuel Pepys, "Diary," March 10, 1666.

Early in their marriage the couple were thrilled to be able to purchase their first house. They still live there 15 years later. The deed reads "… Hal H. Higgins and Wendy L. Higgins, husband and wife, as joint tenants with right of survivorship."

For purposes of this illustration we'll have to interrupt this pleasant life, and have Hal go to his heavenly reward. Upon his death, Wendy becomes the sole owner of all of the property they owned jointly. She takes the house because of that language in the deed: "… right of survivorship." The same terminology is on the savings account card she and Hal signed when they set up that account. The household goods go to Wendy because they are also owned in that style.

There are several benefits to this type of ownership with a spouse.

➤ The ownership transfer is automatic

➤ There is no probate (which means no delay, and no costly lawyers)

➤ There are usually no income tax consequences on a transfer to a spouse

Let's look at a different scenario. Even more unfortunately, Hal and Wendy die in an automobile accident. Wendy survives a few minutes longer than Hal. Then Wendy's estate will include their jointly held property. If there is no evidence as to which one of the two survived the other, then the property is divided and one half is included in each person's probate estate. Using their house as an example, one-half ownership of that residence would go into Hal's estate, the other into Wendy's.

Tenants in Common

Here is another marital ownership style.

This applies to Sam and Ann, to take one example, a couple who also purchased a home a few years back. The deed *they* received read "… to Sam R. Black and Ann Decatur Black, as tenants in common…"

If Ann dies before Sam, then Sam does not automatically become the sole owner of their home, because tenancy in common does not transfer ownership to the surviving spouse. In other words, tenancy in common does not have the same result and advantages as joint tenancy with right of survivorship. Survivorship results do not apply to tenants in common. It is the deceased's will that provides for the house; because of the way it is owned, it does become part of the deceased's probate estate. Ann would have to deal with the home in her will.

While joint tenancy with right of survivorship can be used by married couples or single persons, tenancy in common more often is confined to couples who are not legally married.

Family Property Laws: Every Province in Difference

The way married couples share property varies according to each province's family law rules. Provincial statutes provide that some marital property is automatically shared, or excluded from division with a spouse as family property. In most circumstances family property (including pensions) acquired during the marriage is shared equally. This may depend on how it was acquired. A gift or inheritance during marriage, for example, may not be subject to division under the family property rules.

Why exactly are we talking about this?

Provincial family laws protect the property rights of legally married spouses. These laws restrict how married people can deal with their own property.

You cannot prepare a will or an estate plan without taking your spouse's property rights into consideration.

Division of Marital Assets

Legislated rules for the division of marital property vary from province to province. They provide for married couples in cases of death and divorce. Those in unmarried opposite sex and same sex relationships do not have the same property rights. This is even more reason to have a will.

Claims to property, if not set out in a cohabitation contract, would need to be asserted through the courts. This is to be distinguished from the Income Tax Act, which grants common-law spouses tax deferral advantages equal to those of married couples.

Avoiding Family Property Rules

If you have a home or other assets and plan to remarry you may want to avoid the automatic application of a province's family property sharing rules. This is often done by entering into a marriage or domestic contract. This is the "prenuptial agreement..." or, in Hollywood terms, just the "prenup."

Most jurisdictions allow you to enter into an agreement with your intended spouse before or even during the marriage. The husband and wife would agree that the normal application of family or community property rules for division of assets would not apply except as may be specified in the contract.

A prenuptial or domestic contract can also deal with child or spousal support, appreciation of a business, family assets, or an inheritance.

Most people with children from a prior marriage or with a business or inheritance will want to modify the division of family property rules. Protection of this property can be achieved by a

Quote...Unquote

Property has its duties as well as its rights.

—*Benjamin Disraeli*

Wedlock, a dead-lock.

—*English proverb*

marriage contract that excludes some assets from sharing in the event of a spouse's death or a divorce.

You've seen how fond I am of using examples to illustrate certain points I want to make, or explanations to put forth. I'll use another one now for family property rules.

Norman and Esther marry in Prince Edward Island. Both are in the entertainment business. Esther is a star, but Norman is a struggling actor. Since this is only a story, we'll say they have no prenuptial agreement, although these days that might be un-likely given their vastly unequal incomes.

During the marriage Esther purchases a house in her name only. It is used as a home for both spouses. She then goes on to buy a vacation property, with title in both her name and Norman's.

Norman, of course, is not earning anywhere near the major bucks Esther is bringing in. But "struggling" does not mean sacrifice for the young thespian. Thanks to Esther's income and generosity, his lifestyle is quite grand. He knows, too, that all of the property Esther purchases during the marriage, no matter if titled in her name alone, is shared with him under the province's family property laws. If it is sold, one half of the proceeds are his, too.

Of course, it should also be noted that Norman's property acquired during the marriage is shared with Esther.

While mulling his good fortune, and quite delighted with Esther and his present life, Norman gives the tiniest thought to all that he missed—monetarily—by not marrying the star sooner. He calls his lawyer aside one day for an off-the-record chat. The lawyer informs him that whatever Esther owned before the marriage is her separate property and Norman has no claim on it. *But*—always an important word in per-sonal finance—if this property increased in value during the marriage, he could share in the "appreciation."

What's This About "Separate Property?"

Well, *separate property* is whatever is owned by either spouse before marriage. Excluded property may be acquired after marriage as a gift, or perhaps through an inheritance. What a spouse has or acquires as separate property usually belongs exclusively to him or her. Each province has its own family property rules and definitions that its residents must be aware of.

Do Family Property Rules Last Forever?

They might not. The spouses may agree to convert their assets into separate property. That can be done with a written agreement signed by both parties. The parties can agree that they each would be free to deal with their own separate property as they see fit.

More About Those Prenuptial Agreements

Prenuptial agreements between celebrities make headlines. However, it isn't only the famous who scribble their names to these documents. It can be any two people about to marry who are, well, perhaps just a tad concerned about what will happen to what's theirs in the course of the marriage, and even in the event of

> **Quote...Unquote**
> When poverty comes in at the door, love flies out the window.
>
> —*Anonymous, 17th century*

a divorce one day. I say two people. Sometimes it is only one half of the couple that wants—demands—the "prenup." The other party goes along or there is no wedding. This is a legal guide, so I won't will not get into who should and shouldn't have a marriage contract, and who should or shouldn't break an engagement over the request by the other party to sign one. That's for advice columnists. Obviously the best situation is when both parties want that document (or neither wants it). Let's get on with the other considerations of this arrangement.

A *prenuptial agreement or marriage contract*, signed by both parties, spells out any aspect of ownership in the marriage that the two parties can think of. It is a legally binding agreement. A prenup can go into property ownership, salaries, pension plans, and issues about existing children from prior marriages, specifically noting what belongs to whom going into the marriage, and perhaps for the duration of the marriage.

A prenup can take precedence over some, but not all, family property laws. However, prenups generally cover non-jointly-owned

Briefs

It was said the document signed by Jacqueline Kennedy and Aristotle Onassis before their 1968 wedding was quite hefty, providing weeks of work for both parties' lawyers (and bringing in an okay to the agreement by Jackie's brother-in-law, Ted Kennedy). It was rumoured there were even clauses about where each would maintain a permanent residence, and how often the two would spend time together. But then, there was a good deal of property, real and personal, involved on both sides of this famous union. There was a business owned by Onassis, and children from previous unions to be considered.

Did Jackie's son John Kennedy Jr. and his bride Carolyn Bessette have a prenup? If they did, no doubt bits and pieces of *those* clauses will eventually surface.

property—that *is* the point of having one of these documents—so that does not often become an issue.

In case you have a prenuptial agreement in mind, or might some day, or are just plain curious about what is contained in such a document, below is a specimen agreement for you to page through. This form is intended for a couple who have each been married before, and who both have children. That can make for a few extra pages. You will see there are even provisions for the distribution of the engagement and wedding gifts between the couple in the event of a divorce. A prenup can be quite thorough.

There is more about marriage contracts, especially how they are treated in contested wills, in Chapter 13.

A cautionary note here: If you are considering adopting this form for your own purposes, better check with your lawyer first. Every province, particularly Quebec, has different family laws and requirements for legal documents to be effective within its borders. This warning holds true for all of the forms in this book you might want to use, but I'll remind you again when we come to those documents in upcoming chapters.

PRENUPTIAL AGREEMENT

THIS Prenuptial Agreement made this _____day of _____, 1998, by and between _____, of _____, (City, Province) (hereinafter referred to as "Wife"), and _____, of _____, (City, Province) (hereinafter referred to as "Husband"), both of whom are also referred to herein individually as a "party" and together as the "Parties," THE PARTIES AGREE AS FOLLOWS:

1. BACKGROUND

1.1 The Parties believe that this Agreement will enhance and encourage a harmonious marital relationship between them.

1.2 The Parties intend to be married on _____.

1.3 The Husband has been previously married and has _____ children; Wife has been previously married and has _____ child. Each possesses or will possess wealth derived from their respective families or as a result of their respective employments.

1.4 The Parties have disclosed and discussed their mutual rights and obligations, in furtherance of which the Husband, through <u>Exhibit A</u> hereto, and the Wife, through <u>Exhibit B</u> hereto, have disclosed their respective assets, liabilities, and sources of income to each other, which disclosures each represent to the other to be substantially accurate and which include copies of their respective most-recently-filed Income Tax Returns.

2. PURPOSE OF AGREEMENT

2.1 The Parties desire to clarify what their respective rights are:

(a) to share in the property belonging to each other;

(b) to limit their respective rights in the property of the other during the marriage relationship and upon its termination by dissolution or death; and

(c) to accept the provisions of this Agreement in lieu and in satisfaction of all such rights.

3. PROPERTY COVERED

3.1 The property of the Parties as listed in their respective exhibits, and business property, real, and personal, which they have inadvertently omitted therefrom, and all interest, rents, profits, and increased value which may in time accrue or may result in any manner, or any other property owned or to be owned by each party, shall be owned as separate property of each party during the marriage, except as elsewhere provided herein.

continued

3.2 Each party hereby waives, discharges, and releases all right, title, and interest in and to the property of the other party presently owned, or hereafter acquired, except as elsewhere provided herein. Each party shall have the absolute right to sell, transfer, convey, or otherwise dispose of his or her property as he or she sees fit. Each realizes that although the other now has property, there may be an increase or a decrease in the value thereof, or ultimately, there may be no property at all.

3.3 Each party shall, if requested, join in the conveyance or other transfer of the other's property to a third person, but shall not be required to assume personal liability in connection with any such transaction.

3.4 Joint use of separate property shall not give rise to joint ownership of that property, unless the Parties agree otherwise in an amendment to the contract in writing signed by each of them. Notwithstanding the provisions of this Agreement that allow the Parties to maintain their separate income and assets, the Parties recognize that it is possible, through accident or intent, for their respective separate income or assets to become, or appear to be, commingled. It is the Parties' intention that such commingling or pooling of assets not be interpreted to imply abandonment of the terms and provisions of this Agreement.

4. RELEASE OF CLAIMS

4.1 Except as otherwise provided herein, each party with respect to the other party's property and estate now hereby waives, renounces, relinquishes, and releases all rights as surviving spouse, heir, executor or administrator, survivor, or next of kin, whether by common law or by statute, provincial or federal, now in effect or hereafter enacted to all claims, interest, estate, title, or otherwise, right to elect against the will, statutory dependant's relief allowance, or to the property, real and personal or mixed, or preferential share of the other party.

4.2 Each party shall, on the demand of the other party or his or her heirs, devisees, administrators, executors, or assigns, execute any and all assurances, deeds, releases, instruments, receipts, and other documents that may be necessary to accomplish the foregoing. The rights of each party herein described as released and renounced are hereby assigned to the other party, his or her heirs, devisees, legatees, administrators, executors, successors in the interest, guardians, and assigns.

5. PROVISIONS FOR EACH OTHER

5.1 Except as elsewhere provided herein, each party shall make no provision for the other unless he or she voluntarily elects to do so. Each party may in his or her sole discretion, make additional provisions for the other, whether by

continued

lifetime gift, by future will or codicil, by joint or family property, by insurance, or otherwise.

6. MARITAL RESIDENCE

6.1 Husband owns the real estate located at _____, _____, _____, individually. Upon the death of either party, or divorce, Husband or his estate shall become the sole owner of the real estate. The household furnishings located therein shall be divided equally between the parties in the event of divorce. Upon the death of either party, the survivor shall become the sole owner of the household furnishings.

7. ADEQUATE PROVISION

7.1 The Parties hereby agree that the provisions made herein by each party for the other are fair and equitable under the circumstances.

8. GIFTS

8.1 Either party may make a gift to the other party, which gift shall be the separate property of the other party.

9. MARRIAGE BREAKDOWN

9.1 The Parties, in the event of marital discord resulting in the breakdown of this marriage, renounce and release, except as elsewhere provided herein, all rights, present and future, each may have with respect to the other's assets now owned, including all business ventures and property owned by the Parties, as well as any inheritance they may acquire during the marriage. Each party renounces and releases all rights he or she may have with respect to the other party for spousal support, alimony, property settlement, legal fees, and court costs.

10. AFTER ACQUIRED ASSETS AND LIABILITIES

10.1 The Parties agree that if they separate or divorce that all assets and liabilities acquired or incurred by either party in joint name during the marriage shall be shared equally between the parties, but not including: any inheritance; and increase in the value of the Parties' pension funds; or any other increase in the value of other property owned by either party prior to the marriage (including, but not limited to, increases in net value attributable to the retirement of any outstanding indebtedness with respect to such property during the marriage).

10.2 Wedding and Engagement Gifts.

(a) Death. If either party dies while the Parties are married, then all wedding and engagement gifts received by the Parties from third parties shall belong to the surviving party.

continued

(b) Divorce. In the event of a divorce, said wedding and engagement gifts shall be distributed between the Parties so that each party receives wedding and engagement gifts which, in the aggregate, have a value which is as close as reasonable to being equal to the value of all the wedding and engagement gifts to be distributed to the other party.

10.3 Employee Plans and Employee Benefit Rights. Except as may be otherwise provided herein, each party (as "Releasee") hereby elects, and the other party (as "Releasor") hereby consents to a waiver and release of any and all benefits, including without limitation, the qualified pre-retirement survivor annuity form of benefit under all pension, retirement, death benefit, stock bonus, or profit-sharing plans, systems, or trusts (hereinafter collectively called "Employee Plans") of which the Releasee is, or may become, a participant, beneficiary, or member.

11. SPOUSAL SUPPORT

11.1 Each of the Parties acknowledges that, taking into consideration, among other things, each spouse's private estate, education, work experience, health, age, and ability to work and earn a living, each is fully capable of being self-supporting. Accordingly, if a Breakdown of Marriage occurs, each of the Parties waives, relinquishes, and releases any and all rights and claims as against the other and their respective successors to receive support, alimony, maintenance, or any other payment of a similar nature whether permanent or temporary.

12. PROPERTY SETTLEMENT

12.1 The amount of the property and support settlement Husband shall pay to Wife shall be based upon the length of the Parties' marriage and equal to _____ Dollars for the first year of the Parties' marriage, and _____ Dollars per year for every completed year thereafter of the Parties' marriage, with no maximum, and determined as follows:
Length of Marriage   Total Settlement Amount

_____   _____

12.2 The first installment payment of the property and support settlement shall be in the sum of $_____ and made on the 30th day after the dissolution occurs. The balance of the property and support settlement shall be paid yearly in $_____ increments. If, when Husband dies, there are remaining installments of the property and support settlement owed to Wife, then the remaining payments shall be accelerated and paid to Wife within a reasonable time after the settlement of Husband's estate. If Wife predeceases Husband, then any remaining installments of the property and support

continued

settlement shall be paid to Wife's estate as the installments come due. The property and support settlement will be made as and on a tax-free basis. Husband shall not deduct said payments or any part thereof on his income tax returns, and Wife shall not be obligated to include such payments or any part thereof in her taxable income on her income tax returns.

13. VACATING RESIDENCE

13.1 Wife acknowledge that Husband owns the residence located at _____, _____, _____, where she and Husband expect to reside immediately after their marriage. In the event one of the Parties files for separation or dissolution, within thirty (30) days after the filing for said separation or dissolution, Wife shall remove herself and her property from the _____ residence and give Husband all keys thereto, and consents that thereafter Husband shall have exclusive use and possession of all other rights pertaining to such residence. In the event of Husband's death, Wife shall be allowed to remain in the residence for her lifetime (a life estate) or until she remarries. Husband's Estate shall be the owner of the residence upon Husband's death.

14. LIABILITY OF DEBTS

14.1 The debts contracted by each party hereto prior to their marriage are to be paid by the party who shall have contracted the same, and the property of the other party shall not in any respect be liable for the payment thereof, except as elsewhere provided herein.

15. INDEPENDENT LEGAL ADVICE

15.1 The Parties hereto both stipulate that they, and each of them, have been represented by legal counsel of their choice in the preparation and execution of this Agreement; they were advised to and have read this Agreement and have had its contents explained to them by such counsel. In addition, the Parties were advised not to and did not execute the document until they fully understood the terms, provisions and legal consequences of this Agreement.

16. CHILD SUPPORT

16.1 Nothing in this Agreement shall be construed to limit or in any way decrease any child support which might be awarded pursuant to a dissolution of the marriage, should a child or children be born to or adopted by the Parties together.

17. GENERAL PROVISIONS

17.1 (a) This Agreement shall become effective upon the date of the marriage.

(b) This agreement and the provisions hereof may be asserted as a bar and

continued

estoppel in any court of law or equity to the claims of the surviving party in the estate of the first to die.

(c) The parties may amend, revoke, or rescind this Agreement only by written mutual agreement.

(d) The Parties hereto and their respective heirs, devisees, delegatees, administrators, executors, guardians, successors in interest, and assigns, shall be bound by the provisions of this Agreement.

(e) The domicile of the Parties at the time of the execution of this Agreement is the Province of _____, and the law of such province shall govern. The Parties recognize that they may change their domicile to another jurisdiction by agreement. The Parties agree that all questions arising under or with respect to this Agreement and its interpretation or enforceability shall be governed by the substantive laws of the Province of _____, where Husband and Wife are presently residing and Province where the Parties expect to reside after their marriage.

(f) At those places in this Agreement, including this sentence, except Exhibits A and B, where there appears a recitation of property, ownership rights, survivorship rights or interests, or otherwise which list shall be by way of illustration and not by way of limitation.

(g) In the event a provision of this Agreement is held to be unenforceable for any reason, it shall be considered severable from all other provisions of this Agreement and the Agreement shall be binding upon the Parties in the same manner as it otherwise would have been, had the unenforceable provision not been inserted herein.

(h) The Parties acknowledge and agree that it is difficult to value equity interest, agree to accept the valuation of such interest as set forth in this Agreement, and waive any right to secure an independent valuation thereof and to otherwise present any challenge to the values as set forth herein.

(i) The Parties hereby agree, and state their intentions that, this Agreement shall be followed by, and considered binding upon, any judicial or quasi-judicial proceeding in any way concerning a dissolution of this marriage or death of one or both of the parties.

(j) The parties have fully disclosed to the other the value of all significant assets and debts and that full particulars have been provided to each other and their respective counsel. They acknowledge that they are satisfied with the financial disclosure.

18. COMPLETE AGREEMENT

18.1 The Parties hereby agree, represent, and warrant that this Agreement

continued

comprises the entire understanding of the Parties regarding this matter and no promise or inducement not contained in this Agreement has been offered to either of them by anyone and that this Agreement is executed without reliance upon any statement or representation not contained in this Agreement by either the Wife, the Husband, their attorneys, or any other person or entity.

IN WITNESS WHEREOF, the Parties have executed this Prenuptial Agreement on the day and year first above written.

_____   _____
Witness   "Wife"

_____   _____
Witness   "Husband"
[Exhibits A & B]

The Least You Need to Know

➤ Most couples hold property as "joint tenants with right of survivorship."

➤ What couples earn, buy, or otherwise acquire individually during a marriage generally becomes family or community property that belongs to them equally.

➤ It is possible to exclude specific or all property as family property.

➤ A prenuptial agreement can take precedence over some forms of property ownership. The agreement can override provincial property laws so your spouse will not automatically share in your estate.

Chapter 4

Life Insurance: You Need It!

In This Chapter

➤ How insurance can help your estate grow

➤ A term or whole life policy?

➤ How much will you need?

➤ Your beneficiary(ies)

Do you have enough life insurance? No, no, come back, I'm not trying to sell you a policy. I ask because life insurance is an integral part of estate planning.

So force yourself to read this chapter and give the subject some thought. Then you will almost certainly want to take steps to make sure you (a) know what your own coverage entails and (b) beef it up in areas where it needs emphasis. Or perhaps buy insurance in the event you have none.

What Life Insurance Can Do for You

You are probably underinsured. Remember, I am not an insurance salesman, so I have no vested interest in making such a statement.

Sadly, many of us view life insurance like a bad lottery: If we win, we're dead. We often have little regard for life insurance sales agents as well (although I believe they still rank slightly higher than lawyers). Still, there are those folks who wisely look and plan ahead and do buy insurance.

There are several reasons why coverage is a worthwhile expenditure. Life insurance:

➤ increases your estate, building wealth with a relatively small outlay of cash in the form of premiums

➤ provides ready cash for loved ones upon your death

➤ is received by the beneficiary free of income tax

➤ may be owned by someone besides the insured and not be subject to probate fees or the claims of the insured's creditors

➤ can be used to fund a business buy-out plan, and

➤ could serve as a savings account, if it is permanent cash value insurance

Let's look at these statements in more detail.

Building Wealth

Most of us would like to have as substantial an estate as possible so our loved ones can live comfortably after our death. Unfortunately, most of us, me included, don't have a rich relative about to pass away and leave us their fortune—or rich relatives eager to share their wealth during their lifetime through generous gifts. We have to build up an estate the old fashioned way: by earning money and saving it, or investing it very wisely.

Your estate can be substantial with the inclusion of life insurance. Take Al, for example. He is 52 years old. His company pension and his house are his biggest assets. When he dies, his wife will own both. But he is concerned that she and their children will not have enough to live comfortably, so several years ago Al bought term life insurance (I'll talk

Quote...Unquote

Lack of money is the root of all evil.

—*George Bernard Shaw*

about this in detail in the next page or so) with a face value of $350,000. That's in addition to the group term life insurance he has at work. Al knows that his family will be financially more secure because of that insurance.

Al pays approximately $380 in quarterly premiums for his coverage. He hopes he and his wife have many years together, and he's certainly content with the insurance company keeping the premiums. That's a small investment for his family's financial future.

Ready Cash

Life insurance people like to emphasize that your estate may not be "liquid." That is a genuine concern, and one that some form of insurance protection can address.

Let's take Adam and Eve as an example here. The couple, in their mid-thirties, have two young children. They own their own home in Winnipeg, have a small savings account, a little invested in stocks and mutual funds, and they each have a small contributory retirement plan through their jobs. Adam earns considerably more than Eve, although it could be the reverse with other couples.

If Adam suddenly dies, his salary stops, but bills won't stop coming in. Revenue Canada in particular isn't all that patient if you owe it money. The cost of a funeral might be around $5,000 and up, and funeral directors want to be paid, too.

Adam could solve those immediate problems with life insurance, at very little expense. Since he is young, the premium for coverage similar to Al's policy will be considerably less than what Al is paying. Eve can deal with her grief and not have to worry about where the money is going to come from—it's in the mail from the insurance company.

Not so incidentally, single people and couples without children can make use of an

Watch Out

Beware of skimping in this area. Two-income couples with children should each have an insurance policy. Look at it this way: If one party's death would result in a serious financial hardship for the family, then both husband and wife should carry insurance.

insurance policy, too, and for the same reasons: immediate cash for beneficiaries and money to pay funeral expenses and that individual's other bills—repayment of loans, credit card balances, and any other debts that would have to be satisfied from the estate.

Taxes, Probate Fees and Creditors

The beauty of life insurance is that the beneficiary receives the proceeds free of income tax. Eve, for example, does not have to pay a cent in taxes. The proceeds will also escape probate fees if paid directly to Eve. The insurance proceeds will not be subject to claims from Adam's creditors, unless Adam's estate is the beneficiary of the policy. Adam should always have a contingent or back-up beneficiary in case Eve dies before him.

Business Plans

If you are the owner, or part owner, of a business, you also need to consider life insurance. The business could purchase insurance on the life of the owner, and the proceeds could be paid to the business. The business that has an owner/key employee who dies suddenly might experience a financial crunch for a short time, or perhaps even longer. That could be alleviated by the insurance proceeds. Or, the owner's family may need cash, but can't sell the business interest to generate the necessary money. Life insurance can be an answer there too. (Chapter 6 contains a good deal more info about having your own business.)

> **Tip**
>
> Some folks purchase a life insurance policy as a gift, perhaps to a grandchild, making that individual the beneficiary. Money left in this manner goes directly where you want it to after your death and is not held up as part of your estate.

Savings

If you choose whole life insurance—explained in detail in a couple of pages—your premiums are divided into two parts. One part pays for the insurance coverage, while the other becomes a savings account. If you have trouble saving money, this feature can help you build a nest egg.

Which Policy Is Best for You

There is life insurance coverage to fit practically every reader of this book, and at a variety of costs too. You just need to determine the type of policy that's best for your purposes.

We can divide most policies into two categories: temporary and permanent insurance.

Temporary or Term Policies

Term policies have one common feature: there is no cash value built up by your premiums. This is simple life insurance, offering the most coverage for the least initial amount. You can select whatever that amount will be, perhaps $50,000, maybe $500,000, or any other number. You pay an annual premium. If you die while the policy is in force, your beneficiary receives the money.

You cannot borrow against a term life insurance policy because, of course, there is no cash value. The policy expires on the date specified in the insurance contract.

The premium you pay is based on the amount of insurance you purchase, your general health and your age when you first buy the

Briefs

Life insurance is one of the staples of the mystery novel (another is the will). When police investigate a murder, the first question they ask is "Who benefits from this crime?" Why, the murderer, of course, and that's rarely the butler. It's often the insurance beneficiary. Timing the purchase of life insurance may allay or enhance suspicion about that buyer.

Then there is the serial wife killer, who takes out an insurance policy on each new bride. Sadly, too, there is also the bomb that explodes on an airline flight. Investigation leads to a relative of one of the passengers, who had purchased a large policy of flight life insurance before the departure—or straight life insurance back home. So much havoc and heartache caused by a few pieces of paper.

policy. The term premium rises as you grow older. Also, insurance costs vary the way prices of other products do, so it pays to shop around to find the best, safest coverage with a company offering the lowest cost to you. As a gauge, keep in mind Al's age and the fact that he pays $380 a quarter for a $350,000 policy.

Here are some varieties of term policies.

➤ **Annual Renewable** This type offers one year of insurance, usually renewable every year with an increased premium (because you are growing older). This has the advantage of giving you the greatest coverage at the lowest initial cost to you. Read carefully any policy you are considering to see what your renewal rights are.

➤ **Level** Coverage here is for a guaranteed term, such as 5, 10 or 20 years, with level premiums. That means they reach a certain plateau and stay "level" until the next change, or the premium remains the same but the coverage decreases from one level to another. Some insurance companies will allow cost-of-living increases at proportionally the same premium.

➤ **Mortgage or Credit** With this style, coverage decreases as the debt you are insuring is paid down, but with a level premium. This is expensive, so you will want to consider purchasing another form of term insurance if you want that debt paid off at your death. Buy this only if you are otherwise uninsured.

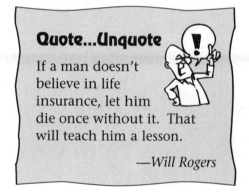

Quote...Unquote

If a man doesn't believe in life insurance, let him die once without it. That will teach him a lesson.

—*Will Rogers*

Permanent or Cash Value Policies

Another option, *cash value life insurance,* is sometimes referred to as *permanent* or *whole life insurance*. Most of these policies have, as mentioned earlier, a savings account feature, with variables in investment returns. Here are some cash value policy styles.

➤ **Whole (ordinary)** Coverage is guaranteed at a fixed amount, with level premiums. Part of each premium goes into a savings account at a predetermined amount and investment return. You can borrow against the cash value of the policy.

Tip

If you have child support obligations under a divorce decree, you might want to consider a life insurance policy, to protect their financial future and your estate and your child's financial future should you pass away.

➤ **Universal** The term and cash value portions are split into two accounts. Depending on the insured's allocation, the savings can increase or decrease. It does have the flexibility of changing coverage as needs alter, but is more expensive than term if the insured uses most of the premiums for savings.

➤ **Joint First-to-Die or Second-to-Die** This is life insurance coverage for two people, usually spouses and business partners. It is less expensive than buying two separate policies. The proceeds are payable according to the first- or second-to-die provisions. This form of coverage is available on term and permanent products.

There are some hybrid forms of insurance that blend qualities of term and permanent life insurance. Some develop cash value and some don't. Talk to your insurance representative.

Discuss policies you are considering with your financial adviser. (Remember, you are going to call often on your estate planning team.) He or she can probably be more objective than a life insurance agent. Have your adviser read the fine print of policies. What the large print giveth, the small print often taketh away.

How Much Coverage You Need, and Where to Find It

First, you need to determine how much insurance coverage is sufficient for you. A life insurance representative and your financial adviser can help you here. After your purchase, you will want to review your calculations periodically, perhaps once every year or two, to be sure your coverage matches current needs.

These things are quite subjective, but usually the main purpose of life insurance is to provide money that will replace the deceased's income. If you want a quick calculation, here's a suggestion. Keep in mind that your future income may vary considerably from these estimates.

Step l. Calculate your annual income (reduced by personal expenses for you alone, such as clothing, lunches, etc.)

Example:
Bob earns $45,000 after taxes and spends $5,000 on himself = $40,000

Step 2. Divide that amount by your expected rate of return from investing the life insurance proceeds

Example:
$40,000 divided by 0.05 = $800,000

Step 3. Subtract your current total savings and investments.

Example:
$800,000 minus $30,000 = $770,000, which covers Bob's life insurance needs.

The rough method Al (our example from a few pages ago) used for *his* life insurance was to add up all his debts—and don't think that's not a depressing experience—then determine how much money which, when invested, would be needed once all those debts were paid.

Example:

Debts to be paid	$100,000 plus
Investment needed (at 5 % return for family—$30,000)	$600,000
Total needed	$700,000

Yes, I know the $700,000 Al listed above as what he needed is far from the $350,000 term life insurance policy he carries. He does, however, have another policy—group life insurance through his

Tip

Do you have more questions about insurance? You can call the Canadian Life and Health Insurance Association Inc. in Toronto at 1 (800) 268-8099. This is a consumer service sponsored by a number of insurance industry trade associations. The Helpline operates from 9 AM to 5 PM, Eastern Time, Monday through Friday.

Watch Out!

Naturally, you'll want to choose an insurance company that's in good health. Some are in better shape than others. Company financial strength ratings are published by A.M. Best, Standard & Poor's, and Moody's & Trac. Your public library's reference department can help you access those reports, or you can check with your financial planner.

place of business. However, Al would concede he's still underinsured.

Don't forget, if you have university expenses coming up for one or more children, those costs could considerably alter the amount you will need.

Who Owns the Policy? Who Is the Beneficiary?

If the insurance is on *your* life, then probably you own the policy. It works that way for most of us. We can control the premium payment and beneficiary designation because it is our policy.

If you are married, you probably have named your spouse as primary beneficiary of the policy, and if you have children have named them as alternate beneficiaries.

You ought to review your beneficiary designation at regular intervals, especially if your family needs and life situations change. Always make sure that you have an alternative beneficiary, because if the primary beneficiary dies before you do, without an alternative named, the proceeds become part of your probate estate. That is generally not desirable, because it will delay distribution of the proceeds and be subject to probate costs. You can change your beneficiary designation by using the insurance company form provided for that purpose. If you have an irrevocably designated beneficiary you must have that person's consent to change beneficiaries.

Quote...Unquote

I have enough money to last me the rest of my life, unless I buy something.

—*Jackie Mason*

If you have minor children, then consider establishing a trust for them to receive the proceeds, and to manage the assets until they become more mature. Chapters 9 and 12 talk about trusts for minors.

Easy Go the Taxes

Keep in mind that life insurance proceeds paid to a beneficiary because of the death of the insured are tax free.

There may be several pay-out options for insurance proceeds, such as a lump sum or a periodic payment over a number of years. For example, if Al's wife chooses the latter, part of each cheque will include interest on the amount left with the insurance company. The interest portion is taxable.

If the proceeds of an insurance policy at your death are payable to your estate, this amount will be subject to probate fees. The insurance proceeds will also be subject to any claims from your estate creditors. You can avoid this situation by designating a beneficiary for your policy other than your estate. Then the proceeds will no longer be included in your estate.

> **Watch Out!**
>
> Don't transfer a life insurance policy without consulting with your estate planning team. The potential tax savings may not be as important as the insurance coverage payable to the beneficiaries of your choice.

Is There Anyone Who Should Not Carry Insurance?

Healthy empty-nest couples, with a debt-free home and sufficient investment income, may consider this option. If one or the other dies, and they are well off financially, they *might* want to reduce their life insurance coverage, or not take out a policy in the first place. But don't forget possible capital gains and the tax consequences of dying. Insurance can help pay these liabilities.

If you do some number crunching here and see that you can do without your term life policy, all you have to do is notify the company that you are cancelling and not continuing payments. Dropping a cash value policy is more complicated, because while those policies are part death benefit, they are also part savings. Check with your financial planner or accountant to see if this is a wise step for you. If you are in poor health, for instance, it might be wise to keep the policy in effect. You could be considered uninsurable if you go to purchase another one some day.

Think about it, though. You pay a reasonably small amount in premiums for insurance, and the return on this investment can be very large. In Al's case, for example, so far he has invested approximately $5,000 in premiums, but his policy will pay his wife over $350,000 when he dies. Of course, he prefers not to think about the downside should that happen, but at least he knows the money will be there for his wife if he's not.

The Least You Need to Know

➤ Life insurance can increase your estate significantly at very little expense.

➤ Work the numbers to determine what your specific coverage should be.

➤ Term insurance is straight insurance, payable at death. While you are young, it has a low cost compared to the coverage it offers.

➤ Permanent cash value insurance is a combination of term insurance and a savings account.

➤ Insurance proceeds paid directly to your beneficiary at your death are not included in your estate when calculating probate fees.

Will You Have a Pension?

We're all certainly trying. A recent survey by the U.S. accounting firm KPMG Peat Marwick LPP found 91 percent of employers with 200 or more employees offer some kind of retirement plan. Many smaller employers have specific savings programs for workers, and some employees make contributions on their own for retirement.

Here in Canada, we look to our futures with similar concern. No one wants to rely solely on the Canada Pension Plan after retirement, but many of us have trouble saving on our own. Fortunately, a variety of pension plans have been developed, with attractive tax incentives as well. This is a complex area, but after you've read this chapter you'll better understand your own choices, and have more confidence in building savings for your—let us hope—"golden years."

Registered Pension Plans (RPPs)

A *pension plan* is simply an employee compensation program where the worker receives his or her benefits upon retirement.

What does *registered* mean in the context of pensions? That's a pension plan in which the employer can claim a tax deduction for contributing to the plan. These pension plans must be registered and comply with Revenue Canada's rules. The accumulated income and contribution will be taxed only upon distribution, which is usually a monthly payout to the employee after retirement. Those payments are *tax-deferred*, a term you'll read often in this chapter. In the context of pensions, that means taxes on that money are not due and payable until the employee has retired, when he or she will presumably be in a lower tax bracket and will have to pay less than when he or she was employed.

Quote...Unquote

Who hath so entire happiness that he is not in some part offended with the condition of his estate?

—*Boethius (AD 470–525)*

Here are the styles of qualified retirement plans I'll talk about. The two major pension programs are either a defined benefit or a defined contribution plan. Let's take them in that order.

Defined Benefit Pension Plans

The *defined benefit pension* is one in which the amount of the monthly cheque an employee will receive at retirement is specified. Defined benefits are usually calculated based on years of service and salary. So if Joan walks into her company's human resources department and asks how much she will be entitled to at retirement, the staff could do some calculations and perhaps tell her. Once vested, the promised benefit is guaranteed. That means, simply, if you meet the conditions for vesting and leave your employment, you will still get a benefit based on a benefit formula.

Joan is enrolled in a defined benefit pension plan because it clearly states her retirement income. It might have some variables, such as a cost-of-living adjustment, or a reduction equal to her Canada Pension benefit when that kicks in. But essentially Joan can count on a specific pension benefit coming to her each month at retirement.

Joan's husband will receive her pension benefits if she dies before him because she has a joint-with-survivor pension. If her husband had waived his right to that money, then her pension would be larger. But it would only have been paid during her life rather than over two people's lives.

Generally, a husband or wife has a right to at least a 50 percent survivor benefit in the other spouse's qualified pension, unless that right is waived in writing in a prescribed form. (A prenuptial agreement won't always ensure that a spouse has waived his or her pension rights.) If spouses agree to a waiver to those rights, then an employee can ask to fill out an employer waiver form, which can be picked up at his or her place of work.

Defined pension benefits are determined by a formula set out in your plan. It could be a flat rate of years of employee service or final or best compensation during your career. The employer is supposed to set aside enough money to fund your benefits, using actuarial calculations of how long you and your spouse are expected to live. There are limits to annual benefits but you probably won't have to worry about that unless you are a retiring senior executive with a Fortune 500 company—or a pro athlete.

Defined Contribution Pension Plans

In this plan the monthly benefits you receive on retirement are not defined. What is defined is the amount of the contribution that is to

> **Tip**
>
> Government employees and some others might have pension types not discussed in this chapter. If that applies to you, check with your human resources office for information about *your* retirement program. Federal and provincial public sector workers may fall under special government legislation for regulation.

> **Tip**
>
> To get information about your workplace pension plan, try your employer's human resources department or pension administrator. Your province may also have a pension commission. Information can usually be obtained without cost from your province's finance ministry or the Canada Pension Plan benefits department.

Tip

Some companies offer employees no say at all in how they invest pension funds. But yours might allow you to select the type of investment you prefer. For growth you might want a selection of stocks, while bonds could be your choice for a fixed return. Discuss your options with your financial adviser and consider a combination of different investments. Your choice will depend on factors in your personal and financial life.

be paid into the plan. It is not the amount of money you'll get out at retirement, but how much money—usually a fixed percentage of your income—you put in before retirement. In a *defined contribution pension*, benefits are based solely on the amounts contributed by the employee and employer and the account's accumulated income. Each plan participant has his or her own account, which is much like a savings account. Usually the employer makes a contribution as determined by the plan. Upon retirement, the employee's amount available for retirement living is easily determined, and usually will be reported on a semi-annual basis.

A "money purchase plan" is another name for a defined contribution pension. It is difficult to predict what pension benefit an employee will get under a "contribution plan." There is no guaranteed benefit related to earnings or years of employment. When you retire, the money in the fund is used to generate a pension benefit.

For example, Ken is employed by Medium Company. He is enrolled in a defined contribution plan and contributes four percent of his salary, which is matched by his employer. The semi-annual statement on his retirement account shows his contribution, his employer's con-

Watch Out!

If you leave your company, you are entitled to all employee contributions you made to your pension and, depending on plan vesting requirements, the employer contributions. A direct rollover payment from your ex-employer's pension to your LIRA avoids Revenue Canada's requirement of a withholding tax on the pension cheque if it is paid directly to you.

tribution and the accumulated income. Neither his nor his employer's contributions are taxed when he earns the money, nor is the accumulated income. Ken only starts paying taxes on the money when he begins receiving retirement payments.

Vesting Requirements

Vesting means you have met the particular plan's legal requirements to receive pension benefits, based on your years of service. Your benefits start at retirement age, which is usually 65. In most new plans, an employee is vested after two years of contribution. Once vested, your benefits are locked in until your plan entitles you to draw them down.

To use the jargon, you are 100 percent vested in, or own, what you contribute to that plan. If you move to another employer before you retire, you usually have options to transfer your accumulated benefits to a new plan. A "rollover" of funds into a new plan must usually be done within a specified time frame to avoid any tax penalty.

If you leave the company, the employer's contribution that is not vested remains in the pension plan. You take with you whatever you put into the plan.

Check your own retirement plan, and consult with the appropriate office at your place of employment if you have any questions.

> **Quote...Unquote**
>
> When I was young I used to think that money was the most important thing in life; now that I am old, I know it is.
>
> —*Oscar Wilde*

> **Words, Words, Words**
>
> **COLA** is not for sipping, at least not when you're speaking pension talk. It stands for Cost of Living Adjustment. Check to see if your pension plan provides automatic or periodic COLAs. Or, too bad for you, no COLAs at all.

Other Deferred Compensation Plans

Deferred Profit Sharing Plans

A *profit sharing plan* is just what it sounds like: a program where employees share in any profits the company makes. It's set up by the employer,

Watch Out

Since the retirement account in a stock bonus plan consists of the employer's company stock, there is no diversification of portfolio. With this plan, market fluctuation in that stock will have an impact on your retirement benefits. In other words, your eggs are all in one basket, and that basket is your company.

who contributes part of the company's profits to separate employee accounts, as determined by the plan. The law generally treats a profit sharing plan like a defined contribution pension. When the profit sharing plan makes a distribution to the employee, then the employee is taxed on the money he or she receives.

Stock Bonus Plans

An *employee stock ownership plan* is another type of contribution plan. The employer contributes money so employees can purchase shares of its company stock. The plan is subject to some requirements similar to a profit sharing plan. When the employee sells the stock, he or she is taxed on its value.

Other Great Ways to Save

You've got several choices if you don't have a pension plan, or you want to put away for retirement more than what your company is providing.

Registered Retirement Savings Plans (RRSPs)

The most common retirement plan available to individuals who have no employer-sponsored pension plan is the registered retirement savings plan (RRSP).

➤ Contributions can be made by deducting money automatically from your pay (through a payroll deduction plan). You're less likely to miss money you never see

➤ RRSPs can be used as a tax-deferred savings plan that has nothing to do with your retirement

➤ When you withdraw money from an RRSP, you'll be taxed on your contribution to the plan plus the accumulated earnings. But that tax is usually paid when your income bracket as a retired person is lower than it was when you were working

➤ Plan distributions can be delayed until age 69, when you may be in a lower tax bracket

Locked-In Retirement Accounts (LIRAs)

LIRAs were formerly called locked-in RRSPs. They allowed you to transfer vested benefits out of a registered pension plan to a locked-in retirement account. The funds in an LIRA are locked in and can only be used to provide a pension benefit.

There are some limitations on your choice of investment vehicles in an LIRA, which are regulated by the pension authority in each jurisdiction. If you exercise your portability rights and transfer pension benefits, the funds are tax-sheltered in an LIRA. You should allow them to grow to increase the funds available to provide you with retirement income.

Distribution must take place no later than age 69. Funds can also be used to purchase an annuity.

Individual Pension Plans (IPPs)

Individuals are eligible to receive qualified retirement benefits under an IPP. The coverage requirements, contribution limitations, and levels of taxability upon distribution are similar to defined benefit plans. The high cost of these plans tailored for a specific employee make them attractive to those with high incomes.

Is There an Annuity in Your Future?

Here's another way to save for retirement. Whether through your place of employment or on your own, you can put as much money as you like each year into an annuity. An *annuity* is an investment vehicle that brings a fixed, periodic return for a specified number of years, or for a lifetime (or, if desired, the lifetime of a spouse). The annuity grows without taxation. But the amount you deposit is not deducted from your reported earnings.

Joe purchased an annuity from an insurance company for $20,000 in 1996. The company promised him that he will receive $3,000 a year for 10 years (a fixed term), beginning in the year 2006, when he will be retired and in a lower tax bracket.

Each one of Joe's annual payments starting in 2006 will include income earned from his premium. His investment was $20,000, with an expected return of $30,000. His annual payment will be $3,000, but because $2,000 of that will be considered one-tenth of his investment, and not earnings on that investment, only $1,000 will be taxable to him each year.

The advantage of the annuity is, as you've read so often here, is to defer payment of income earned until the future, when your tax rate is likely to be less. Contrast that with Joe putting his $20,000 into a Certificate of Deposit. Each year the interest earned from the CD will be taxed, while the income from the annuity will be tax-deferred until payout begins.

Annuities are considered safe for future needs, but with limited returns. That should appeal to the conservatives out there.

Variable Annuity

You say you want something a bit more daring? There is also what is known as the *variable annuity*, which puts your principal into the stock market. Now your annuity has become as responsive to the current economy as the performance of any stock or mutual fund. And any earnings are tax-deferred.

Building Wealth at Revenue Canada's Expense

The bottom line, you are probably saying about now, is, "Just tell me how much all of this will save me."

The answer is, "Well, that will depend." For one thing, it depends upon how much you can afford to put into your retirement plan. Of course, there are limits.

The tax deductible limits for RRSP contributions are frozen until 2003 to a maximum of $13,500. How much you can contribute to a plan includes a maximum of 18 percent of your previous year's earned income after subtracting any pension adjustment if you are a member of an employer's pension plan.

Here is an example of how one employee is working her pension to her advantage.

Hope has an RRSP plan. She earns $50,000 annually, and wants to contribute 5 percent of her salary to her plan through a payroll deduction plan. Hope's taxable salary for a year will then be $47,500 ($50,000 salary minus her $2,500 salary contribution, which is 5 percent of her income). Into her RRSP goes her $2,500 contribution, which is tax-deferred. Hope has reduced her taxable income by the $2,500 she herself contributed.

When Hope retires and starts receiving distributions from her RRSP, they will be taxable, but by then she will be making less money, so her tax rate will be less.

Compare the results in Hope's RRSP account with her putting her contribution into a savings account. She would have to earn approximately $3,500, depending on her tax rate, to save $2,500 (since the savings account is funded with after-tax dollars), and any interest earned each year would be taxed. She is, therefore, saving at Revenue Canada's expense. And you would be, too, if you had an RRSP.

What you save in your retirement account is tax-deferred, and the income earned by the account is tax-deferred. I don't know about you, but I personally prefer paying taxes some time in the future—when I retire, but certainly not now!

Early Withdrawals From Your RRSP

Most of us look at our assets and see that a big chunk of money is sitting right there in a retirement plan, doing absolutely nothing. What a crime! If we are short of cash, there is the temptation to withdraw some money to pay off debts.

Quote...Unquote

Life does not begin at the moment of conception or the moment of birth. It begins when the kids leave home and the dog dies.

—Anonymous

Quote...Unquote

There are two times in a man's life when he should not speculate: when he can't afford it, and when he can.

—Mark Twain

Early withdrawals from qualified RRSPs are subject to a withholding tax. In addition, you must report the amount you withdraw to Revenue Canada as income in the year withdrawn for taxation at your individual tax rate.

Uh-Oh Department: Will Your Company Pension Be There When You Need It?

Well, we certainly hope so. During the coming few decades the baby boomers (those born between 1946 and 1964) will earn larger and larger incomes, rack up more years with their company and, as all of us must, approach retirement. Employers will have to make larger and larger contributions to their pension funds. Some experts fear that some companies will cancel that benefit when faced with the increased amount they must spend.

"Gee," you say, "Can they do that?" Yes, I'm afraid they can. A company does not have to file for bankruptcy, or even be in financial trouble, to justify terminating its pension plan. Most companies replace it with some form of employee contribution plan.

Quote...Unquote

Those who work too much do not work hard.

—*Henry David Thoreau*

Whatever the future holds for you—and your company—your pension is probably safe, although its benefits might be frozen at the date the plan was terminated.

Nailbiting about Canada Pension and whether *that* system will be around for us when we retire should get all of us busy putting away as much as we can in savings and investments. Just in case.

The Least You Need to Know

➤ A company retirement plan can sometimes be tailored to fit your own particular needs.

➤ If your company does not provide a pension, you can set up your own RRSP or non-tax-deferred savings plan.

➤ Money you put into your RRSP doesn't get taxed until it's distributed to you at retirement, when you'll probably be in a lower tax
bracket.

➤ Your company pension will probably be alive and well when you
hit retirement age, but it still makes lots of sense to save as much
as you can on your own.

Chapter 6

Got Your Own Business? Then This One's for You

In This Chapter

➤ In business by yourself?

➤ When others are involved

➤ Tax savings

➤ The importance of a buy–sell agreement

This chapter is for you if you own a business, or perhaps are considering starting one. Your choice of entity—how you set yourself up to conduct that business—is important. It can impact the success of your enterprise tax-wise. And it can affect your estate as well, as you will see in the explanations and tips woven throughout the next several pages.

What we'll talk about first is how you might choose to set up shop (or office, plant, shopping mall kiosk, etc.). You have several choices.

Sole Proprietor

If you are the only owner, with no partners or anyone else in the picture, that makes you what is known as the *sole proprietor*. That means you are personally responsible for your business's debts and all of its income (or losses). If the business is profitable, you include the net income in your personal tax. If the business incurs losses, they can be used to offset other sources of income.

A sole proprietorship is easy to set up because most provinces only have a few legal requirements to get started. Well, all right, there are a few exceptions. For example, if you are opening a store, you will need a retail merchant's licence, and some other professions might call for a local licence. Someone like Harry, who is carrying on business (c.o.b.) as Harry's House of Wicker, must register his business stating his c.o.b. name so that the public knows who is the owner behind that store.

> **Watch Out!**
>
> Better check the name you want to give your business with your provincial business registrar's office. Duplicates are not allowed within a province, so if the name you want is taken, it's back to the drawing board to come up with something else.

However, as a lawyer I don't have to secure anything from city or town hall to start my business, and many other enterprises don't either.

Of course if you have anyone on your payroll then you must follow the reporting requirements of Revenue Canada and meet provincial employment standards.

If it is simple to set up a business in this manner, it's as easy to exit one. Just take down your sign. There is usually nothing to file with any agency.

If you die while owning your business, that asset is treated like any other. It goes into your will, passed on to whomever you choose. (That individual won't personally be obligated for any business debt, but the estate will be. That means the business debt will have to be satisfied before any distribution of assets is made to heirs.)

The Buddy System: A Partnership

Let's say you and two or more associates co-own your business. If you haven't incorporated, you probably are a partnership, whether or not you have a formal partnership agreement. A *partnership* is a recognized form of business ownership in which who owns what and how much is set out in the partnership pact. That agreement controls each partner's share of the profits or losses, assets, and management. If there is no agreement, then each partner has an equal interest in those profits and losses and in management decisions.

Violet, Rip, and Mark have joined forces to become partners in a detective agency. They have no specific partnership agreement. Each contributed $5,000 to set up the agency. Therefore, each partner, according to the law, has an equal share in the profits and losses, and an equal voice in management decisions. Each has his or her $5,000 capital contribution on the partnership books.

Let's say the partnership computed its net income for 1997, which was $21,000. Since each partner has an equal share in the profits, each will report $7,000 income on his or her personal income tax return.

This trio should have a specific written agreement, particularly if they want to divide profits or losses or management *unequally.* For example, Rip runs the partnership into $15,000 of debt by buying expensive disguises. Unless they have such an agreement, each partner will have to contribute $5,000 to the partnership so that $15,000 debt can be paid. It is not just Rip's bill.

Breaking Up: Hard to Do?

Our detectives might dissolve the partnership for several reasons: the death or retirement of a partner, consensus termination, or involuntary termination by a court. Usually the latter involves bankruptcy.

In this case Mark, while on a stake-out, chokes while eating a doughnut and dies. Since the partnership has no agreement, it has to terminate business, pay its creditors, then distribute any balance left to Violet, to Rip, and to Mark's estate. If they had a partnership agreement, then it could have provided that the business would continue on the death or retirement of a partner. It could also contain clauses for the selection of Mark's successor.

If you die while in a partnership, your partners are likely to buy out your share in the business, sometimes with periodic payments to whoever inherits from you. That comes from their having a buy–sell agreement, which I'll describe in detail later in this chapter.

Another Style

Also under the partnership umbrella is a *limited partnership*. This type of partnership involves two types of owners: general partners, who are personally liable for the business debts, and limited partners, who are not. The general partner runs the entity.

General and limited partners are taxed on the business income or take its losses, subject to some tax restrictions.

Are You the Corporate Type?

Many small businesses incorporate. Most do so because incorporating makes the business, rather than the owners, liable for its debts.

A *corporation* is a separate legal entity, owned by its shareholders, with policy set by a board of directors and managed by the officers. There can be one shareholder (you), or as many as there are in Canada's largest corporations. The corporation is liable for its debts unless the shareholders personally guarantee a corporate obligation.

In most provinces, forming a corporation is pretty simple. You prepare a form called Articles of Incorporation, which you can get from a legal stationer, and then file the document with the government's corporate registrar. If you are setting up a one-shareholder corporation, you can probably fill out the form and obtain and prepare any other corporation documents needed. You should at least have a lawyer review your work to make sure it is properly prepared.

Corporate Tax Advantages

There are several tax pluses to incorporating. The first is that income splitting may be achieved by having shares owned by family members who use their own money to acquire them. Therefore, dividends paid or capital gains realized are not subject to the attribution rules.

The second is that the corporation may benefit from a low rate of tax (approximately 22 percent in Ontario) on $200,000 of active business income, which is income other than dividend, interest or other income from passive activities.

The third tax plus is the benefit obtained if the shares are disposed of and a capital gain is realized. Provided the rules are met, the shares

Tip

Always have a lawyer prepare corporate papers when there are two or more people involved. Disputes can arise later, so you need to ensure proper documentation.

Quote...Unquote

How happy the life unembarrassed by the cares of business!

—*Publilius Syrus*
(circa 42 BC)

Tip

Provincial laws on business entities vary. Always consider where you will be carrying on business, because some provinces require that you have an extra-provincial licence to operate. You may want to investigate the advantages of incorporating a federal corporation.

owned by individuals may qualify for a lifetime capital gains deduction of $500,000. That means that the tax on $375,000 of taxable capital gains can be avoided. If the individual taxpayer is in the 50 percent tax bracket, the saving is approximately $180,000.

There are complex rules associated with eligibility for the $500,000 lifetime capital gains deduction as well as planning opportunities. Accordingly, the advice of your professional tax adviser should be sought.

Mike and Sharon have decided to form a corporation as consultants for TV and radio stations. The Articles of Incorporation are filed, by-laws are drawn up, and the shareholder and board of directors' minutes are recorded. The stock is issued: 49 shares to Mike, and 51 shares to Sharon. Since Sharon has control of this business, Mike will probably want a contract detailing his employment and other rights in the corporation.

If you are terminating a corporation, most provinces require you to file an Articles of Dissolution form with the provincial corporation branch.

If you die while part of a corporation, what happens? Well, your fellow owners will consult *their* buy–sell agreement (which was mentioned in an earlier section on partnerships and will be described in more detail shortly). Your share of the corporation is represented by stock, which is now considered part of your estate.

The buy–sell agreement may require the corporation to buy a deceased's share, perhaps with funding from a life insurance policy. Proceeds, of course, go to your heir(s).

Here is a chart that can help you differentiate among these various ownership styles at a glance.

COMPARISON OF BUSINESS ENTITIES

FACTOR	PARTNERSHIP	CORPORATION	PROPRIETOR
Owner	Partners	Shareholders	Sole-Proprietor
Formation (setting up)	Agreement	Articles of Incorporation	Business name registration
Liability for business debts	Partners liable	Shareholders not liable	Individual liable for business debts
Income and deductions for tax	Partners	Corporation	Individual
Division of Individual	Agreement	Dividends based on stock ownership	Individual
Tax Loss Deduction	Partner, with limitations	Corporation, with limitations	individual, with limitations
Limits on ownership	Agreement	Number of shareholders restricted by Articles of Incorporation	Individual
Transfer of interest	On Partner approval	Usually freely transferable except if stock restriction agreement	Individual
Continuity of life of business	See Partnership Agreement	See Operating Agreement	Ends with individual
Gain on sale	Capital and ordinary	Capital	Capital & ordinary
Management	Partners	Board of directors	Individual

Even More Tax Talk

You have seen some tax consequences for you in selecting a business entity. Naturally, you will want to consider all the tax ramifications of setting up your organization.

Tax-Free Formation

Sole proprietorships, partnerships and corporations are formed without incurring a tax when established.

Reporting to Revenue Canada

The sole proprietor reports income (or loss) on his or her personal tax return. Partners calculate the income or loss of the operating business at the partnership level. Then it is allocated to the partner's account to share and be reported on each of their personal tax returns. The partners are taxed at rates for individuals.

The corporation reports its income (or loss) on a corporate tax return, and pays a tax on income. The corporation shareholders only report dividends received from the corporation on his or her personal return.

Partnerships and limited liability partnerships report passed-through income as being of the same "character"—that is, ordinary income or capital gain—as its source. For example, capital gain created by a partnership will be passed through to the partners as capital gain.

Briefs

A little boy looked up at his father and asked, "Papa, what does it mean, 'business ethics'?"

"Well," explained the father, a merchant, "It's like this. A man comes into the store and makes a purchase. He gives me a clean, new, five-dollar bill, which is just the right amount. He starts to leave the store. I'm turning to the cash register when I discover that it's not one, it's *two* five-dollar bills stuck together. Now comes the business ethics—should I tell my partner?"

To sum up, only the corporation pays its taxes, not its shareholders (except on dividends received). All the other owners report and pay income taxes on their share of the entity's income.

Why a Buy-Sell Agreement Is Vital

Ah, now we come to that buy–sell pact, which is also called a shareholders' agreement.

Whether you are nearing retirement or just starting out, you ought to have a plan for succession upon your death, disability or that longed-for retirement. Your work is a valuable asset, probably more so as a going business than just the sum of its assets.

Every partnership, limited liability partnership, and multi-shareholder corporation should have a *buy–sell agreement*. This is a contract among the business owners that usually (1) restricts transfer of each owner's interest and (2) provides a procedure to purchase an owner's interest upon death, disability or other departure.

The agreement keeps ownership among the original owners, unless they want to allow in new people. The old group may be relatively compatible; a newcomer is an unknown quantity.

The agreement also provides a means of "cashing out," or paying those who no longer want to own the company or who have become disabled. A buyout—perhaps through a life insurance policy—can also step in to pay the estate of a deceased owner for his or her share of the business, or pay a disabled owner.

Usually the *buy–sell* agreement provides for annual payments to a retiring owner over several years.

If you and your co-owners do not have a *buy–sell* pact, you are courting disaster, particularly if the death of an owner is involved. The deceased's heirs may need money right away, which may not be available if he or she has not planned for that possibility.

Tip

Any business, sole proprietorship, partnership or corporation provides an opportunity for income splitting to reduce taxes if a family member is legitimately employed by the business.

Remember: Time Marches On

Many owners select one form of ownership style, go on to do business and forget about that setup. That's not a good idea. Their choice might always be the best one for them, but then again, maybe it won't. Decisions made initially in a business do not have to last forever. Indeed, some of them should be revised somewhere along the way.

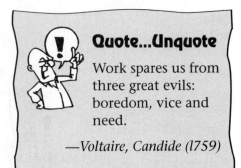

Quote...Unquote

Work spares us from three great evils: boredom, vice and need.

—*Voltaire, Candide (1759)*

A business is a living, evolving entity. Tax and business laws are constantly changing, too. When it's your business, consult your accountant and lawyer every few years to be certain the ownership style you have chosen is still the most beneficial for you.

Will, Evan, Jeff and Carlos have gone the partnership route with their marina. They are concerned about personal liability for business debts, but they like the pass-through tax aspect of partnership. They might want to consider changing to a corporation, which eliminates personal liability.

Treating Yourself Well as the Key Employee

Indeed, if you aren't good to yourself, who will be? Here are some points to consider with a growing business.

The key employee is you, the owner. You can only improve your financial picture by either increasing your income or lowering your expenses. But you may be able to add more fringe benefits. Discuss benefits with your accountant, who will be able to help you determine if you can afford them. Many on the list list below are tax free, and all are quite good at making a weary businessperson feel a little more prosperous and coddled. Some will make your employees feel better taken care of, too.

➤ group term life insurance

➤ medical and dental insurance

➤ business-related entertainment

➤ tax-sheltered retirement plan

➤ cafeteria plan of benefits (employees select what they want and can afford)

Watch Out!

Want to operate your business from home? Many munici-
palities have zoning bylaws that prohibit home businesses
in some neighbourhoods. Often those laws are directed at
the obvious: converting the front of a home to a shop, for
example. Keep in mind any exterior alterations and parking spaces
you will need. You might have to apply for a zoning variance—and
you could be turned down.

➤ use of corporately-owned or leased
vehicles

➤ disability insurance

When You Want to Sell

When the time comes to sell your business, your choice of entity will make a
difference, tax and otherwise.

➤ As a *sole proprietor*, you're simply
selling individual assets, and the
classification of gain or loss depends
on the nature of the assets. Capital
assets, such as land, create capital
gains, and ordinary income assets,
such as inventory, create ordinary
income.

Drew and Elsa, for example, are
partners in a business selling art works.
The art is inventory, which results in
ordinary income, while the building
that the partnership owns and sells at an
amount over its original cost is a capital
gain. When the two sell their business
assets, part of the sale will result in ordinary income, and part will be capital gain.

Quote...Unquote

Some will rob you
with a six gun/
And some with a
fountain pen.

—*Woody Guthrie,*
"Pretty Boy Floyd"

Quote...Unquote

Perpetual devotion
to what a man calls
his business, is only
to be sustained by perpetual
neglect of many other
things.

—*Robert Louis Stevenson*
(1850–94)

➤ *Corporate shareholders* own a capital asset—their stock—so when it is sold, they have a capital gain.

Taking a Broad View

For your information now, and your plans for a future that might be years down the road, sit back and do a little thinking about these aspects of your work, keeping in mind what you have just read.

➤ *Analyze the current status of the business.* Most have a life cycle: beginning, turning the corner, and maturity. The business likely will be less valuable and have significant debt at the beginning. When it turns the corner and starts becoming profitable then its value increases, although the debt may still be considerable if the business is expanding. The mature business is profitable and thus attractive to others.

Where is *your* business at this point? Ask yourself again when you are considering retiring or selling. And ask yourself when you are putting together an estate plan. What would happen to the business, and your heirs, if you were to die suddenly?

➤ *Consider the cash value of the business.* It could be at a stage where you may have few purchasers for it, and it also could be valuable only if *you* are able to run it. Again, you need life insurance and disability insurance to provide an adequate estate for your family. If there are purchasers willing to pay its fair market value, and you are ready to retire or sell, then less insurance may be needed.

➤ *Review your buy–sell and other business arrangements, if you have co-owners.* Your heirs may not want to continue owning a share of the business after your death, so a plan to "cash out" your interest upon death should be an ingredient of your estate plan.

➤ *If you have a family business, plan for an orderly transfer of ownership when you want to retire.* Your retirement funds might come

Tip

If you would like to ease into retirement and start letting your successor take over, it is likely he or she will want some ownership interest in your business. A corporation may issue shares to the successor. A partnership could increase its number of partners and rearrange profit sharing to accommodate him or her.

from your withdrawal from the business. You may be able to restructure the business ownership to provide for a gradual withdrawal, with the minimum of adverse tax consequences.

Talk over all of your prospective business moves with the appropriate members of your estate planning team—certainly your accountant and lawyer.

Keep in mind your will, trust and other estate planning documents may be virtually useless if you haven't considered how best to arrange your business to maximize your estate while minimizing taxes. This is the "bottom line." I'm afraid it gives you plenty of work to do, but it's time and energy worth investing.

Finally, there are suggestions specifically for physicians, accountants, lawyers, and other professionals licensed by the province and in business for themselves, and for those engaged in farming, in Chapter 14.

Tip

Family corporations can restructure stock ownership to create a new class of stock for the retiring owner. Consult your corporate lawyer for the best means of doing this.

The Least You Need to Know

➤ You have several choices of business entities to choose from; study the legal ramifications of each carefully.

➤ Examine your pay and fringe benefits because you, the owner/employee, may be missing some tax-free benefits you could have at little cost to you.

➤ If you and another person, or several other people, are in business together, then sign a *buy–sell* agreement to protect yourself and the business.

➤ Always keep in mind your business's current status, and how it figures in a typical business cycle.

PART 2
About Wills, Trusts... and Probate

Now we come—ta-da—to one of the most important parts of this book. In the pages that follow you'll learn all about what should go into your will, and you'll see how to examine your family and financial situation so that you can prepare a solid document. You say you've never heard of a trust, at least not for those who don't have incomes somewhere up there in the stratosphere? You may be surprised to find that not only is that not true, but also that a trust is just what you need right now. Or, perhaps not right at the moment, but that it is something to consider down the road, when you've built up your assets a bit more.

Probate is what happens to your will once your heirs have it in hand and turn it over to the courts to be acknowledged as your last will and testament. Probate is an interesting, and to many mysterious, process that transfers your assets from your estate to your heirs or beneficiaries. What exactly goes on here? I'll tell you. The mystery will be gone, but I'll replace it with a few interesting, sometimes quirky, probate stories.

Chapter 7

No Will? No Good!

In This Chapter

➤ How your property is distributed

➤ Guardians for minor children

➤ Who administers your estate

➤ Remarriage and children

If you're with me so far you're making good progress in your planning. You have just analyzed and recorded what you own and how you own it, in the process getting a clear idea of exactly what constitutes your estate. We're coming soon to one of the most important parts of this book—having a will prepared.

Are you at all reluctant about making your will, perhaps because you're put off by all the decisions and details that it entails, or maybe because you just don't like to even *think* about the inevitable? You're not alone; many people feel that way. But by the end of this chapter, I guarantee you'll feel differently.

As you will see, when you don't have a will things can get pretty sticky, with a string of complications that could someday, if you'll excuse the expression, have you turning in your grave.

Dying Intestate Is About As Bad As It Sounds

If you do not have a will when you die (that's what dying "intestate" means), you may have given your family another reason to mourn your loss. Without a will they must turn to provincial statutes to determine who your heirs are and how much of a share in your estate they are entitled to inherit. The state poking its nose into your family affairs? Yes indeed, that's exactly what it will do, down to your last penny.

Watch Out

Just as bad as having no will is having an outdated one. If there has been a marriage, death, birth, or maybe a divorce or two in your family since you wrote yours, then get thee to a lawyer for a new one.

When you don't get around to making a will, you give up the right to:

➤ select the beneficiaries of your estate

➤ make gifts to close friends

➤ name the executor of your estate

➤ designate a guardian for your minor child

Here are a few other complications you may leave behind if you die intestate. All will be covered in depth in upcoming chapters.

➤ Federal income taxes could be higher

➤ Savings may be lost

➤ Probate expenses will be higher

Ah, Probate

There's that word you often hear in the same breath with "wills" and "estates." It's usually said with a shudder. What does it mean, and can it really be that terrible?

Probate is commonly referred to as a court procedure to administer a deceased person's estate. Legally speaking, probate only describes estates with wills. If you die intestate, without a will, your estate is not probated but administered by a court-appointed administrator.

Most people are familiar with the term probate. I will use "probate" to describe the court process to administer an estate's assets whether the deceased died with or without a will.

The laws are designed to apportion your estate according to your own wishes if you have a will, or according to how the state sees fit if you don't. Naturally, the law ensures that your creditors are satisfied and that any legitimate taxes due on your estate are paid before assets are disbursed to your family and friends.

If an individual dies with a will, the presumed beneficiaries bring it to the estate court. They apply for "letters of probate" confirming the will. If a person dies intestate, again heirs come in, this time with a list of the deceased's assets that comprise the estate, in order to begin administration. In Ontario, they file an "application for a certificate of appointment of estate trustee *without a will*." In some provinces this application is called "letters of administration." This is a simple form that contains information needed by the court, such as the name and address of the deceased, and names and addresses of relatives and likely heirs.

Most times the family member or other individual wishing to settle an intestate estate through administration must post a bond, to cover any loss to the estate caused by their negligence or malfeasance. That might be, oh, let's say a bond of $100,000, for which the executor might pay a fee, or a premium, of maybe $500 a year until the estate is settled (and most estates are settled within 12 and 24 months because of tax clearances). That cost varies, however. The executor would go to a local insurance company that has bonding power to purchase the bond, and then would return with it to the court. The premium cost comes out of the estate, not the administrator's pocket.

(You'll find out more about probate in Chapter 10. I thought you needed to know a little about the process right now, in the context of dying intestate.)

Estate Exceptions

There seems to be an exception to almost every explanation. There is one with probate, too.

A *probate estate* is defined as property distributed by a court-supervised process. This includes assets that pass by will (or, as I explained, "intestate" laws), which are subject to court filing or probate fees. But there is property that *doesn't* go through probate. That's what you own jointly with right of survivorship, which I discussed in Chapter 3. Also, if you have a life insurance policy, a pension fund or other investments with a named beneficiary, or jointly-owned assets, then those assets are part of your estate but they also skip probate and go directly to the person named.

As a matter of fact, what with the above-named exclusions, sometimes there is little that *is* subject to probate these days. That might be done on purpose by the deceased, to avoid having his or her heirs spend time and money in probate court. Sometimes, though, it's just a coincidence on the part of the deceased.

Speaking of heirs, I'll digress a little here for a brief explanation. Technically, the word *"heirs"* is used for those who inherit in an intestate estate, *"beneficiaries"* for those who inherit from a legitimate will. Sometimes the terms are used interchangeably. I'll try to keep them separate throughout these pages, but once in a while you'll probably find I've just used one word or the other. Also, although probate legally only refers to estates with a will, I'll refer to probate fees to describe the estate court fees that are levied to administer estates even if there is no will. You cannot avoid "probate or estate court fees" by not having a will. Chapter 19, Probate Fees, looks at specific probate-saving techniques.

How the State Determines Your Heirs

Once your assets—minus a will—land in estate court, the process of settling the estate begins. Here is an example of how that court might proceed, again noting there are slight differences among provinces.

Let's use a typical family as an example. Albert is married to Susan. They have three adult children: Ken, Betty and Clark. Ken has one child, Alice; Betty has no children; Clark has two, Chloe and Charity. Albert's father is deceased, but his mother is alive.

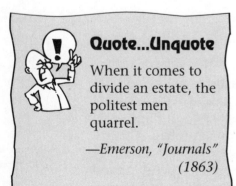

Quote...Unquote

When it comes to divide an estate, the politest men quarrel.

—*Emerson, "Journals" (1863)*

Albert dies without a will. Who inherits his intestate estate?

Albert's spouse, Susan, receives a specified amount of money from the estate. This amount is referred to as the preferential share and it varies in each province. Then the rest of the estate is divided between Susan and each of their three children.

In Ontario, for example, Susan's preferential spousal share is the first $200,000 from the estate, after all debts are paid. If there is anything left over after the preferential share goes to a spouse, it is divided as follows:

➤ if Albert only had one child, one half would go to his spouse and the other half to his child.

➤ if he had more than one child, one third would go to his spouse and the other two thirds would be divided among his children.

Albert's mother and his grandchildren would receive nothing.

If there is no surviving spouse, but there are children, then the children receive the entire probate estate. The court also appoints a guardian for minors and administers their funds. Wouldn't you prefer to have someone you know do this for your children?

Grandchildren inherit their deceased parent's share. So if Clark were deceased at the time of Albert's death, his two girls, Chloe and Charity, would inherit Clark's share of his father's estate.

➤ If Albert were single—leaving no surviving spouse and no surviving children—then most provincial intestate laws would divide the estate between his parents. If the parents are deceased, then it would be divided just among his siblings. If Albert had no brothers or sisters, the estate could be divided among his grandparents, if they are living, and his aunts, uncles and cousins.

➤ If Albert had no spouse, no children and no next of kin his estate would become the property of the Crown.

➤ If Albert were single but had been in a 10-year relationship with Lee, then since Albert died without a will Lee would come in for no portion at all of Albert's estate. (There is more about relationships outside of marriage in Chapter 14.)

If you're preparing a will, you can apply all of the above family situations to your own position and discuss with your lawyer just who you want your heirs to be.

The State Specifies the Guardian, Too

If you have minor children (under the age of 18) and your spouse survives you, then you won't need a guardian. However, if the other parent is not alive, or is not capable of caring for a minor child or a child of any age with special needs, then a guardian is necessary for them if you die.

Naturally, parents of young children should appoint a guardian for them in the event they both die at the same time. Naming a guardian is especially important in a one-parent situation.

Let's consider Jane's situation. It is a potential guardianship nightmare because there is no will. Her husband passed away several years ago. Jane has two minor children, Jason and Joan, both in their early teens. Since Jane doesn't have a will designating who will be guardian, then provincial law takes over.

Whom would the court appoint? Well, the children's grandparents or aunts and uncles are usually in line for that appointment. If they agree on who will care for the child, fine. But if they cannot, then a court battle may ensue.

It's bad enough to have relatives fighting over child custody. Worse yet is when *no* family member wants the child or children. Perhaps both sets of grandparents in Jane's situation define their golden years as not including child rearing. And Jane's siblings might have children of their own and say, quite frankly, that they don't want to be responsible right now for a couple of teenagers.

What happens then?

Jane could have a close friend who would be competent and quite capable and willing to serve as guardian. But the friend might not be able to take on that role without being nominated in Jane's will. Can Jane's kids recommend that friend? Sure, and since they are older children, the judge is likely to listen to their recommendation and seriously consider that nominee.

But if there is absolutely no one to take Jane's kids—and surely if the situation became that desperate one would hope that a set of grandparents or a sibling would step forward—the kids become wards of the

Crown, and are then placed in foster homes. They are, after all, orphans.

If you have a will, name a primary and an alternate guardian to be sure that one will serve. Always get that family member's or friend's permission before naming him or her as guardian. A person is not required to serve as a guardian just because you name them in your will.

You can see that a will matters with property, but that it is absolutely vital when it comes to the welfare of your children. You will read more about guardians when I talk specifically about kids and your estate in Chapter 12.

Watch Out!

It's trendy, but is it legal? Only in some American jurisdictions can you shoot a video will, which is a videocassette recording of a person reading his will out loud—and probably making comments throughout. But remember, in Canada a will must always be in writing. No "shooting" allowed.

The Administrator: It Could Be a Stranger

The *executor* or *estate trustee* is a person nominated in a will to handle the disposition of that property according to the wishes of the deceased. We'll get into that role in more detail in Chapter 10.

The *administrator* of an estate is an individual appointed by the probate court to handle that function for the deceased who dies intestate.

While you are apt to ask a relative or friend to be your executor, if you die without a will there could be a stranger handling your estate and dealing with your family on estate-related, certainly personal, matters. The judge has quite a bit of leeway in appointing an administrator, and could name a person you consider inappropriate to that position.

The executor or administrator is usually paid for his or her services. Fees run quite a wide range. I hesitate to offer even a ballpark figure, because so much

Tip

Here's another good news/bad news reason for having a will. The good news: If you die in an accident of some kind, a court could bring in a sizable judgment, payable to your estate. You'd certainly want that money to go to specific loved ones. (The bad news? You're not around, of course, to enjoy the windfall.)

depends on the size of the estate and the amount of work facing the administrator. But I'd say that fee could perhaps be as much as 5 percent of the estate's worth. It is paid from the estate before any part of it is disbursed to heirs.

The administrator handles the paperwork of an estate, such as composing a list of the deceased's assets, hearing from likely heirs, processing claims from creditors, and the like.

Divorce, Remarriage—and No Will

There are complications here, too, as you might imagine.

Consider Hank and Wanda. The couple are legally married and both work outside the home.

Wanda had been previously married and has one child from that union, Willie, who is under 18. Hank likewise had an earlier marriage, and he has two minor children: Hank Jr. and Karen. Hank and Wanda together have one minor child, Holly.

Wanda has custody of Willie; Hank does not have custody of his children from the prior marriage.

Wanda dies suddenly. She does not have a will. Let's look at possible consequences:

➤ **Inheritance** Wanda owned the house where she and Hank lived. She had a substantial investment in stocks and bonds in her own name. All of this is part of her probate estate. What happens to that property?

In Ontario, for example, the surviving spouse, Hank, will have to divide ownership of the house and investments with Wanda's child of her previous marriage, Willie, and Hank and Wanda's daughter, Holly, as follows: Hank receives his preferential spousal share of $200,000 and then divides the remainder: one third of the balance for himself and two thirds for the two children.

Whether Hank can continue living in the house is a question; he may have to pay rent to the children for their share, or the estate may have to sell the house. Is this what Wanda would have wanted?

➤ **Estate Administration** The surviving spouse is usually, but not always, appointed administrator. If Hank is named to that position, it's very likely his administration will be closely scrutinized by the children's legal representative. If they are underage, each province appoints a "Children's Lawyer" or "Official Guardian" to protect their interests. Because of a potential conflict there, estate expenses could be considerably higher than they would have been if Wanda had had that will.

➤ **Guardianship** Hank and Wanda's child will have Hank around to serve as her guardian. Wanda's son from her prior marriage may have his father appointed as guardian. If the father has been out of Willie's life for years, that may not be a viable option. Hank could be the seemingly likely choice, but he might not be chosen by the court, which could favour the biological father. This could be quite a lengthy, even messy, issue.

An additional worry: The guardian normally manages the minor's money until he or she is 18 years old. What if Wanda's previous spouse had made a career of maxing out credit cards?

➤ **Income Taxes** The tax situation can be worse for Wanda's estate since she has no will. We'll get into tax unpleasantries in detail in Part IV of this book.

➤ **Simultaneous Death of Spouses** Finally, we must consider what could happen if both Hank and Wanda died at the same time—in a boating accident, say, or a car or plane crash. Of course, neither has a will. All of the problems we just discussed remain, or are magnified. Now we also have an orphan—their child, Holly.

The intestacy rules would likely split the house and investments that Wanda owned solely as follows: one half to Willie and one half to Holly.

Any property that Hank owned solely at his death (which in this example is simultaneous with Wanda's, remember) would likely be shared by Hank Jr., Karen

> **Tip**
>
> A written (or typed or computer-printed) witnessed will is best. However, some provinces recognize a holographic will—handwritten, dated, signed and unwitnessed. Using will forms with blanks that can be filled in is not likely to be useful if you have a large or complicated estate. Also, problems can occur if the document is not filled out and witnessed properly. Check with a lawyer to be sure what you have in mind is acceptable.

Watch Out

Stepchildren have no inheritance rights under state intestacy laws. Children inherit from you if you are their biological parent or adoptive parent. If you want to make provisions for your stepchildren, that's another good reason for making a will.

and Holly. However, those children may or may not have a claim for child support from the estate during the rest of their minority, so they may be in financial distress. Children in some provinces can make a claim for child support from an estate, sometimes until they are 18, sometimes up to age 21, which can include university expenses. Naturally, Wanda's son Willie could make the same claim against Wanda's estate.

Any property the couple owned jointly as spousal property would be equally divided and put into each estate.

For example, Hank's estate would be distributed this way: one third each to Hank Jr. and Karen (children of a previous marriage) and one third to Holly (child of a current marriage).

Wanda's estate would be divided equally between Willie and Holly.

You'll learn more about simultaneous death of spouses, both with and without a will, in Chapter 11.

Adoption

Adopted children inherit from their adoptive parents. In most provinces the adopted child will not automatically inherit through the biological parent, unless that parent is married to the adoptive parent.

So let's look at Ali, who adopted Kim, the daughter of his wife, Tracy, from a prior marriage. He and Tracy have a child of their own from their marriage, a son, Cory. Ali has no will. If he dies, his estate in Ontario will be divided like this: preferential share to his wife and then one third to his wife and two thirds divided equally between the adopted child (Kim) and the biological child (Cory). If he had not adopted Kim, she would have received nothing from his estate.

And Children Born Out of a Legal Marriage

Child support, survivor's rights and inheritance are but a few heavy legal issues swirling around these youngsters.

Clearly, a child born out of wedlock can inherit automatically from his or her mother. What is less certain is the child's inheritance (not to mention support) rights from the father.

A child may inherit from the father if paternity is established in court or the father marries the mother and acknowledges the child born out of wedlock as his child.

A *paternity suit* is a court action to have it acknowledged that a man is the father of a specified child and, usually, to secure financial support for that child from that father.

Paternity actions require the assistance of the mother, who is often reluctant to bring the lawsuit for a variety of reasons. The mother may deem the father unfit to fulfill his parental role, or the father could simply have left the scene. If a paternity action is initiated, today's genetic tests can determine whether that man is the biological father.

If there is no paternity action or marriage between the biological parents then the child will not be able to inherit automatically from the father or the father's parents without a will.

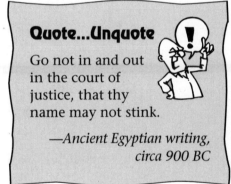

Quote...Unquote

Go not in and out in the court of justice, that thy name may not stink.

—*Ancient Egyptian writing, circa 900 BC*

Have I motivated—or perhaps scared—you into writing a will yet? Good. Now you're ready for the next chapter, in which I'll explain to you just how to go about it.

The Least You Need to Know

➤ If you die without a will, provincial law specifies who inherits your property, which passes through your estate.

➤ If you are married when you die and you have no will, your spouse will usually receive a preferential share of your estate and then share the remainder with your children.

➤ The court appoints an estate administrator and a guardian for your children if you have no will.

➤ Adopted children do inherit automatically from their adoptive parent, but stepchildren do not when there is no will.

Chapter 8

The Basic Will, and a Few Extras

In This Chapter

➤ Identifying yourself

➤ Bills and taxes get paid first

➤ How to determine who gets what

➤ Avoiding snags

Now we come to the most important element of your estate plan: your will. Here you will decide (a) who will inherit your property (beneficiaries); (b) who will administer your estate (executor); and (c) who will take care of your children (guardian).

For the person with an average estate and a rather uncomplicated business and family life, this is not difficult work, and the document needn't be long, as you'll see. Short, but important. Let's start.

First, Do You Know Where You Live?

That's certainly a silly question. Or is it? Some of you might have a home here and another one there, perhaps a vacation home—or two.

For purposes of your will, you must clearly designate your legal residence. That is likely to be your voting address, where you have your driver's licence and where you file tax returns. It is important to use that address—and have evidence backing it up in the form of those documents—to determine the province where your will will be submitted to probate court administration.

Every province has different family law requirements. It is important to know your place of domicile if you are married. Your province's family laws dictate what your spouse is entitled to under your will.

Where you live and make a will, however, does not matter when it comes to realty. Real estate investments are controlled by the laws of the jurisdiction where the land is located and not the law where the will was made. As well, your capacity to make a will and the laws allowing you to make a will are governed by the place of domicile. If you are moving to another province, you will need to have your will revised when you take up a new residence.

Incidentally, you may not know that if you own real estate in more than one province or outside the country, probate proceedings are required in that second jurisdiction to transfer title to your beneficiary. This means that if, for instance, you are a legal resident of Manitoba and have a second home, say, in Florida, probate will occur in Manitoba for all of your estate except that Florida house. There will be a limited probate, or *ancillary administration*, for the Florida property.

You should look to a Florida financial institution, or a trusted relative living in Florida, to be your ancillary executor for the property located there. A Florida bank or Florida attorney can help you.

> **Words, Words, Words**
>
> Lawyers use the word *domicile* a lot. In legal documents it means your permanent residence.

> **Tip**
>
> You can pay anywhere from around $150 to $500 and more for a will. The fee depends on how complicated the will is, the time spent and the price range and experience of your lawyer.

The Simple Will

It helps to see what's being described in text, so on the next few pages I've reproduced a specimen will for you to follow along with me. It's a basic, very brief document that I call "bare bones." It's for a woman who is rather typical in that she leaves everything to her next of kin, which in this case is her spouse and children. There are no other bequests.

You will see from time to time in this chapter and in a few others that I suggest clauses that should be added to any will. Heed my advice. They are not included in the will reproduced here because, as I said, this is a bare bones document just to show you what absolutely must go into a will, not necessarily what also should or could. It is not a will that you would want to copy for your own use.

I'll explain this will practically line by line so that it's crystal clear to you. Immediately following the will you'll see another document called "Affidavit of Execution." It is attached to a finished will, and I'll explain its purpose after discussing the bare bones will.

First, though, I'll issue the caution you're expecting when you come across a legal form in this book that you or anyone else can fill in: Since provincial laws to make an enforceable will vary, do not adopt this as a will form for yourself without legal advice that confirms it is valid where you live.

I haven't tried to cover Quebec's laws regarding wills and estates, which are quite different than those in other parts of Canada. If Quebec is your legal residence, consult a lawyer experienced in Quebec law.

Introduction

This seems clear enough. It introduces the name and residence of the person making the will, and—very important—revokes any prior wills and codicils by that individual. A *codicil* is an amendment to a previous will. (*A warning here*: If you begin re-arranging assets and beneficiaries in a codicil, you're running the risk of having your will challenged, or contested, by a beneficiary—or whoever. If you need to make a codicil, keep it short and simple, such as changing your executor from one person to another.) If it's much more complicated, then write a new will. Codicils (like wills) must comply with all the laws of execution of your place of domicile.

Use your legal name on your will, of course. That is the name that should appear on all of your official papers, such as deeds to real estate, stock certificates, insurance policies and the like. Problems for your

LAST WILL AND TESTAMENT OF Christine Pilar

I, Christine Pilar, of the Town of _____, in the Province of _____, do make and declare this to be my Last Will and Testament.

1. Identification and Definitions

    (a) I hereby revoke all Wills and Codicils heretofore made by me.

    (b) A beneficiary must survive me by thirty (30) days to be entitled to receive a devise.

    (c) "Issue" is to be construed as lawful lineal descendants, and includes adopted persons. Issue shall receive any devise by representation.

2. Personal Representative and Estate Trustee

    I hereby appoint _____, referring to him as my executor or estate trustee and personal representative. If he cannot serve, I appoint _____ as personal representative. I request that the personal representative serve without bond, or if a bond is required, that a minimum bond be required. My personal representative shall have all necessary powers enumerated and granted to personal representatives under the Trustee Act, and any other power that may be granted by law, to be exercised without the necessity of Court approval, as my personal representative determines to be in the best interest of the estate.

3. Debts, Expenses, Encumbrances, Taxes

    (a) I direct that my enforceable debts, illness, and funeral and administrative expenses of my estate shall be paid by my personal representative from my residuary estate. In his or her discretion, my personal representative may continue to pay any installment obligations incurred by me during my lifetime on an installment basis or may prepay any or all of such obligations in whole or in part, and my personal representative may, in his or her discretion, distribute any asset encumbered by such an obligation subject to the obligation.

    (b) I direct that all income, capital gains, gift, estate and succession duties or taxes (including interest and penalties thereon) payable by reason of my death in this or any other jurisdiction which shall be paid out of and be charged generally against my residuary estate without reimbursement from any person.

4. Specific Devises

    I devise all my personal effects and household goods, such as jewellery, clothing, furniture, furnishings, silver, books, pictures, motor and recreation vehicles to _____. If he does not survive me, I devise said property, in equal shares, to _____. If a child does not survive me, then his or her share devolves to the deceased child's issue, or if none survive me, then the share devolves, equally, to the surviving children.

5. Residuary Estate

    I devise my residuary estate to my spouse, _____. If he does not survive me, I devise my residuary estate, in equal shares, to _____. If a child does not survive me, then his or her share devolves to the deceased child's issue, or if none survive me, then the share devolves, equally, to the surviving children.

6. Miscellaneous

    If my spouse and I executed Wills at approximately the same time, this Last Will and Testament is not made pursuant to any contract or agreement with my spouse.
    I have signed this Last Will and Testament in the presence of the undersigned witnesses on this _____ day of _____, 199 ___.

    _____
    testatrix, Christine Pilar

The foregoing instrument, consisting of two typewritten pages, this included, was at (city, province) _____, this _____ day of _____, 199 ___, signed, sealed, and declared by the testatrix to be her Last Will and Testament, in our presence, and we, at her request and in her presence and in the presence of each other, have hereunto subscribed our names as attesting witnesses.

residing at _____

AFFIDAVIT OF EXECUTION
ESTATE COURT

In the matter of the Execution of the Will or Codicil of Christine Pilar

AFFIDAVIT

I, Christine Pilar, of the Town of _____, in the Province of
_____, MAKE OATH AND SAY:

1. On the _____ day of _____, 199___, I was present and saw the
    document marked as Exhibit "A" to this Affidavit executed by Christine
    Pilar.

2. Christine Pilar executed the document in the presence of myself and
    _____ of the Town of _____ in the
    Province of _____.

We were both present at the same time, and signed the document in the testator's presence as attesting witnesses.

SWORN before me at the Town of _____,

in the Province of _____,

this _____ day of _____, 199___.

_____
A Commissioner, etc.

Tip

Do you have legal fees you paid in connection with writing your will? I know what you're probably thinking now, but no, you can't deduct a lawyer's bill for preparing a will document.

Words, Words, Words

The word *testament* means a disposition, or distribution, of personal property to take place after the owner's death, according to his or her desire and direction. It is used, of course, in the expression "last will and testament."

estate *could* arise if, for example, you were to refer to yourself on a legal document as Biff Hanover instead of Barton T. Hanover.

1. Identification and Definitions

Careful identification of your beneficiaries by name and their relationship to you avoids possible confusion. Fathers and sons often have the same name as cousins. There is a boxer who has given all of his sons the same first name as his. In his will he will probably have to label them by order of birth for separate designations.

Paragraph 1(b) seems self-explanatory, until you get to the word *devise*. In legal terminology, that means "gift." The first sentence in paragraph 1(c) is understandable. But what is that legalese in the second sentence? (Could it, by chance, have been written by a lawyer?) Essentially it means that "issue" (or "children") shall receive any gifts by taking their deceased parent's share that happens to pass on to them through the will.

2. Personal Representative

Here's another section that seems pretty obvious. I'll talk more about these executors or estate trustees in Chapter 10. "My personal representative" is the executor. In an Ontario will, for example, the term used for this person is "estate trustee." Legal representative, estate trustee or executor are used interchangeably throughout this book.

3. Debts, Expenses, Encumbrances, Taxes

In Paragraph 3(a), that first sentence seems clear. "Residuary estate" means what is left in an estate after debts, taxes and other expenses are deducted and other gifts or bequests made.

Here you are asking your executor to keep paying installment bills, such as a mortgage, perhaps, until the estate is settled. Let's say you own a cabin by the water, or a cabin cruiser *in* the water. You leave it to your son. It has a financial obligation or debt, perhaps a bank loan, mortgage or other lien, against it. Your son may inherit that property subject to that mortgage or lien. If you want him to have the property free of debt, then you need to specify in your will that the estate is to pay off that debt.

Paragraph 3(b) directs that all due taxes be paid from the estate. I'll get into what those taxes are likely to be in subsequent chapters.

4. Specific Devises

Here we talk about particular gifts you want to make. This can be the almost-fun part of making a will, where you look at your possessions and, like royalty, proclaim "I bequeath my stamp collection to ..." and so on and so on. You will read more about some different kinds of specific devises later in this chapter.

Listing a current home address after the names of your beneficiaries is not necessary for family members. Believe me, if someone is in your will they'll hear about it and will be there to come forward for their bequest. Besides, people do move frequently and addresses become outdated. Friends might be another matter. If you are leaving your sterling silver tea set to a good friend, you might include her address. It will give an executor a place to start with a search, since your family might not know your friend or have kept up with her moves over the years.

Tip

You can forget about awarding a family member $1 in your will so that he or she cannot contest the document and claim the right to more. That $1 business is the legal equivalent of an old wives' tale.

Watch Out!

You can make a separate list for special gifts, to be attached to your will. It may not be legally enforceable, though. If you want valuable or specific items to go to certain individuals, then specify that in the will. Many courts do not consider the separate list part of the will, and do not allow your estate trustee to honour the list.

5. Residuary Estate

This seems pretty clear. In the third sentence, the word "devolves" means "goes to."

Remember, no one can be awarded anything from your will until your debts and taxes have been paid.

6. Miscellaneous

What does that first sentence mean? To explain briefly, it is there so that no one interprets the survivor's will as unchangeable, written with the spouse as a two-will package. Christine's spouse's will, if he has one, is a separate document. And Christine *can* write another version of her own will at any time she chooses.

Your lawyer will bring in two witnesses from his or her office. They or their spouses must not stand to inherit from the will, and they must "witness"—at the same time— your signing of the document in their presence. Witnesses do not need to read your will to sign it.

Words, Words, Words

Alas, legal terminology remains politically incorrect in some ways. For example, *executor* is used for a male in that position, *executrix* for a female. A *testatrix* is woman signing her will, a *testator* a man. For ease in reading, I'm using "executor" and, if the occasion arises, "testator" throughout this book.

Finally, here, there is the document titled "Affidavit of Execution" filed along with Christine's will. A similar form is reproduced here. It is a common page that goes along with a will these days. It avoids the need to locate witnesses to identify the signature of the deceased on the will.

How to Distribute Your Worldly Goods

In Part I you read about how to list your assets and how you own them. What you need to do now is see in black and white what property you can leave in a will, and think about exactly what you'd like to bequeath to family and friends before making out that document.

Take a look at the Estate Planning Information Sheet you prepared in Chapter 2. You know that property owned jointly with right of survivorship goes automatically to that other owner and need not be mentioned in a will. Property that names a beneficiary, like a life insurance policy, also skirts probate.

However, if you have any of the following:

➤ solely-owned property

➤ property held as tenants in common

➤ life insurance, RRSPs, pension or employee death benefits, or any similar asset with no named beneficiary

then those assets are distributed in your will. There's a worksheet on page 102 that you can fill in to help you sort out what you can bequeath, and whom you would like to receive that property. You might want to work this out in pencil—you could change your mind a few times before deciding on final dispositions.

Tip

You've read about a video will. Can you present your will out loud, just by speaking it? Not in Canada, you say! But an oral will, usually in the presence of witnesses, is recognized by a few states in the U.S. Usually it is limited to those on their deathbed, or in military service. It may dispose of personal property only, and is limited to no more than $1,000 of that property.

Who Gets What

If you are single, you will probably leave assets owned by you alone to anyone you choose—parents, siblings, a significant other, friends or charity. There is no usual "order" here.

If you are married, then you probably want your spouse to inherit, and can so specify in your will. Your children are likely to be next in line. Who receives what and in what percentage is up to you—almost. Please read Chapters 12 and 13 about spousal and family rights before finalizing your disbursements to see if the information there will affect your decisions.

How They Get It: The Specific Devise

You usually provide for the distribution of tangible personal property, such as household goods, automobiles, antiques and collectibles, tools, jewellery and sporting equipment, in the specific devise section of your will.

WILL WORKSHEET

Here's some homework. Doing it will help you see what assets you have to leave in a will and, if you bequeath them to anyone at all, whom you would choose. This is just a scratch sheet to help you in thinking about bequests, so mark it up as much as you like—and perhaps use pencil so that you can easily erase and make changes.

In column one, "Asset," you might, for example, list your condominium. In column two, you could jot down 'solely.' In the third column you might write 'no.' Then, under 'I'll leave it to:' in column four, you can name the person you'd like to inherit the property if you do not own it jointly, or if you have not already named a beneficiary.

Asset	How I own it	Does anyone automatically inherit?	I'll leave it to:

A client owned an extensive collection of Royal Doulton figurines. She bequeathed each one to a different family member or friend, a list that ran two single-spaced legal size pages. That was her prerogative, of course, and many do leave specific items that do not necessarily have monetary worth but perhaps have heirloom value. Or people might want to pass along particular mementoes to close friends.

> **Tip**
>
> If you have keepsakes or family heirlooms, consider asking your children now if they wish one day to inherit specific items that might have special meaning for them.

Specific devises may be for specific property, for a sum of money, or from a specific source. For example, you could say:

I devise my diamond wedding ring to…

I devise the sum of five hundred dollars to…

I devise one half of my Trustworthy Bank savings account to…

Often you will have several beneficiaries sharing in your specific devises, such as your adult children. You should consider how amicably they will divide that property. If you believe amicable won't enter into it, then your will should carry a provision specifying a method of selection, such as rotation among the children, with specific dollar limits for each rotation.

That could work like this. Your children, Sandy, Ginger, and Toni, are each allowed to select $1,000 worth of personal property from your estate. They can make their selection in whatever order you like, perhaps with Sandy, the oldest, going first, then Ginger, and finally Toni, the youngest, choosing. The next $1,000 worth of property is rotated, with Toni now having first dibs on the remainder of the property, with Ginger next and Sandy following her. That should keep everyone happy and not bickering over the tea towels.

Oops: When Beneficiaries Die Before You Do

You need to consider that the person given the specific devise might not survive you. The provision "I bequeath my Rolex watch to my cousin, Fay Summersby, if she survives me" is preferable to just bequeathing the watch to Fay. If you don't name an alternative to Fay, the watch will go to the beneficiary of the residue of your estate.

Ask your lawyer if your province has an *anti-lapse law,* which provides that another person will receive the specific devise from your will if the person you named did not survive you.

Here's how that works. Suppose that this list represents your family:

You and Your Spouse

Your Daughter, Debbie

Your Daughter's Child, Geraldine Carole

Your Daughter's Grandchild, Georgia Gloria

In your will you left a specific devise of your grandmother's ruby ring to your daughter, Debbie. If your daughter predeceases you and you haven't made a new will, then the anti-lapse statute would automatically provide that her child, Geraldine Carole, your granddaughter, would receive the ring.

The anti-lapse statute only applies to descendants and a brother or sister. For example, if in your will you leave me $1,000—for which I truly thank you—and if I die before you do, since my descendants aren't yours they receive nothing. If no one is alive to receive that ring, it goes to the residuary beneficiaries in the will. Most provincial statutes specify that you can exclude the operation of the anti-lapse provisions by a specific reference in your will.

Or When You No Longer Own What You've Willed

Let's leave the anti-lapse statute, and consider another potential problem with wording in a will. Let's say you leave your collection of hockey cards to your friend, Michel. But then your mother, in a cleaning frenzy, tosses them out at some point (an often-told tale of woe). Or you sell the collection to the Hockey Hall of Fame and you die without changing your will.

Common sense (not always applicable in the law!) would dictate that Michel gets nothing. Your will only distributes what you own at your death, and the cards are now long gone. But more than one court has held that the equivalent amount in cash should be distributed to that beneficiary.

You might want to put in the will the phrase "… if I own the collection at my death."

That should take care of that.

Here's still another occasion for misunderstanding. Let's suppose you want to leave "100 shares of ABC Co. to my friend, Ted Foster." In these days of mergers and business tremours, strange things have happened to corporate stock. Perhaps the best solution is to word this as follows: "I devise to Ted Foster the amount of stock I own in ABC Co., or its corporate successor, at my death." That's better.

Watch Out!

Be very careful to identify beneficiaries specifically. No one receives anything from your will unless he, she or it (such as a pet, which we'll get into later in this chapter) is named: Ian Carl Turner, Spot or your favourite charity. You can identify a person as "my child" or "my aunt" if you have only one of each, but if there are others, use the specific name and correct legal relationship.

Finally here, add up all your specific devises to determine if they significantly reduce what the residuary beneficiaries receive under your will. After all, they are the people you want to receive the bulk of your estate. Don't shortchange your family by being too generous to others in specific gifts.

How They Get It: The Residuary Devise

You may have an extended family of the "yours, mine and ours" variety. You and your spouse each have children from a prior marriage, as well as children from this union.

Let's consider the possibilities here. Remember that the residuary beneficiary receives the balance of the estate after your special devises, and, of course, after debts have been satisfied.

Perhaps you want everything to go to your spouse. Fine, just say that in the will. What about the children? Therein might lie some difference of opinion between spouses (but remember, your will can be different from your spouse's). If you name your spouse as residuary beneficiary, but don't specify further, then you have a problem. Your estate could go intestate because you do not have a surviving beneficiary by name. It's best to name an alternate beneficiary to your residuary estate. That might read like this:

"... if my brother, Seth A. Baker, does not survive me, then his share devolves to his children who survive me."

Do you think you might have more kids one day? Then you should provide for them in your will too. The safe practice is to specify that possibility with a phrase like this:

"to my daughter, Rose, and to any afterborn or adopted children of mine..."

Here's a reminder in passing: Children *can* be cut out of a will unless they are dependants. I tell my college students they had better be *very* nice to their parents.

Also here, you may choose to divide the residuary estate into several shares going to different persons or institutions. For example:

"I devise my residuary estate as follows: 45 percent to my brother,

Briefs

Jack Kelly, self-made Philadelphia millionaire and father of the actress Grace Kelly, wrote his own will. "For years," it went, "I have been reading Last Wills and Testaments, and I have never been able to clearly understand any of them at one reading. Therefore, I will attempt to write my own will in the hope that it will be understandable and legal. Kids will be called "kids" and not "issue," and it will not be cluttered up with "parties of the first part," "per stirpes," "perpetuities," "quasi-judicial," "to wit," and a lot of other terms that I am sure are only used to confuse those for whose benefit it is written. This is my Last Will and Testament and I believe I am of sound mind. (Some lawyers will question this when they read my Will; however, I have my opinion of some of them, so that makes it even.)"

Seth A. Baker; 45 percent to my sister, Charlene C. Dewey; 10 percent to a charity selected by my executor."

Hey, What About Rover?

Oh, yes, your pets. I wouldn't think of forgetting them. If you are married, your spouse will probably take over caring for Fluffy and Spot. But if you are single, you had better give some thought to who will care for those animals after you're gone.

Remember, if you die intestate, a judge will decide who gets the animals. If you have a will, you have more control over their fate.

It's smart to ask the person you'd like to be responsible for your pets before including him or her in your will as "beneficiary," if you will, of the animals. An even smarter move is to name an alternate in the event your first choice is unable to come through. You might want to include a small (or large, if you can afford it) sum of money as a gift to that individual for taking over the care of your pet. If you have a quite sizable estate, you probably have a trust and can authorize payment to that person periodically for Pyewacket's care.

If you find no one willing to take your animal(s), you might look into humane societies in your area that accept household pets, giving them a home for the remainder of their lives. Ask your veterinarian about places like that in your region, then give them a call.

If there's any doubt about who will care for a beloved pet, resolving that concern can bring you as much peace of mind as having a will made. Perhaps more.

Now you know what a simple, and slightly more complex, will is. But before you run out to have one prepared—a quite commendable step— you will want to read the next chapter, about trusts. A will with a trust could serve you better than a simple will, which immediately distributes your estate. Also, there is more information in upcoming chapters that could have some bearing on the contents of your will. So continue reading and gathering information before having that document drawn.

Incidentally, if you keep your original will in a bank's safe deposit box tell your executor. Banks will usually allow access to boxes to locate a will. You can keep a will in a waterproof and fireproof box or safe in your home. Or you can keep it at your lawyer's office.

The Least You Need to Know

➤ A will can be the simplest of documents, or as complex as your needs and wishes require.

➤ You have quite a bit of latitude in leaving what you solely own to anyone you choose, subject to the claims of your spouse and dependants.

➤ Wording is important in seeing that your gifts go to the beneficiary you select.

➤ Don't write your will just yet—continue reading.

Chapter 9

A Trust and a Will (The Best of Both Worlds?)

In This Chapter

➤ How a trust works

➤ Who's a trust for?

➤ Living and testamentary trusts

➤ Selecting a trustee

➤ But you also need a will

Depending on the size of your estate, and what you would like it to accomplish for you, a trust can be an excellent financial tool.

A trust will see that your estate directives are carried out now, or that your assets are passed along to your beneficiaries. It can save you money, through your own funding of it and in tax strategies. And it has some other advantages that you'll learn about a little later in this chapter. Drawbacks? Well, of course there are a few. I'll talk about them as we go along too.

Definitions, Please

A *trust* is a legal instrument to hold and manage your real property, and your tangible and intangible personal property. Putting all of those

Quote...Unquote

Money, big money (which is actually a relative concept), is always, under any circumstances, a seduction, a test of morals, a temptation to sin.

— *Boris Yeltsin, The Struggle for Russia (1994)*

assets into a trust transfers them from your ownership to the ownership of the trust. That trust will hold the property for your benefit, or for that of anyone you name.

Trusts can be set up and run while you are alive, or you can prepare a trust as you would a will, to take effect upon your death. For example, in this chapter I'll talk about a *living* (or *inter vivos*) *trust* and a *testamentary trust*. Generally speaking, as you can pretty much determine from their names, one is set up for use in your lifetime, the other (the testamentary trust) comes into existence after your death, when your will is probated. More about them later.

A trust used to be just for the very wealthy, or at least that's what most of us thought. But in the last decade or so the use of trusts has grown significantly in popularity as more and more folks of less than millionaire means take advantage of their benefits. However, the workings of a trust are still not that well known by the average person. How a trust can help in estate planning is also a mystery to many.

What a Trust Offers That a Will Does Not

A trust has several advantages over a will. It:

➤ manages property for you while you are alive

➤ can reduce your taxes

➤ easily transfers your assets to beneficiaries after death

➤ could allow you more flexibility in how you dispose of your assets—for example, passing your money on to your children from a prior marriage while bypassing your present spouse

➤ avoids probate and its time and expense

➤ protects your privacy: A trust is not filed and open to public scrutiny the way a will is.

Tip

You can, if you like, skip generations in your trust, with income going to your children and the principal secured for future grandkids.

Who Would Want—or Need—a Trust?

People establish trusts for a number of reasons, but these are the main ones:

➤ **Minor children** Parents might use a trust for minors after their death, or for the special needs child of any age throughout his or her life. You'll read about trusts for kids in Chapter 12.

➤ **Spendthrift children** A trust can be set up for a child of any age thought to be unable to manage money prudently. I'll talk about a trust for the adult child (sounds like an oxymoron, doesn't it?) in this chapter.

➤ **Retirement management** If you want a trust to manage your funds during your retirement, no problem. It can take care of you and your spouse if a time comes when you can no longer look after your affairs.

➤ **Tax planning** A trust can help you in a number of ways here, not the least of which is legitimate tax savings—always a welcome benefit of any estate plan.

➤ **The charitable trust** You may be philanthropically inclined and want to establish a trust, perhaps for worthy university students attending your alma mater. Or you might have a charity you'd like to contribute to in an ongoing way. Or you could participate in a trust that's already established by your favourite charity. The choice is yours. I'll explain charitable trusts in Chapter 18.

Who Doesn't Need a Trust

Would a trust be right for you? That would depend on the size of your estate, and your plans for it. If you have few assets right now—say you're young and single, or newly married and just starting out—you can skip a trust for a while. If none of the earlier-mentioned family or lifestyle situations quite fits your needs at the moment, you probably do not need a trust.

Keep in mind that a living trust is likely to be more expensive to set up than having a will drawn. You might have to pay around $2,500 for a trust versus a few hundred dollars, or less, for a will. So a trust's cost alone might put off some, which could be another good measuring device for deciding whether or not you need one. There

Words, Words, Words

Tenant, as used in the ownership styles discussed in this chapter, means owning and not renting. Of course, "tenant" more commonly refers to an individual or company that is leasing real property.

will also be the ongoing costs of filing separate tax returns for the trust.

(Speaking of cost, by all means comparison shop when looking for a lawyer to set up a trust for you. You should be able to do better than that figure cited above.)

A Caution on Trusts

Trusts exist not just because of their tax advantages. A trust can hold property for the benefit of the trust's beneficiaries who, by reason of their age, incapacity or lack of experience, are unable to deal with the trust assets personally.

Management of the trust property is left to the skilled trustee who administers the trust. A trust can benefit the beneficiary but keep the trust assets beyond his or her reach.

Here's the Lingo

More words! Each area of the law has its terminology, of course. You've been introduced to many terms so far in this book. Here are a few more words having to do with trusts that I'll be using in this chapter, with an explanation of each, to help you as you read on.

➤ **Settlor** This is the person who establishes, or sets up, the trust. That's you, in other words. The settlor can also be called the grantor, donor, creator or trustor.

➤ **Beneficiary** You probably have a handle on this term by now— it's the person who receives property, in this instance from the settlor, according to the provisions of a living trust.

➤ **Trustee** This is the individual or institution entrusted to carry out the terms of the trust. So it's the person (or institution) who turns property owned by one person (you) over to another, in accordance with your wishes as settlor. A trustee also invests property for the beneficiary's benefit. A trustee can be a relative, friend, lawyer or trust company (which could be stand-alone or bank owned); these are the most common choices.

➤ **Contingent Trustee** This is the second-string trustee, also known sometimes as the surviving trustee. He or she continues to manage assets in the trust should the primary trustee die or become incompetent.

➤ **Trust Estate** All the property legally transferred to the trust by the settlor for the benefit of the beneficiary or beneficiaries.

➤ **Trust Agreement or Deed** This is the legal document itself, spelling out the terms of the trust and how it is to be administered.

One Choice: The Testamentary Trust

A *testamentary trust* is a directive established in a will and is effective when the will is probated. It isn't a separate document, it's incorporated in that will. Your assets are just transferred to the trustee as if that trustee were the beneficiary of the will (which he is in a way, because he's holding your property for the real beneficiary). For example, the wording might be "I devise my residuary estate to ABC Company as trustee for my sons, John and Jeffrey."

The trust survives probate and goes on to exist as long as you, the settlor, have designated and the law permits. A standard will, which does not contain a trust, of course, is wrapped up and the assets

Briefs

The Roman Emperor Augustus (63 BC–AD 14) is said to have instituted trusts. They first appeared as a method of apportioning assets, for the most part to family members other than the oldest son, who otherwise was always the sole inheritor. There are records that credit Augustus with using a trust to try to make inheritance fairer for younger sons, who often suffered financially from that custom.

And Thomas Jefferson set up a trust to avoid passing his estate to his bankrupt son-in-law, who would control Jefferson's daughter's property (those were the days before women could own property in their own name).

Tip

Keep in mind a trust, by law, can't exist forever. It can last until a date you specify in the trust document, or upon a particular event—the date a young child reaches a particular age, for instance.

distributed after probate proceedings. Most wills should contain provisions for a testamentary trust in case a minor inherits any portion of the estate. This allows the minor's interest to be held "in trust" until he or she reaches majority, and avoids having to pay the minor's inheritance into court.

Downside to This Kind of a Trust

Well, with a testamentary trust your assets have to go through probate, and are subject to creditors' claims. So if your goal is to avoid probate, you can consider setting up a living trust if it is appropriate.

Another Choice: The Living Trust

The client was reluctant to sign her will, thinking it her death warrant. The sagacious attorney suggested she might sign a "living trust." She signed.

The terminology is simple here. A *living trust* is a legal instrument established during its settlor's life. It might serve as a partial substitute for a will. At the death of the person creating the trust, his or her assets are distributed to beneficiaries according to the terms specified in the trust.

You designate a trustee, who can be your spouse, another person, or a financial institution, such as a trust company. It's your choice (you'll read about determining a choice later).

Watch Out

Don't confuse a living trust with a living will. The latter relates specifically to health matters. There's more about living wills in Chapter 23.

A living trust would also be an option for what I referred to earlier in this chapter as your adult child who perhaps spends too freely. Or you might have an older child who, at the moment, is involved in drugs or alcohol. The umbrella term for a solution in those situations is known as the "*spendthrift trust,*" and is set up to prevent a child from spending a legacy foolishly. With this trust, specified amounts of money are released periodically to the beneficiary rather than as a lump sum, as in the case of most bequests. There are other restrictions, too, to that child's access to his or her inheritance.

A living trust can be established in either of two styles: the revocable living trust or the irrevocable living trust. You must determine which you want at the time the trust is set up.

Revocable Living Trusts

This type of trust gives you the freedom to sell, spend or give away your assets while you are still alive. You can change any of the trust's conditions, too.

A revocable living trust isn't for everyone, but it does have some features that warrant your attention:

➤ assets in the trust pass to the trust beneficiaries outside of probate

➤ settlor(s) can serve as trustees or select another to serve

➤ the alternate trustee can serve when the settlor/trustee is no longer capable

➤ the trust can receive assets from the settlor and the settlor's estate

The revocable living trust does not have any special tax advantages, since all capital gains and income are taxed to the settlor under the attribution rules. The assets are also subject to income taxes upon the settlor's death.

Care must be taken when you create a revocable trust. A transfer of property other than cash can immediately result in capital gains tax to the settlor if the property has appreciated in value. A tax liability can be triggered just by transferring legal title of an asset to the trust.

The tax rules of a deemed disposition would apply to make the settlor liable for payment of all taxable capital gains. This is not a desirable situation. I'll

Tip

If you act as your own trustee, you are likely to specify that the alternate trustee begin serving when you become incompetent. Who makes that decision? You might put into the trust agreement a clause stating that there will be medical evidence of incompetence from your own physician. A lawyer can help you with the wording, in accordance with your wishes.

discuss the tax rules in Chapter 16, but one other point should be made here about revocable trusts. The income and capital can't be distributed to a beneficiary under the trust during the settlor's lifetime without tax consequences. Furthermore, Revenue Canada attributes the income from a revocable trust back to the settlor of the trust to be taxed. For all of the above reasons, revocable trusts are not used as commonly as our next topic, irrevocable trusts.

Irrevocable Living Trusts

This trust, which is not as popular, allows you to make a gift of property while you are still alive. Here, however, you forfeit all control of it in order to receive a deferral from federal income taxes. So you'd better be careful: Once this trust is established, it is impossible to revoke.

The irrevocable trust is often used to minimize income for the wealthy, who can afford to give away assets to others, such as children or grandchildren.

Funding the Living Trust

You might want to *fund* the trust, which simply means putting some assets in it to begin with. Once a trust does exist you can add to it if the document allows you to do so. You can set up a fund with just $1 to get it going. Trust language calls this the trust *res* or *principal* (depending on whether you prefer the Latin or English version).

A living trust can be partially funded at the time it is established, with later additions. A trust can also be funded at the settlor's death from his or her probate assets through the will.

The trust principal is invested and generates income, which the government likes to see because it can tax that money. That principal may be used by you if you have established a revocable living trust and made yourself a beneficiary.

Taxing Trusts

Trusts are not like corporations, which are separate legal entities. The Income Tax Act deems a trust to be an "individual" when it comes to paying taxes. Trusts are taxed as separate taxpayers but are not entitled to any personal credits. The primary disadvantage to living trusts is that they are taxed at the highest marginal personal tax rate, as I'll discuss more below.

Trustees must file separate T3 trust tax returns and pay tax on the trust's earnings. What tax rates are applied to trust investments? There are two different individual rates:

➤ **Testamentary Trusts**

A trust created by a will on death is taxed at the varying or graduated individual's rate. This can be lower than the highest individual rate. Testamentary trusts can defer capital gains if the beneficiary of the trust is a spouse. Qualified spousal trusts are entitled to benefit from spousal rollovers.

➤ **Living Trusts**

Living trusts, on the other hand, are taxed at a flat rate, which is the top combined federal and provincial rate (depending on the province) of about 50 percent.

Retiring? How a Trust Can Simplify Your Life

Let's look at an example of a couple who could make good use of a living trust. Reed and Shirley are in their late sixties. They own their home, have household goods, cars, retirement plans, and significant investments in stocks and bonds. They have two adult children who are both married and have children.

The couple have assets worth over $500,000, not counting their home. They truly want someone else to handle their estate so they can enjoy their retirement days in other pursuits. Their trust could have the following features:

➤ Reed and Shirley as joint trustees

➤ Trustworthy Trust Company as the alternative trustee if the two become incompetent or choose to resign as trustees

➤ trust income paid to Reed and Shirley

➤ trust principal possibly used by Reed and Shirley as they see fit

➤ assets added or withdrawn by Reed and Shirley

➤ trust revoked by Reed and Shirley at any time, except after the survivor becomes incompetent or dies

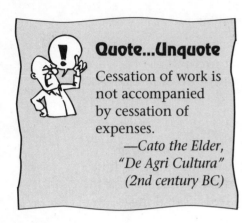

Reed and Shirley may choose to put some or all of their property in the trust. If one of their goals is to avoid probate upon the death of the last of them, they can put their assets, such as their home, household goods, cars and investments into their trust. If they have retirement pension plans that they want to keep out of probate, they can add successor beneficiary designations, such as their children, to these plans.

If the house is put into the trust, then a deed must be prepared to reflect the trust as holding legal title. Household goods and cars placed in trust have to be accounted for if sold, exchanged or abandoned. Those complications should be considered before the couple contribute real or tangible personal property to a trust. Certainly putting their *liquid investments*—stocks, bonds, mutual funds and the like—in the trust would be simple.

The Downside to a Living Trust?

Well, one "down" is explained in the foregoing paragraph—all that personal property in the trust could cause a lot of record keeping and expense, too much for some. For instance, would you want to keep records of household items sold at every garage sale you held? And file paperwork to the trust every time you bought or sold a car? Some assets, like these, can well be kept outside the trust.

How to Select the Right Trustee

If you establish a trust, you name the trustee. His or her duties are specified in the trust and by law. Naturally you will want to be sure your choice is willing to serve in that capacity.

A trustee's duties may include

➤ administering the trust according to its terms

➤ managing trust property, which can include reinvesting assets

➤ investing the trust principal

➤ maintaining trust accounting records

➤ making tax decisions and filing tax returns for the trust

➤ distributing assets to various beneficiaries

➤ terminating the trust at the time specified by the trust agreement

If you are creating a revocable living trust, then you and/or your spouse, if you are married, may be the logical choice for trustees.

Or you might consider appointing co-trustees, where one would be a person who understands what you intend the trust to accomplish, and the other would be an institution. The institution is going to be around, while the individual may retire, become incapacitated, or die. Review the trustee duties. Do you have a relative or friend who would be capable and willing to perform them?

Since most trusts are not supervised by a court, there is always a danger of misappropriation. If you decide on an individual as trustee, consider including an annual accounting to the beneficiaries, and a bond taken out by the trustee to protect you from wrongdoing.

If you elect to name an institution as your trustee, investigate the various trust companies in your area. Discuss their fees (usually a small percentage of the trust assets, probably no more than 5 percent). Inquire about their investment policies and who in the department is likely to invest your assets. Be wary of a trust company that assigns inexperienced employees to your size of trust, or has a high rate of employee turnover. You want continuity and sound investments.

> **Watch Out!**
>
> It's smart to provide in the trust a way to replace the institutional trustee if the beneficiaries are not satisfied with his or her performance because of poor investment return or other problems. The replacement should be another institutional trustee.

"So, I Need a Trust Instead of a Will?"

No, no, no. You almost certainly need a will, even if you have a trust. For one thing, as you have read in this chapter, you probably don't want all of your assets to be placed in a trust. It can be a nuisance to do that with some personal property. There are also items you may inherit or receive as gifts after the trust is established that you elect not to put into it.

So those assets remain outside the trust, even if one day they are subject to probate. You need a will to cover that residue. Probate, as you will see in the next chapter, is not the money gobbler people perceive (or fear) it to be—and there are other legitimate ways around that expense.

Be wary of anyone who suggests that all of your problems will be solved by establishing a trust. That just isn't so. On the other hand, if it's right for you, a trust can be an excellent ingredient in a comprehensive estate plan.

Don't forget, though: You still need a good old reliable will.

The Least You Need to Know

➤ You don't have to be very wealthy to set up a trust. In some cases, regardless of the tax issue and trust expenses, trusts may be attractive to use for other reasons.

➤ A testamentary trust is part of a will. This is the most common trust that you need to consider.

➤ A revocable living trust gives you some freedom; it allows you to change your mind. An irrevocable living trust, on the other hand, is etched in stone, so to speak.

➤ Even with a trust you need a will.

All About Probate

I gave you a brief overview of probate and estate court in Chapter 7, pointing out what happens if you have no will (and you won't let that happen, will you?).

There's more to probate than that concise explanation, of course. Quite a bit more to this frequently puzzling and misunderstood judicial arena.

Let's Bring This Court to Order

As you learned in Chapter 7, probate provides for an orderly transfer of property under a will from the deceased to his or her beneficiaries.

Let's go on from there.

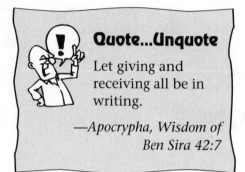

Laws governing probate procedures vary slightly from one province to another, and so can the court itself. Estate or probate courts come under provincial jurisdiction. In some provinces there is a special court to handle probate and guardianship issues only.

There is always a judge presiding in estate court, to oversee proceedings, review various documents—a will, inventory of assets, requests from possible heirs (we'll get into that later)—and make decisions where necessary. However, this is basically a supervisory role; the major decisions come in when a will or claim is contested, or when a guardian issue must be decided.

Is It Really That Formidable?

Of course not. You may have read or heard over the years that folks seem to run from probate or even the mention of it. The court has had a reputation for being time consuming when reviewing an estate, and expensive, because legal disputes take a chunk of the estate. The message you may have picked up in your general reading has probably been "avoid probate at all costs."

Well, let's see.

If you die without a will, it's true that your estate's administration can be longer and more costly for your heirs. This situation can be avoided by having a will.

On the other hand, some folks easily avoid probate because all of their property consists of jointly held assets, life insurance, pensions and other assets with named beneficiaries, which ordinarily are not subject to probate. You'll recall all of that from my explanations over the last few chapters. Other people use a trust, which also does not go through probate. So, you see, not everyone makes use of the probate court.

Probate really isn't a problem for the average estate, and especially where practically all of the deceased's worldly goods go to his or her spouse. There might be a few bequests to other family members, and to friends, but then the estate is usually distributed within twelve months after the date of death. Provincial laws do vary, and complications arise, particularly if there is no will or there are numerous heirs, complicated property holdings, business interests, will contests or complex tax issues.

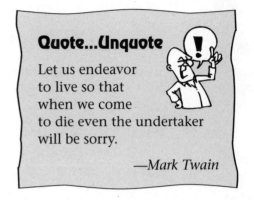

The probate process is fairly simple, although again, each province varies its system a little. In Ontario the term probate is no longer used, for example. Your estate trustee would not file a court application for probate. Instead, it would be called an application to obtain a certificate of appointment of estate trustee with a will.

When a person dies owning solely owned property, or other property that will be in his or her probate estate, someone—usually a relative—contacts the court and asks to open the estate. If there is a will, the family will have read it, and usually it is the executor named in that document who hires a lawyer to file the papers for the court to probate or confirm the will.

If there is no will, the court appoints an administrator, as you will recall from Chapter 7. (Since an executor and an administrator serve the same function, I'll use the term executor from now on to avoid confusion and save ink. You might want to keep in mind, though, that some jurisdictions use the generic "personal representative" or "estate trustee" for that individual. I'll still stick with executor.)

Simply put, the executor collects the assets of the estate (a written list), pays the estate's debts and taxes, and distributes the balance to the beneficiaries or heirs. I'll talk more about those duties in just a little bit.

How do creditors know you've died? Well, not very likely by being invited to the funeral! What happens is that your executor places a notice in your local or regional newspaper, giving that information and asking anyone with a debt to come forward. You might have seen those news items in your local paper. If not, I've reproduced one here to give you an idea what they look like. Incidentally, the fee to run that sort of news brief is paid by the estate.

No Supervision? Whee!

Some provinces provide for "unsupervised" probate administration, which involves minimal court involvement. It makes the process

---

NOTICE TO CREDITORS AND OTHERS

All claims against the Estate of _____, late of the City of _____, in [county or district], who died on or about the ____ day of _____, 199__, must be filed with the undersigned personal representative on or before _____, 199__; thereafter, the undersigned will distribute the assets of the said estate having regard only to the claims then filed. Dated _____, 199__.

_____, Executor

The Estate of _____
by her Lawyer

Typical legal notice placed by executors, asking creditors to come forward and file a claim against a deceased's estate

Words, Words, Words

Legatee is a word you might occasionally come across in preparing for, and reading about, a will. That is a person to whom money or property is left in a will. However, "beneficiary" is the more common term for that individual.

quicker and less costly than if the administration is supervised, which frequently requires court orders and detailed accountings of assets and court appearances.

Duties of Your Executor

Here is an outline of what an executor will be required to do, which coincides with what is involved in the probate process:

➤ file an application with the court to admit the will

➤ notify all beneficiaries to the will, or intestate heirs of the administration of the will

➤ notify all creditors of the deceased to file claims (that's putting the legal notice in the deceased's local paper)

➤ obtain a bond, if required, to insure performance (check back in Chapter 7 for details here)

➤ collect the deceased's assets and list the assets in an inventory

➤ seek court approval, if necessary, to sell any assets

➤ determine and pay claims against the estate

➤ pay any federal income taxes (there's more about these taxes coming up in Part IV of this book)

➤ distribute the estate's net assets, according to the court's order, to the will's beneficiaries, or to the heirs if there is no will

➤ close the estate

Those are the basics. Of course, the estate might have complications that require additional work, such as operating a business for a time and/or selling it, defending a will contest, petitioning the court to interpret a will or to determine the appropriate heirs, contesting tax determinations, and accounting to the court and beneficiaries.

There may be additional legal obligations, but the ones I have listed are the executor's primary tasks.

Selecting an Executor

Often your first choice will be your spouse. The second may be an adult child. I'll discuss having family versus professional executors later, but keep in mind that the more complicated the estate the less likely that your immediate family may want to serve as executor.

Here are some questions that might pop into your mind about now regarding an executor. I've added answers.

➤ *Should I ask the executor to serve before I put his or her name in my will?* By all means, approach that individual to be sure he or she is willing to take on that responsibility. A trust company must consent as well.

➤ *Do I need a back-up executor?* Yes, definitely. The person you name as executor may not be willing or able to serve when the time comes, so always name an alternative executor.

➤ *Does an executor have to know about taxes to do this work?* He or she ought to have a minimal knowledge of paying taxes, although a lot depends on the size of the estate. If it's small, and the executor knows enough to do his or her own taxes, that should constitute sufficient tax smarts.

Watch Out

Some of the trickiest parts of an executor's job are tracking down all of the deceased's assets, and putting a dollar value on some of them, like antiques. Keep that in mind when preparing your will and inventory of assets.

Quote…Unquote

What's a thousand dollars? Mere chicken feed. A poultry matter.

—*Groucho Marx*

➤ *Will the executor be able to do the work required if he or she has a full-time, or even a part-time, job?* Certainly—although that, too, depends on the size of the estate. If the deceased has left a multimillion-dollar business, feuding relatives and complicated tax issues, there could be quite a job waiting for the designated person.

➤ *Does the executor have to put up any money to take on this assignment?* No, that performance bond you read about in Chapter 7 is paid out of the estate's assets.

You also need to consider the following when thinking about who might be best suited to handle your estate when you're out of the picture:

➤ **Organizational skills** If your candidate keeps a good chequing account record, he or she should make out fine here. The executor sets up an estate account, and writes cheques and receives money through that account for the estate.

➤ **Experience in managing assets** That depends on the size and complexity of the estate. You'll want someone who has at least written a cheque in his or her life, but the typical estate doesn't present especially tough challenges for anyone you're likely to be considering.

➤ **Investment expertise** Yes, you might well want someone with experience in this area, if the estate is large enough so that money will have to be invested until the estate administration is completed, which can be twelve to twenty-four months. Your executor will want to keep a close eye on your other investments, too.

➤ **Ability to get along with your heirs** This is very important. You want a person who will be contributing to the solution and not be part of the problem. Choose someone who gets along with everyone involved here, or who at least has the kind of temperament that can calm everyone down if voices get a little loud.

➤ **Fees to be charged** What, if anything, is your candidate likely to charge for performing an executor's duties? Take that into consideration.

Those are some qualities and points to look for in an executor. Sound like anyone you know? Below is a worksheet to help you determine who among your family and friends might fit the bill to handle your estate.

If you think the requirements are a bit heavy for those in your circle, you might want to look to outside assistance.

Help! Bring in the Pros

Most trust companies (either stand-alone or owned by a bank) provide estate administration services. Instead of appointing a relative as executor, you could select Trustworthy Trustco. You might also want to take that route if the assets of your estate are substantial, if there are business interests involved, or tax issues are particularly complex. Probably a

---

SELECTING AN EXECUTOR

Sometimes choosing an executor is easy: Your spouse wins that slot. Other times the choice can be difficult, as you might find when you mentally run down the list of family members and good friends. Here's a worksheet to help you decide whom you might ask—and who would be a good choice for alternate executor.

Name	Organizational Skills?	Experience Managing Assets?	Gets Along With the Family?	Likely to Expect a Fee?	Will Accept the Job?

Best Choice(s) _____

_____

_____

Tip

If the trustee you have chosen for a family trust is a trust company, then that same institution should be the executor for your will, to ensure continuity of management between the estate and the trust.

trust company will only be interested in handling your estate if it has at least $200,000 in assets (not counting your home). They're likely to charge a percentage of the estate: maybe 5 percent, perhaps less if the estate is substantially larger, say, several million dollars.

If the beneficiaries of your estate are likely to squabble, then you may well want to select an impartial and professional executor. After all, if Johnny and Janey haven't agreed on anything since they were in elementary school, there's no reason to believe they'll get along now handling your estate.

Ch-Ching: Probate Costs

Administering a probate estate costs money. Generally speaking, we are talking about these expenses:

➤ **Court filing fee** This fee can vary significantly from province to province. For example, in Ontario it is 0.5 percent on the first $50,000 in estate value and 1.5 percent on every thousand dollars of value above that.

➤ **Executor bond premium** You've already read about this. Here's an example of what a bond cost in a recent case in my office:

Value of estate: $300,000.

Cost of Bond calculated as follows:

(a) for the first $100,000	$310
(b) for the next $200,000	$400
(c) administration charge	$250
TOTAL PREMIUM COST	$960

A bond may not be required in all cases; for example, if assets are just being transferred to a spouse who is the executor.

➤ **Executor's fee** Perhaps nothing, although it could be as much as 5 percent of the estate.

➤ **Lawyer's fee** If your executor chooses a lawyer, an uncomplicated estate should not take a lot of that lawyer's time (many use law clerks to do most of the work). Some charge a flat rate, others a percentage of the estate. Again, I'll mention that 5 percent figure. Make sure you understand just exactly what will be included in that fee.

Keeping Those Costs Down

Your estate cannot do much about the filing costs, which are relatively minor anyway. But other fees can be reduced.

➤ Name a family member as executor, if that is appropriate in your situation, because he or she may serve for no fee, or at just a small charge.

➤ If you're dealing with a large estate and opt for a corporate executor, try to negotiate the fee. Many such fees are set, but it's worth shopping around a bit or at least asking the executor you've chosen if she or he will negotiate. As I have mentioned, the larger the estate, the more that fee should come down a bit. The institutional executor usually does not have to pay for a bond, which is a small saving to your estate.

The institutional executor also brings professional management and investment expertise that may allow the estate to earn more income than would the individual. Too, the corporate executor can use its tax department to make tax decisions which could save the estate considerably in income taxes.

Words, Words, Words

Here are some words you might hear around medium- and large-size law firms. *Associates* are fully qualified lawyers who usually spend several years working for a firm, waiting to be tapped to become a *partner. Students-at-law (or articling students)* are trained in some legal work, but are sort of interns and not lawyers. They are usually involved in research and rough-drafting documents. *Law clerks* are legal assistants with special skills who are not lawyers.

Tip

If you are concerned that the institutional executor will ignore your personal concerns, like dividing up family mementoes, consider appointing a family member as co-executor to the corporate executor. Then you'd have professional management with a personal touch.

How to Avoid Probate

You say you'd like to skip the whole probate process, no matter how much money you can save here and there on expenses?

More than 20 years ago there was a book published in the U.S. called *How To Avoid Probate*. It became an instant best-seller. Probate then was to be avoided or reduced to a minimum. It could be done. It can now, too, and is almost certainly just as good an idea now as it was then.

All you need to do is put your assets in a form of ownership that would not be distributed in your will at your death, or go to your heirs if you die without a will. I've dedicated Chapter 19 to detailing some techniques you can use to reduce probate costs.

Here is a summary of those ownership styles that will avoid probate on your death, if your co-owner or beneficiary survives you:

➤ Joint owners with right of survivorship

➤ Life estate and remainder

➤ Revocable or irrevocable trust

➤ Life insurance with named beneficiary

➤ Annuities with a successor annuitant

➤ Pensions and RRSPs with named beneficiary

Joint ownership only avoids probate if an owner survives. Too often the surviving co-owner doesn't get around to putting another person's name on that document as a new joint owner. Then at the death of that survivor, the property goes into his or her probate estate.

Life insurance policies and many annuities and pension plans permit the owner to name successor beneficiaries.

As long as a beneficiary survives to receive the life insurance proceeds, annuity or pension benefits, those payments will not be included in the deceased's probate estate.

There's another way around probate: the living trust that you read about in Chapter

Tip
Review beneficiary designations for life insurance, pension and annuity benefits periodically to make certain that everyone you currently want to receive those proceeds is named.

10. Using a trust avoids probate for all assets put in the trust, assuming that the beneficiaries named are living. Since most trusts go as far down as the second and third generation from the person establishing the trust, this usually isn't a problem.

Of course not every person and every asset is suited for a trust, as you will recall. Too often we become so fearful of probate that we buy a "canned" living trust, fill it out, then forget about it. We assume that our estate is in order. While it just may be, it is more likely we have created chaos for our heirs instead. Determining which property is and is not in the trust (and therefore in and not in the probate estate) can take a great deal of unravelling and can be very expensive.

Trusts do have an important role in estate planning. Your lawyer and tax advisers can tell you if you are a candidate for one. But avoiding probate shouldn't be your only goal.

Besides, as I have just explained, between having assets in forms of ownership that avoid probate, perhaps having a trust, and taking advantage of the money-saving tips just listed, your heirs' experience with probate shouldn't be that traumatic—or costly.

The Least You Need to Know

➤ All estates, with and without a will, must pass through a province's estate court, for distribution of assets and payment of necessary taxes.

➤ Many of the assets in your estate do not need to go through probate at all.

➤ Choose an executor wisely, according to the demands of your estate.

➤ You *can* shave probate costs—and even avoid the process altogether.

Chapter 11

Some Unique Probate Situations— Maybe Yours?

In This Chapter

➤ Void marriages

➤ Estate puzzlers

➤ Getting an "advance" on an inheritance

➤ Crime *doesn't* pay

Now you know about probate and that court process. It all seems rather clear-cut, doesn't it—at least I hope I've presented it that way!

Ah, but if probate court walls could talk! There are many twists and turns in estates that can force a judge into the role of present-day Solomon. Sometimes it's a grave Solomon, at other times it's a judge fighting to hide a smile at a particularly amusing situation or folly of humankind. Here are some variations on simple inheritance issues. Perhaps one applies to you—or might one day.

Love and Marriage(s)

All jurisdictions recognize solemnized marriages requiring a cleric or a judge. Common-law relationships receive some form of legal recognition as well. That is when a man and a woman do not have a legal marriage ceremony, but do live together as husband and wife.

Honey, Where Are You?

Throughout this book we have discussed spousal rights in a deceased person's probate estate, and assumed, quite understandably, that the spouse was readily identifiable. Well, not every case is that simple.

Arnie, who was ready to retire from the military, had a dilemma that called for legal advice. His pension required him to name his spouse as beneficiary. He had been in the Armed Forces, and over the course of his career had been stationed at about nine different bases around the country.

It happened to have been Arnie's habit to select a new wife when he arrived at a new posting. He simply left the previous "spouse" and didn't bother with the formality of a divorce. Sometimes he went through a wedding ceremony with his new bride, but on other occasions the two just began living together as husband and wife.

Arnie's lawyer reminded him of the law against having more than one wife at a time, and he acknowledged that yes, he had heard something about that. He was told that whatever relationship had come first was his legal marriage, and the rest were void marriages, which means that no judicial action was necessary to establish that the marriages were invalid.

That might have simplified his problem until Arnie realized his first "marriage" was a common-law relationship. It would be extremely difficult to determine if he were married or simply cohabiting, since there is no record of a common-law

Tip

Remember, lawyer–client privilege does exist. A client will tell his or her lawyer "I'm a bigamist," and the lawyer will go on from there. You need not fear talking with your lawyer about a tangled life that has perhaps even taken you down a legally questionable road or two.

Words, Words, Words

Legally, an *annulment* is a court ruling that says a supposed marriage was never valid. The most common ground for annulment: fraud.

marriage, whereas with a legal marriage there is, of course, a marriage certificate that can be produced.

The predicament in Arnie's case? His executors were never able to determine which "spouse" was which. Actually, Arnie could not even remember the names of some of his blushing brides at those new military assignments!

In the event of Arnie's death, could one—or more—of his wives apply to court for spousal rights? The law recognizes dependants' claims for support and constructive claims to property. Of course, one can *try*. And maybe even win. So it isn't a foregone conclusion that a person would be left in the cold financially on the death of their common-law spouse.

I know *you* will never enter into multiple marriages without making that little side trip to divorce court, but keep in mind that bigamy violates civil *and* criminal law. Any "marriage" you enter into without a previous divorce is void. However, children born of a bigamous marriage are entitled to inherit from their parents, even though the marriage was invalid.

Death and the Law

Death used to be defined as the stopping of the heart. That is no longer an adequate definition in a medical era that permits life to be artificially extended by machines.

At the moment of a person's death, the inheritance rights of the heirs or beneficiaries to that individual's will are fixed and determined. A moment sooner or later may make a difference.

I'm not about to discuss the "legal" moment of death—the date and time listed on a death certificate. However, I will examine here the problems involved when related persons die at the same time.

Most provinces have legislation to deal with simultaneous death. If there is no evidence that one person survived the other (even for a brief time), then the statute may set out the following rules:

➤ **Wills and intestacy** The beneficiary or heir is treated as having not
survived the deceased. This is subject to anti-lapse rules for certain
family members or contrary intention in the will

➤ **Life insurance** The beneficiary is
treated as having predeceased the
insured

➤ **Jointly owned or tenants in
common** One-half passes through
each owner's estate

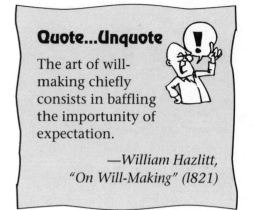

Quote...Unquote

The art of will-
making chiefly
consists in baffling
the importunity of
expectation.

—*William Hazlitt,
"On Will-Making" (1821)*

The deceased could have provided in his or her will or life insurance policy that the legislation will not apply in the event of a simultaneous death with a spouse. The will could state "in a simultaneous
death, my spouse is deemed to have survived me."

Let's Not Forget Greed

You might recall the biblical parable of the prodigal son (Luke 15:11).
This younger son wanted his share of the family estate before his father
died, an event that didn't look like it was going to happen any time
soon (Father was in fine health, and seemed nowhere near approaching
his final days). The son wheedled his portion from the older man, left
home, and proceeded to waste the money. Finally, after living in de-
grading conditions, he came to his senses
and returned home. His father welcomed
him and forgave him.

In modern legal terminology, the
father of the prodigal son had made a
gift to the young man against his further
inheritance. That is called the *law of
advancement.* It could affect what the
prodigal would later receive—if his
father had intended the gift to be an
"advance" against the son's share of the
father's estate.

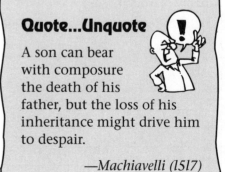

Quote...Unquote

A son can bear
with composure
the death of his
father, but the loss of his
inheritance might drive him
to despair.

—*Machiavelli (1517)*

Tip

If there is any inequity in how you leave your children your assets—and there shouldn't be, except for the special needs child—be sure to spell out your reasons, such as advancing money over the years to one of them. If you do not explain, you'll cause bad feelings among the kids—and resentment toward you.

Here is an example of how advancement is taken into account in dividing an intestate estate, again using our wayward son.

Assume that the young man received a $10,000 advancement. Then his father dies intestate, leaving a probate estate of $50,000. The prodigal son's advancement would be figuratively added to the probate estate for purposes of division between him and the elder son. That would make the probate estate worth $60,000. It's to be divided equally. Since the prodigal already received $10,000, he would be given only another $20,000 from the estate, with the older brother taking $30,000.

That should please the older brother. In the parable his nose was quite out of joint at his father's good humour—even celebratory feasting—over his brother's return.

You might want to note here that if the father were to make a will, he might want to follow the same division of his estate. But now that

---

WHAT COULD BE A PROBLEM FOR YOU IN PROBATE

Is it real property that could cause you some concern about your estate? Is it a particular relative, who might be concerned about an asset of yours? Or maybe there's a grey area in your estate you're just not sure about. Jot down where likely alarms might go off with your will, or later in probate, and think about what you can do to head them off.

Asset	Possible Problem in Will/Probate	Can I Handle It?	Better Check With a Lawyer
_____	_____	_____	_____
_____	_____	_____	_____
_____	_____	_____	_____
_____	_____	_____	_____
_____	_____	_____	_____
_____	_____	_____	_____

---

he's setting down his wishes on paper, he could explain a little. To his younger son, after his bequest he might add, "I am reducing his share because I have provided for him… etc." The younger brother might have forgotten that gift or gifts over the years. Perhaps the other brother didn't. An explanation is called for.

Abandoned Spouses and Adultery

The spouse who deserts the other, or commits adultery, is not denied the right to inherit from that partner. Adultery has no impact on an estate—or, I should say, very likely no impact at all.

Unless there is a written separation agreement in which a spouse releases claims to an estate or a divorce, a married partner will share in your estate.

Not to be confused with the mate who has genuinely moved out—or abandoned his or her spouse—the missing person is, well, just that. There are jokes about the disgruntled spouse who went out for a pack of cigarettes one evening and was never heard from again. On the far more serious side, there is the adult who disappears, perhaps not by choice. Has he or she met with foul play? Years go by with no answers.

The next of kin in those cases would probably ask the court, after the required period of time, to have that person declared legally dead, for inheritance and other purposes.

Murder and Profit? Never!

Most laws bar those who feloniously and intentionally kill from receiving any inheritance from their victims. The law bars those found guilty of murder or voluntary manslaughter.

If you watch television news shows and notice a spate of parental killings from time to time, you will be interested to know that those who become orphans by their own hand cannot inherit from their parent-victims.

> **Words, Words, Words**
>
> **Corpus delecti**, as any mystery fan knows, means the "body of the crime," or proof that a crime has been committed. It does not necessarily mean, as is often assumed, that a body has been found.

This bar applies not only to intestate laws, but also to wills and life insurance policies. The killer is treated as if he or she had predeceased the victim. If the killer and victim had jointly owned property, one half would go to the deceased's estate and the other half would be owned by the killer. The killer has no further claim to anything solely owned by the victim and his or her half of anything jointly owned.

Obviously the majority of these cases and examples of problems in probate can be considered pretty rare. The more usual probate estate is quite uncomplicated, causing hardly a flicker of interest in probate court. May your beneficiaries have just such an experience!

The Least You Need to Know

➤ No matter how strange or shady your story, your lawyer must keep it confidential through lawyer–client privilege.

➤ An advancement to an heir can reduce his or her share of an estate.

➤ Abandonment and adultery do not affect a married spouse's entitlement to share in an estate.

PART 3
All in the Family—and Just a Little Beyond

What is all this planning for? Or should I say whom is it for? It's for your family, of course, immediate and extended, and perhaps a few very close friends.

So it's important that while you are being so diligent in this work, you anticipate what could call for more attention than usual. Everyone's life is different, of course, with ingredients not quite like the next person's.

In Part III you'll learn about some special living situations that might affect you. You will also find out about a few specific, not run-of-the-mill, family circumstances that could have bearing on your will and estate. It certainly pays to anticipate what could go wrong and head off at the pass potential arguments among relatives or—heaven forbid—court decisions one day based on your choices now.

Chapter 12

Looking After Your Minor Children

In This Chapter

➤ The importance of naming a guardian

➤ Choosing the right person

➤ A trust to manage assets

➤ A child's entitlements

Q: Kids. Do we ever stop worrying about them?
A: No, probably no matter how old they—and we—are.

If we are overwhelmed by all that could harm our minor children, what could happen to them if we were not even *here* becomes incomprehensible. What I'll help you with in this chapter is keeping your kids safe, or as safe as it's possible to be with the paperwork anyway, if by some chance you are not around to look after them.

Grim? Sure. But if you grapple with the issue now, you'll feel a lot better knowing your directives are written down and will be followed. Then you can get on with other things relating to the kids that are more fun, like figuring out where the money for university is going to come from!

A Minor Issue of Major Importance

You read in Chapter 7 how important it is to have a will, not just so your assets will be passed on to whomever you choose, but also for arranging the care of your minor children. (If you have a special needs child of any age, that is certainly a concern to you, too. I'll cover that topic in Chapter 14, although you will still want to read this chapter since there's probably a good deal that will apply to you here as well.)

A *guardian* is a person appointed by law to be responsible for the food, housing and other needs of a child until he or she reaches legal age. (Of course, guardians are also named for adults who can no longer look after themselves. I'll talk about the elderly adult who becomes incapacitated in Chapter 23.)

Usually your will names a guardian and the court appoints that person or couple, unless the court determines it is not in the child's best interest for the named guardian to serve.

As you read in Chapter 7, if you are a single parent and have no will the state decides who'll get to raise your kids. That could be the other biological parent, if he or she is living, or your parents or a sibling. If you're starting to hyperventilate about now just reading some of those choices, then you can see how important it is that your wishes are set down in a will. I'm sure you don't want your children handed about like so many parcels.

If a guardian does need to be appointed for your child, provincial law will list the factors for the judge to consider. While laws do vary, it is common to follow this order:

➤ any request in a will or other written instrument (if you have no will, then of course legally you've got no preference)

➤ any request by a child at least 14 years of age

➤ any request by a relative of the child (grandparents, aunts, uncles, etc.)

The court's overriding concern is the appointment of a guardian who will serve the best interests of the child. The court will do the best it can, but think about how much better it would be for your kids if the judge had your directives to consider.

If you are married, your spouse is likely to assume the legal and actual role of guardian if your children inherit money from you. But there are exceptions. If a surviving parent hasn't taken an active interest in the child or has outright abandoned parent-hood, then he or she may not be the court's choice. A child with serious health problems calls for a guardian who will undertake extra duties.

Quote...Unquote

Rigid justice is the greatest injustice.

—*Thomas Fuller, MD, "Gnomologia" (1732)*

The Guardian's Duties

A guardian has two primary responsibilities:

➤ to rear the child, and

➤ to manage the child's assets

The guardian appointed by the court performs one or both of these functions until he or she is discharged of them. You can also have a separate guardian handle each of the responsibilities. More specifically, the guardian is responsible for:

➤ applying to the court for appointment as guardian

➤ securing a performance bond for him- or herself

➤ preparing an inventory of the child's assets, which could include property from your probate estate (through a will or intestacy), life insurance proceeds and pension benefits, as well as Canada Pension payments due the child

➤ investing and managing the child's assets

➤ providing for the child's support, care, and education

➤ encouraging the child to be self-reliant and independent so that he or she becomes an adult capable of handling the money that will be inherited

➤ periodically accounting to the court about income, expenses, etc.

➤ filing necessary income tax returns on the child's income

➤ closing the guardianship when it is no longer needed

The guardian is responsible for reporting all income and expenses both to the court and to the child. That accounting may be on an annual or biennial basis, depending on provincial law. The guardian is to use the funds for the child's livelihood, which includes necessities and perhaps amenities, like a first car for the youngster when he or she reaches driving age.

In many instances the guardian is not paid a fee—usually it is a family member who takes on that role and does not expect payment.

When the child reaches age 18, the guardianship is terminated. The guardian files his or her final accounting and distributes the assets to the child.

You may want to pause now and contemplate your child receiving your estate at age 18. Is it likely to be large? Do you think he or she could handle the money? Is the child too young right now for you to be able even to guess?

Words, Words, Words

A *ward* is a person of any age who is under the care of a court-appointed guardian. This is an archaic term, rarely heard these days outside of old—very old—movies, where the ward is usually a child or teenager.

Tip

If a home or any other asset is to be kept in the family for the use of the child, you need to specify that in your will. Most provincial laws require the guardian to sell assets that will not earn income.

A trust is likely to be the answer to any dilemma that issue might pose. It can delay distribution of assets until the child becomes more mature. I'll explain how this works in a few pages.

How to Select a Guardian

Let me tell you, this is *hard*. My wife, Krystyna, and I have two sons under the age of majority. Over the course of the years in our various wills we have named different guardians, and many different alternates—most who already had children of their own. While a family member or friend might be willing to be guardian for one child, maybe even two, taking on more calls for a real saint.

You want to select someone who will rear your kids the way you would, and manage their assets wisely. Here are several factors to think about in selecting a guardian or guardians.

Age

This is especially true if you are considering your parents. They aren't as young as they once were (but, hey, who is?). You probably drove them nuts on more than one occasion, but they had the resiliency of youth then, and the energy to meet those demands.

As grandparents, they are wonderful. But they know that when the grandchildren start acting like kids they can send them home. That can't happen if you appoint them guardians. Your parents love your kids, but may want them around only part of the time. One generation gap is wide enough. Two could be a chasm.

On the other hand, grandparents *could* work if they have asked for the job of guardian (and you agree they would do a good job of it), and in some cases if the children are old enough that your parents won't be raising small tykes. Taking in teenagers brings its own, shall we say, challenges. On the other hand, it will be only a few years until those kids are grown. This is a decision that, as you can see, calls for serious thought.

You might prefer to consider a couple closer to your age who already have kids. Their parenting skills, which you will have observed, are well honed by daily use and not, for the most part, out of practice by grandparenthood.

> **Tip**
>
> It's wise to name an alternate guardian in your will, just in case the primary guardian is later unable or unwilling to serve.

> **Quote...Unquote**
>
> If men do not keep on speaking terms with children, they cease to be men, and become merely machines for eating and for earning money.
>
> —*John Updike,*
> *"Assorted Prose" (1965)*

Marital Status

Your child needs to fit comfortably into a family environment. A couple who have a solid marriage and children close to your child's age may be ideal.

We all know perfectly excellent single parents who rear their children to be what you would hope for yours. By all means if you know someone who fits that bill, don't exclude that individual from consideration. The same thing goes for the single person with no children, perhaps a sibling of yours or your spouse's who is particularly close to your child. However, two parents do make it easier on the child—and the guardians.

Here is something you will want to keep in mind, though. If you are naming a married couple as guardians, consider the possibility of their divorce one day. Indicate who should be the guardian in that event, no matter how unlikely it seems to you now.

Lifestyle and Child Rearing Skills

Your child is used to you and your family life. If you want continuity, or as close as you're likely to find it in a guardianship situation, then you'll look for someone who is likely to fit within that pattern. That's not to say that your child can't succeed in a family that doesn't emphasize what matters to you in rearing kids. It's just that it's harder to do. For example, if religion is important to you and your family, you won't want the guardian to be an atheist.

Child rearing attitudes vary, of course. There is no one right way. But if you have your own style, you'll probably want your guardian to follow that sort of system. If firm-but-fair is yours, you're not likely to look for a guardian who believes that children should be "free to do their own thing." Taking a child from a fairly structured family life to a guardian who plans only for the next few minutes could spell disaster for a kid.

Tip

After you have made your tentative choice of guardian, observe your choice interacting with your children, and discuss with the person(s) you've chosen as guardian how comfortable everyone would be likely to feel in that household.

Compatibility

As I mentioned, most courts will listen to a child's wishes if the youngster is at least 14 years of age. If your male teenager detests the very perfume that Aunt Maude wears when she gives him a big smooch at family reunions, and she gives him socks for every birthday, then you may want to rethink Aunt Maude.

Talk with your kids and find out whom they feel comfortable with. That may not decide it for you, particularly if your son likes oft-married bachelor Uncle Dave because he has plenty of "babes" around, but at least their input can move you toward a decision, as it would a judge.

Family Relationships

Your brother or sister may be your best choice. But if there are likely to be squabbles over which brother or sister, that's all the more reason to put your choice in your will.

Favouritism

Some folks do play favourites. If you have three children, and your proposed guardian dotes on one child, giving him more attention, consideration and gifts than she gives to the other two, you might want to give a second thought to your choice. At least have a candid discussion with the kids who aren't the favourite. They probably have noticed the different treatment and won't be inclined to give that person the benefit of the doubt if she becomes the guardian, especially when discipline is administered or money is spent.

Managing Money

Some guardians make superb substitute parents and can manage money wisely. Others can fulfill one of those obligations, but not both. If your guardian choice will be a great parent, but always seems to be just one step ahead of the bill collectors, then take the tradeoff and go with him or her. Parenting should be your first consideration. You can turn to someone else to manage your child's assets. Which brings us now to your other choice: the trust.

First, though, is your head spinning with all the "perfect" traits you're supposed to look for in a guardian? Here is a worksheet to help you sift it all out. Perhaps your choice is an obvious one. If it isn't, putting your thoughts on paper should help you select an individual or a couple who could do a good job of caring for your child, should anything happen to you.

The Trust Alternative

If your proposed guardian is a poor money manager, you may want to establish a separate guardian to control the children's property. You can

---

CHOOSING A GUARDIAN

You've probably given some thought to your kids and a likely guardian, perhaps even before reading this chapter. Still, it helps to see on paper the pros and cons of various family members and friends who might be candidates for guardianship. Take a few moments—no, take as long as you need, this shouldn't be rushed—to set down your thoughts. Your work may lead you to answers that will be satisfying all-around.

Name	Good Points	Any Negatives?	Will They Accept the Job?	Can They Manage Money?	The Kids Like Them?
_____	_____	_____	_____	_____	_____
_____	_____	_____	_____	_____	_____
_____	_____	_____	_____	_____	_____
_____	_____	_____	_____	_____	_____
_____	_____	_____	_____	_____	_____
_____	_____	_____	_____	_____	_____
_____	_____	_____	_____	_____	_____

Best guardian(s): _____

Best alternate(s): _____

---

also set up a trust to manage your child's assets.

You might want a trust anyway—one should be created by anyone who has assets to leave to a minor or special needs child. That could be $100,000 or more in cash, life insurance, stocks, bonds and other savings, not including the value of your house. To avoid having a minor's inheritance paid into court, your will must specify that the minor's share can be held in trust by the executor or guardian.

A trust can accomplish the following for you:

➤ manage the child's property (stocks, certificate of deposit rollovers and the like) and avoid having to pay a minor's interest into court to be supervised

➤ distribute the property later than age 18, if that is your wish

➤ get around a spendthrift child's problems

Chapter 9 gives a complete discussion of trusts. What I'll talk about in this chapter is trusts as they specifically apply to minors.

The trustee you choose can be an individual or a corporate institution, usually a trust company. If you choose a corporate trustee, then you will have the professional management and protection from risk that comes with that choice. Most trustees report to the guardian at least quarterly, and many will assist in filing the child's income tax returns.

You can establish a *revocable living trust* now, which would receive all your probate assets, life insurance and retirement plan proceeds, or you can include a trust in your will—a *testamentary trust*—and accomplish the same thing.

Let's look at Carrie and Steve, who have two small children. The couple established a revocable living trust in planning for their kids, funded only by a life insurance policy on Steve's life, with the trust as the secondary beneficiary (Carrie is first beneficiary). Steve's and Carrie's wills provide for each other first, then the probate estate goes to the children's trust.

The kids' trust could be structured like this:

➤ Trustworthy Trustco as trustee

➤ the children are the primary beneficiaries of the trust, and will receive the income and as much of the principal as is necessary for their support

➤ when the younger child reaches age 21, the trust assets will be equally divided and each child will get one third of those assets (upon written request). The balance of each child's share will be distributed when each child turns 25.

➤ if a child dies before final distribution to him or her, then the other child receives that share

You can establish similar distribution ages to those given above, or any ages you choose, as long as they comply with the laws relating to trusts.

That reminds me of a friend whose son was the beneficiary of the father's trust. The son graduated from university and wandered around trying to "find" himself. He insisted the income from the trust keep flowing. The trustee called the young man in and told him when he got a job the spigot would be opened, but until then it was shut off. He found a job.

There are no tax breaks with a minor's support trust as above; it simply delays distribution of the inheritance until the children are more mature and can make better choices with your hard-earned money.

Special Requests

You can create trust terms that best fit your child or make for differences between your kids.

The heroic woman who consented to be guardian for my two boys was a little concerned about housing the additional brood in her home. I told her we could provide in the trust that the trustee could allow some funds for home improvement.

She then asked about family vacations. We said the trust could specify that money could be used for her children, as well as for our kids, to get away. Indeed, the trust could provide for vacation money for the guardians to go off on their own without the children—a sort of reward for their efforts.

Like ours were, your particular concerns can be addressed when you set up the terms of the trust.

Giving Your Kids Cash Gifts Now

You may have some spare cash that you want to give to your minor children, but don't want them to spend it now. You have some options, but you need to be aware of the income attribution rules for gifts, discussed in Chapter 17.

Your Child and Your Estate: Entitlements

You read in Chapter 7 about a child's rights to inherit under a province's intestate laws when you have no will. In Chapter 8 you saw how to include your kids in that will.

If you are a divorced mom or dad providing child support, you may want to ask your lawyer about your support obligations as they pertain to your estate. The divorced parent's requirement to support a child is not terminated by that parent's death. Support obligations usually bind a deceased parent's estate. The amount of the support may be modified, revoked or commuted to a lump sum by the court.

Quote...Unquote

A father is a banker provided by nature.

—*French proverb*

Most provinces have a statute that entitles your surviving spouse and children to apply in court for support if they require it, whether you had a will or not.

Also, divorce decrees or separation agreements may require the support-paying parent to maintain life insurance on his or her life, which may be the exclusive claim the child would then have against the deceased parent's estate. Whoever the custodial parent may be, the child is the beneficiary.

The Least You Need to Know

➤ You ought to name a guardian, and also an alternate, in your will for minor children.

➤ The guardian is responsible for rearing the children and managing their assets.

➤ Consider using a trust to manage your children's assets, should you die, because of its flexibility.

➤ Child support might be collected from a deceased parent's estate upon death, whether there is a will or not.

GRRRRRR....

Chapter 13

Holy Wedlock: Sometimes a Deadlock

In This Chapter

➤ Property rights after "I do"

➤ Spousal election against a will

➤ Divorce planning and practice

➤ Prenuptial agreements in divorce court

It's bliss. It's a battlefield. It's both—and occasionally at the same time. That's marriage, all right, or so it would seem from all one hears and reads on the subject.

The law has many occasions to intrude into the lives of married couples, from good times to bad moments. All the legal paper shuffling that goes along with marriage, and then perhaps separation and divorce, can also affect an estate plan. Here's what can happen—and what you can do if distressing times hit you.

Spousal Rights

Before we get into the *sturm und drang* of much of this chapter, may I ask if you're planning to be married soon or even just eventually? You

---

GETTING MARRIED? CHECK THIS OUT

Congratulations! This isn't a very romantic suggestion, but before you make that trip down the aisle, you and your spouse-to-be need to review some estate papers, to get your house, figuratively speaking, in order. The marriage licence is proof that you will soon become a new legal entity. It's time to look at some other documents that could—or should—be changed before you trade vows.

➤ *Your wills* Marriage revokes all existing wills except those made in contemplation of your marriage. Both of you need new wills so that you can provide for each other. Please, no joint wills (see more about this in Chapter 15).

➤ *Employee benefits, life insurance policies, RRSPs and qualified retirement plans* You will probably want to change the beneficiary for those investments to be your spouse, or at least review the documents to be certain that you still want the beneficiary you have named.

➤ *Forms of property ownership* Will you be buying a home? Do you already have one in your name? You might want to review Chapters 2 and 3, about ownership styles. Perhaps you'll want to hold real and personal property as "joint tenants with right of survivorship," the most common ownership style for spouses.

➤ *Prenuptial agreement* Will you be having one? There's a discussion of prenups in Chapter 3 (with a sample agreement you can read over). Remember to use separate lawyers for drawing up an agreement, and that marriage contracts can be made after marriage.

---

are? Good for you. My wish is that none of what follows in this chapter will apply to you. Do me a favour, though. Here is a listing for you to refer to in order to make sure the estate paperwork for both of you is in order when you march down that aisle. It affects spousal rights. Keep it in mind and read it again just before you marry.

Now let's get back to the time after marriage, when problems can sometimes crop up.

Tip

Did you recently marry and move to another jurisdiction? Don't forget to update your estate plan to take into account requirements in your new province for wills and other documents.

After the marriage ceremony, each spouse has certain legal rights. The law also specifies certain marital rights upon divorce or death.

Marriage is a fragile institution in modern life for a number of reasons. To ignore that fact is to proceed at your own risk—and possibly to the risk of your financial future. Read on and you'll see what I mean.

A Different Kind of Election

It's your will. You can completely cut your spouse out, or leave only a small portion of the probate estate to him or her. But consider the possible consequences this action will have after your death.

Of course, if you intend to make either of those moves I would suggest not letting your husband or wife view your handiwork unless a divorce is already inevitable, or you have a prenuptial agreement. A colleague's client drew her will and left one-half of her estate to her parents, one-quarter to her private high school, and one-quarter to her husband. Her husband was unaware of his relatively unimportant position in his wife's testamentary scheme. And, of course, the lawyer who prepared the will could not tell him. The couple eventually got divorced.

A spouse who is left out of his or her deceased spouse's will or given a small share of the estate has the right to challenge the terms of that will. This is known as *electing against the will*. It is a strategy for married couples only, and permits the party left out to go to court for a fairer shake. He or she is saying, in effect, "Whatever was left to me, isn't enough. I'm electing against that will." This isn't the same as a *challenge* to the will, which is open to any heir or beneficiary. An election is just for spouses, and already assumes some rights for the survivor.

Quote...Unquote

Marriage isn't a tram. It doesn't have to go anywhere.

—*Iris Murdoch,
A Severed Head (1961)*

The spouse who elects against a will must file that election within the statutory period of time. That time can vary, but might be perhaps no later than six months after a spouse's death. The spouse may also have to commence legal proceedings against the estate within that time period.

Most provincial laws allow a surviving spouse who elects against the deceased spouse's will to receive up to one-half of his or her estate. Usually that is the same share that he or she would receive under existing family property laws prior to the spouse's death.

If the election is untimely (that is, presented beyond the accepted deadline), or improperly made, then unless a court extends the time based on any legislative provisions the surviving spouse receives only what the will provides. However, any property jointly owned by both spouses, and any life insurance or pension with the survivor as beneficiary, would go to the surviving spouse, since those assets are not part of the probate estate in most provinces.

"Bumping Up" an Estate

Several provinces have laws that increase the probate estate for purposes of the spousal election, when certain transfers would otherwise diminish the part of the estate that the surviving spouse would receive. This increase is often referred to as the *augmented estate*. For example, if a spouse owns a matrimonial home as joint tenants with a third person, the law includes the value in calculating the deceased spouse's property. The joint tenancy is deemed ended or severed immediately prior to the spouse's death, causing the spouse's interest to be included as an extra to his or her estate.

> **Watch Out!**
>
> Consult a lawyer before making any property transfers with the intent to thwart your spouse's election against your will. Provincial laws vary as to what is considered part of the augmented estate.

Let me give you an example. Say that, for whatever reason, you don't want your spouse to inherit the bulk of your estate—or maybe not even a penny of it. So you set up a trust and place all of your property in that trust, thinking your spouse will have no access to that money even if she or he decides to elect against the will.

Not so, at least in certain provinces. The court can take that trust property value and deposit it right back into your probate estate—for spousal election purposes, just where you *didn't* want it to be.

Let's look at another example. Meet Ray, who has several assets in his own name:

➤ three expensive cars

➤ a condominium

Quote...Unquote

In the multitude of counsellors there is safety.

—Proverbs 11:14

➤ a substantial savings account

➤ a significant investment portfolio

➤ a large life insurance policy

All except the life insurance proceeds would be part of Ray's probate estate.

But Ray intensely dislikes his wife Michele, and the idea of her enjoying his property and money after he's gone drives him nuts. So he creates a trust and transfers all of his solely owned assets, except the cars, into the trust. The trust provides nothing for Michele. Ray changes the life insurance beneficiary to be his daughter, Eden. Shortly thereafter, Ray dies. His will leaves not a scrap to Michele.

Michele can elect against the will and receive her share of the probate assets, which now consist only of the automobiles. *This is a fine kettle of fish*, the fuming widow thinks. But wait. The family law may either include the trust as valued or as part of an augmented estate, which includes the property in trust. Whether the life insurance proceeds are considered part of the augmented estate may vary with each province. Most pensions are subject to laws that prevent a spouse from being cut out of benefits.

The family laws in her province give Michele the green light to elect against an augmented estate. She *runs* to a lawyer.

Actually, the election could bring a most satisfactory ending to this for Michele. She could get almost one-half of everything, assuming she has few assets of her own. As for Ray... well, we'll never know his response to Michele's good fortune, will we?

The problem with all of this is that Ray's estate plan will be put on hold until a court decides Michele's entitlement. Ray's estate would likely be responsible for all the legal costs of the court proceedings as well.

It's important to note here that a surviving spouse may waive his or her rights to elect against a will by signing a prenuptial agreement. That's our next topic for discussion.

The Prenup as Love Flies Out the Window

They're called prenuptial, premarital and antenuptial agreements, but they all mean the same thing: a document where spouses settle certain property rights before the marriage, in the event of divorce or the death of one party. I discussed prenups in Chapter 3 as they apply to property ownership. Now I'll tell you what happens when problems arise in a marriage.

They're for "Just Folks," Too

Prenups are not used only by millionaires and movie stars. Older couples, or indeed couples of any age, remarrying after the death of or divorce from a spouse, often are concerned about keeping the assets they bring into that new marriage for their children.

A prenuptial agreement will specify that each spouse waives his or her right to any intestate share (if there is no will) and waives any right to elect against the other's will.

Tip

If you have a prenuptial agreement that provides for the bulk of your assets to go to your children, then make sure the title to those assets remains solely in your name.

The provisions of the prenup attempt to keep as separately owned any property brought into the marriage. But spouses frequently will convert their solely owned property into jointly owned property with right of survivorship. That results in the surviving spouse receiving the property, thus reducing the assets going to the deceased spouse's children—and perhaps negating an important part of the prenuptial agreement.

Spouses can agree to modify or revoke their prenuptial agreement. But those wishes must be in writing, signed by each partner after legal advice.

If a married couple does not have a *pre*nup, they can, if they choose, make a *post*nuptial agreement, which could contain the same terms as a document drawn up before the wedding. These contracts are often called domestic or marriage contracts.

A prenuptial agreement can also get into questions of spousal support, into wills and trusts and, as you saw in Chapter 3 and in the sample prenup there, just about any area the couple wants.

Avoiding a Challenge to a Prenup

Joel is about to marry Angelina. It's his second marriage, the first having ended in divorce. Joel's concerned about a possible second divorce and

Watch Out

The person who initiates the prenuptial agreement might be tempted to offer his or her lawyer's services to the other partner. Bad move. That would be a conflict of interest that the courts would probably not look kindly on when deciding whether to enforce the prenuptial agreement. Two parties call for two separate lawyers.

its financial impact. He also wants to make sure that when he dies the bulk of his estate goes to the children from his first marriage. Angelina understands, and she agrees to the pact.

Joel should take the following steps to be sure there are no loopholes in his agreement with Angelina:

➤ hire a lawyer to draft the agreement

➤ completely disclose all of his assets and liabilities to Angelina. Courts will more readily enforce a prenuptial agreement if it is clear that the spouses knew what rights each would give up in the event of a divorce or a death. Hiding assets will almost always guarantee a challenge to the agreement, perhaps a successful one.

➤ require Angelina to hire her own lawyer to review the proposed agreement. She must have independent legal advice.

Finally, remember that when considering the enforceability of a prenuptial agreement, courts do retain the right to alter the effect of a prenup, if there has been a material change in circumstances that was not anticipated by the agreement that creates extreme hardship for either spouse. For example, if both parties assumed that each would be self-supporting upon divorce or the death of the other, and injury or illness precluded that, then the court could specify support payments to the affected spouse.

Divorce

Canada has a no-fault divorce (or dissolution of marriage) law. There is a residency requirement and a waiting period between the petition and the order granting the divorce. But the marriage *will* be dissolved if one party desires it.

For detailed advice on divorce and child custody, why not review *The Complete Idiot's Guide to Winning Everyday Legal Hassles in Canada* by Jerry Levitan; it's got excellent chapters on these issues. But let me go now into financial and tax consequences of divorce, and how divorce can affect your estate here.

Those areas can include

➤ property settlement

➤ child custody and support

➤ spousal support or separate maintenance, and

➤ the tax consequences of all of the above

Remember that a prenuptial agreement may establish the terms of any property settlement, spousal support or separate maintenance for one party. Child custody and support will be set by the divorce court. What follows assumes there is no enforceable prenuptial agreement.

> **Watch Out!**
>
> Separation is sometimes a step taken before divorce. Some folks seem to proceed straight to divorce. However, if you do seek a legal separation, that is certainly a move that calls for a review of your estate plan. Remember, though, no matter how separated you are, and how far away your estranged spouse is, you are still married in the eyes of the law.

Property Division

Mark and Millie are splitting up. The couple have the following assets, with noted market values:

House	co-owned	$100,000 [net, or less mortgage(s)]
Household goods	co-owned	$30,000
Cars	co-owned	$30,000 [net, or less auto loan(s)]
Savings	co-owned	$10,000
His pension		$200,000
Her pension		$50,000

Most divorce courts would add up the assets and divide by two (subject to exceptions in provincial law, of course). Perhaps you've gone through a divorce and are saying "That didn't happen to me! I got the shaft and he (she) got the mine." Be that as it may, most laws require an equitable distribution of the marital assets, however they are defined.

Courts certainly can consider factors that could affect a distribution, such as:

Tip

If you think there might be a problem with your children having regular access to your parents after your divorce, you can make grandparental visits an issue in your divorce settlement.

➤ who acquired the assets and how (gifts, inheritance)

➤ income and property of spouses before marriage and at present

➤ duration of marriage and health of each spouse

➤ need of custodial parent to occupy the home

➤ spousal support

➤ liquidity of assets

➤ financial future of each spouse

➤ spousal fault in wasting assets

➤ tax effects

This list is illustrative and not exhaustive. Certainly each divorce is unique.

Child Custody and Support

Courts award custody of minor children based on what they decide is in the best interests of the child. Naturally, parents should try to work together to establish an amicable custody arrangement that benefits all concerned.

Usually the non-custodial parent provides child support through minority, and often through age 21 if the child is attending post-secondary school (university or college) on a full-time basis. The federal government has established child support guidelines to determine the amount of support to be paid for those divorcing.

Income and Some Other Tax Consequences

Let's return to Mark and Millie's divorce. Mark is an accountant making approximately $75,000 a year; Millie is a public school teacher earning $40,000. They have one child, Manny, age 5.

If one spouse pays the other spousal support, then the paying spouse gets a tax deduction and the recipient spouse reports the payment as gross income.

Mark, who is in the higher tax bracket, might be willing to pay spousal support for a limited time—perhaps as a form of property settlement—to get a welcome tax deduction. Millie, therefore, may receive more from the divorce financially because of the tax saving for Mark.

If the spouses split the property, they can determine which property each is to choose based on the tax consequences that result from the disposition of selected property. For example, if Millie keeps the house and eventually sells it, there will be no capital gain reported for sale of a principal residence.

If Mark relinquishes his share of the house in return for all of his pension (half of which his former wife would otherwise be entitled to), it is likely he will be taxed on all of the benefits when he receives the pension payments. (Chapter 20 offers a more comprehensive discussion of income tax planning.)

If Millie is awarded custody of Manny, Mark will pay child support. The federal child support guidelines apply as of May 1, 1997. Child support paid under court orders or agreements after April 30, 1997, is no longer taxed in the recipient's hands. At the same time, the support paid does not qualify as a deduction from income by the parent paying support.

Complicated, huh? Divorce isn't as simple as marriage. You ignore the tax implications at your own financial peril!

> **Words, Words, Words**
>
> We all know (and a few of us have *experienced*) spousal support as a court-ordered payment from one spouse to another after a divorce. However, these days it is more common for money to be paid to an ex-spouse for property settlement; in other words, for a former spouse to buy out, in periodic payments, the other's share in real estate, investments, and so forth.

> **Watch Out!**
>
> Thoroughly discuss the tax consequences of your divorce with your lawyer and with your accountant, or you could wind up paying more to Revenue Canada than you need to.

Taxes and Divorce

If Mark and Millie divide their assets during the process of divorce, the division will not usually result in any capital gains consequences as long as they are still married at the time they make the transfers. No tax liability arises until capital property is disposed of.

Similarly, if a married couple had a postnuptial agreement that transferred assets from one spouse to another while married, there would be no capital gains to consider.

There is a more comprehensive discussion of income taxes in Chapter 16.

The Least You Need to Know

➤ If a surviving spouse has been left little or nothing in the deceased spouse's will, he or she can elect against that will and receive perhaps one-half of the property accumulated during the marriage.

➤ A prenuptial agreement can limit the rights a spouse has to the other's assets in the event of divorce or death.

➤ Tax planning is an important part of the divorce process.

➤ A divorce calls for another look at your estate plan— specifically your will—because a divorce cancels gifts and appointments to a former spouse.

I'VE GOT SOME BAD NEWS...

Chapter 14

Special Planning for Special Situations

> **In This Chapter**
> ➤ Special tactics for special needs
> ➤ "Living together"
> ➤ Big wins, and major financial losses
> ➤ Parenting your grandchildren
> ➤ Professionals and farmers

Not everyone fits neatly easily into any of the categories and circumstances that I've described so far in this book. Maybe after reading previous chapters *you've* said to yourself "Well, that's true for everybody else, but with me...."

If you feel you're often the exception rather than the rule, then this chapter may be for you. In it I address special situations, and you may well find yourself—and the answers you seek—here.

Planning for the Special Needs Child—of Any Age

Statutes define an incapacitated person as one who has a severe and prolonged mental or physical impairment that is certified by a medical doctor. Some require a guardian, others certainly do not and manage quite well on their own, although they will have certain medical needs throughout their lives.

The range of potential disabilities as they affect a person's work is so significant that no more than general advice can be offered here. Some will be able to earn enough to support themselves, others may be able to work at a minimal level, and still others will never be able to be gainfully employed. Clearly any planning must account for your child's potential economic success.

If you have a child who is physically or mentally challenged, then you well know most of such kids' needs are financial as well as personal. Parents provide a great deal of both, but sometimes the financial part becomes too great, and Mom and Dad must seek government assistance.

To preserve your estate for your other children, and to enable the child with special needs to receive support, it's often necessary to keep family assets separate from that child, especially as he or she grows to legal adult age. This is because government aid is often withdrawn or reduced when a child becomes an adult and has assets that can be used for his or her support.

Watch Out

Grandparents should consider *not* providing for the child in their will if this would raise the child's assets to a level high enough to disqualify the child for public assistance.

Your Child's Assets

Since many entitlements have requirements that limit the income or asset resources of the person with special needs, you need to take those limits into account in your financial planning. Consider doing the following:

➤ review beneficiary designations in your will, life insurance policies, retirement plans and RRSPs, trusts and savings bonds to be sure your child isn't named in them

➤ avoid joint tenancy ownership of property with the child, which creates more assets for him or her

➤ create a special trust for the child, and

➤ name a guardian in your will who is sensitive to the child's special needs.

A Trust May Be the Answer

Instead of giving your child money outright through a will or a life insurance policy, you might establish a trust. You would certainly need to consider the income tax consequences.

Sara was a widow with several adult children. One of them, Alan, had medical problems that held him to a part-time minimum wage job, and would do so for the remainder of his life. Alan lived at home with Sara, and she was concerned that when she died Alan would need a house to live in and someone to handle his finances, even though he probably did not need a guardian.

She could consider—with the advice of her advisers—establishing a revocable living trust. She could place her house in the trust for her life, and thereafter for Alan's life. Her grandchildren would receive the remainder of any assets left after Alan died. Sara should consult her other children before doing this so that they would understand why they would receive very little from her estate, although their kids would eventually benefit.

A trust is established to provide the amenities that government assistance cannot or will not. The goal is to provide a lifestyle for the child that best fits his or her needs. (Alan's needs will, of course, differ from those of others with disabilities.) The trust must be drafted so that it keeps the assets for your child and does not reimburse the government for its basic expenditures.

Government agencies place severe limits on aid for special needs children who are reaching adulthood and have significant assets. To prevent this from happening in your situation, try to obtain a court order appointing a guardian of your choice, naming that individual in your will. He or she might be able to make certain gifts from the child's assets, or establish a support trust like the one Sara set up for Alan. If the child is institutionalized, and you are paying for that care, the guardian and trust can handle payments from your estate.

> **Quote...Unquote**
>
> The joys of parents are secret, and so are their griefs and fears: they cannot utter the one, nor they will not utter the other.
>
> —*Francis Bacon, "Of Parents and Children" (1625)*

When consulting a lawyer about caring for your child with special needs, be sure the one you select fully understands the various federal and provincial entitlement laws.

Living Together/Planning Together

It's also legally called cohabitation, but we seldom see that expression anywhere these days. What we're talking about in these pages is a little more than living together. It's about two people being life partners with a serious commitment on both sides, but having no marriage. With such long-term relationships there is often—maybe usually—the desire to share assets and, of course, incorporate the other person into one's estate plan.

There are few laws that apply to the legal rights of partners outside of marriage. Contract law may apply to some arrangements, and the "constructive trust" or "dependants' relief" suits have been used as a means of trying to enforce support agreements. But the "significant other" has no inheritance rights under provincial intestate laws.

The income tax rules, however, recognize common-law marriages as when a man and woman cohabit for at least twelve continuous months, or they have a child together and publicly acknowledge themselves as husband and wife. Certainly any couple, even if unmarried, can provide for each other in their wills if they choose. But remember, if you are not legally married, you do not have the right to elect against a will (you read about such an election in the previous chapter). Electing against a will is limited to a married spouse.

Challenging your partner's will won't be a victory for you because if you are successful in having the will declared invalid, the deceased will be considered to have died intestate (without a valid will). Then the court will decide who the heirs or next of kin are—and none of them will be you.

Dependant Support

A person who dies without providing for a dependent child or spouse, including a common-law spouse, can be asking for trouble. A dependant has rights under various provincial statutes to obtain a court order for proper support.

In some jurisdictions, for example, a person in need would first have to qualify as a defined dependant and also be entitled to support because the deceased was or ought to have been paying them support. A dependant would have to claim his or her right to support through a court application.

A judge considers the value of the deceased's entire estate, not just the probated one, even if there is no will to assess if the dependant received adequate support.

The court has a wide latitude to resolve the claims based on statutory criteria. But this means a portion of an estate could be carved out and set aside for the support of dependants you fail to provide for in a will or intestacy situation. Think of what this will do to the other plans you had for your estate after the court decides the matter and pays all the costs from your estate!

Keeping Some Assets Out of Your Will

Joint ownership is a possibility here, and it would provide the surviving half of the couple with the property immediately at his or her partner's death. Keep in mind, though, that creating joint ownership in real estate gives both parties an interest in that property that is not easy to alter if the relationship changes.

Tip

Check with your employer. A growing number of companies are providing benefits for same sex—or opposite sex—life partners.

You might also want to consider life insurance, with your partner as the named beneficiary. Do the same with other investments, and they, too, will go directly to him or her at your death, avoiding probate and possible family squabbles.

Only a spouse has a right to the other spouse's qualified pension plan, but that plan could have any beneficiary you name. Consult a professional about any tax or other consequences.

Another wise choice here would be a revocable living trust. You could establish the trust and fund it currently or in the future with life insurance and the assets from a pour-over will (those are assets that go through a will and then into a trust). The partner could be the current income beneficiary of the trust, or the future beneficiary, upon your death.

By all means, it's smart to have a written agreement regarding any financial or property ownership arrangement you have with your partner. That's for the protection of you both, to forestall litigation between the two of you, as well as between a survivor and the deceased's heirs. A cohabitation agreement can record your legal obligations towards each other. In it, you can deal with many of the subjects you would cover in a prenuptial agreement or domestic contract.

The Role of the Custodial Grandparent

Some grandparents are legally in charge of their grandchildren through adoption or guardianship. Others have taken on that responsibility informally, with their son's or daughter's consent.

Are you raising your grandchildren, whether for the moment or until adulthood? You might think you must have legal custody of your grandkids in order to be eligible for services and benefits for the child, but that's not necessarily true. Many of them are available to you without taking that step.

You'll want to review your estate plan if you find yourself responsible for children at this stage of your life. You might want to move beneficiaries around, even if it's just for a time. Or set up a trust for your grandchildren. If you are raising your grandkids because their parent(s) have problems with drugs or alcohol, those conditions might be different one day, and you may want to check your estate plan again. This could be a continually changing situation for you.

Eureka! We're Rich: Handling Sudden Wealth

I don't know your family, so I have no clue if you're likely to come into an eye-popping inheritance from your Uncle Forsyth. I don't know if someone's likely to ring your doorbell and declare you the latest $250,000 winner in a provincial or charitable lottery.

Winning a lottery is a long shot, but obviously there are winners every week. One of them could be you.

In any event, you could wake up one morning to find yourself in the money. By all means allow yourself some champagne and toast your new fortune, while visions of sugarplums with all kinds of fancy price tags dance through your head.

More Money, More Taxes

Quote...Unquote

Wealth is known to be a great comforter.

—*Plato, The Republic (4th c. BC)*

Then stop. Before you make another move, and after the champagne high wears off, think. Income taxes, which were of marginal concern to you before, now loom ominously. You probably will be in a higher tax bracket, so "deduction" and "tax-deferral" become significant words. Yes, you have left behind your middle class tax concerns (and Good riddance, you say). But now you have inherited the rich person's tax worries, which call for a whole new set of strategies.

What you need to do after absorbing your good news is run, don't walk, to your estate planning team (remember those professionals you engaged in Chapter 1?). Do not make any major expenditures or investments without their advice. More than one lottery winner, or inheritor of a small fortune, went from wealth to bankruptcy through unwise spending and investments.

You need to do the following immediately:

➤ analyze all your assets and project your new income

➤ review your life insurance and casualty/liability insurance, now that you have more to protect, and

➤ revise your estate plan.

If you won the lottery, you would have instant cash. If you received a gift or inheritance, it may be in the form of assets that could be difficult to convert to cash, such as stock in a closely-held corporation, real estate, or valuable collectibles. Illiquid assets require special planning. Obviously, cash can be invested in numerous ways to create high-yield, tax-exempt income, or growth in the investment. If you receive non-cash assets, then the income flexibility is greatly reduced.

You may need to add more life insurance, particularly if income taxes will bite into a cash-poor estate. Since you might buy and own

Tip

You might want to give the trustee of any children's trust directives to distribute funds to your kids based on certain incentives, such as gainful employment or a meaningful contribution to society. Inherited wealth need not create wastrel children.

Quote...Unquote

Creditors have better memories than debtors.

—*Benjamin Franklin*

more real property, visit your insurance agent and increase your casualty coverage. If you're involved in an accident with your expensive new car a lawsuit will surely follow, so increase your automobile liability coverage.

Revising your estate plan may require rethinking your goals and the documents executed to further them. That includes who will benefit and by what means. Leaving everything to your spouse may have made sense before when the "everything" was relatively modest, but does it now? Or what about the children? You want to rear loving and responsible kids, not sponges. Perhaps giving something to charity is also possible now.

Tax planning becomes crucial at this time.

Finally, don't forget your will. All your planning may be for naught if your will is not an integral part of your estate file. Remember, everything you own solely is distributed by your will.

About Bankruptcy

Financial distress has a myriad of causes. Some are self-inflicted, like running up credit card balances. With other folks, the problem might be corporate downsizing that led to a job loss. Or perhaps there have been bad investment decisions. Or a divorce.

Obviously the concerns of wealth transfer and high taxes don't apply here, but financial and estate planning are still important.

Budgeting, debt consolidation, cashing in assets and reducing your lifestyle expenses could be sufficient measures to turn things around without turning to bankruptcy. Remember, bankruptcy does clear most of your debts, but it remains on your credit report for years after and can keep you from obtaining new credit for major purchases you may need down the road.

Help! And Perhaps Some Relief

Before taking that initial step to file for bankruptcy, by all means first contact a local credit counselling services office, which you can find in the Yellow Pages of your phone book. Thousands of Canadians in serious debt have been helped to restructure those debts with their creditors. The service continues to assist them during the time it takes them to pay back the money owed. That help is either free or available at a token charge.

If bankruptcy does seem to be the only answer for you, consult a lawyer who specializes in that area of the law. You can find one by calling your local bar association and asking for the names of lawyers who handle such matters. They can refer you to a Trustee in Bankruptcy. Make the call as soon as you have decided on filing. Serious debt can threaten your health, marriage and family, and needs to be quickly addressed.

Better times *will* come. Keep moving forward with your estate plan, and don't for a moment think you do not need a will because you don't have that many assets. You still have some, and you might also need to provide guardianship for minor children.

The Professional: Different Planning Needs

Physicians, dentists, lawyers, accountants and other professionals licensed by the provinces to practise have some unique estate planning needs. For example, they cannot sell their practice in the same way other businesses can be sold because, among other restrictions, the purchaser must also be licensed in that profession.

Usually, the estate planning necessary for those with high incomes and substantial investments applies to professionals. If this means you, here are a few matters you'll want to note.

Disability, Retirement, Divorce and Death

Since your income in this area stops when you are no longer working, it's certainly smart to purchase disability insurance.

The limited marketability of your practice means that you should have a buy–sell agreement if you are practising with others in a partnership or corporation. The agreement can cover both retirement and untimely death, and be a source of retirement income for you or an estate for your family.

If you're a sole practitioner when you opt to retire, you may have to hire a business broker to find a buyer for your practice. The major asset of your business—the client or patient list—may be of limited value to the purchaser. Adequate life insurance is vital to create an estate when the practice doesn't.

The value of a professional licence is, in many provinces, considered marital property for divorce purposes. I hope you'll have other assets to trade off; if not, divorce can seriously impact your estate planning here.

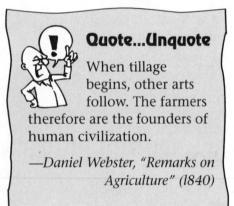

Quote...Unquote

When tillage begins, other arts follow. The farmers therefore are the founders of human civilization.

—*Daniel Webster, "Remarks on Agriculture" (1840)*

Down on the Farm: A Special Situation

Are you a farmer? You may or may not know that you have a unique position, as a number of special rules apply to reducing the tax burdens of transferring a farm. I don't have the space in this book to go into all of them, but here are some planning opportunities.

If you sell "qualified farm property" you could be entitled to a $500,000 capital gains exemption on the disposition. You need professional advice to determine your eligibility.

➤ **Choice of business entity** Many family farms have incorporated to take advantage of tax laws and more limited liability. For example, the farm home not only serves as your residence, but also as a deductible business office.

➤ **Accounting choices** Cash and accrual basis accounting methods are permitted, and you can also use the crop method, which permits the deduction of crop expenses when the income is received.

➤ **Intergenerational Transfer Rules** Any gift or sale of property, even to a family member (other than a spouse) generates a tax consequence. The deemed disposition rule means a gift of a farm would be a sale for its fair market value. The capital gain in excess of your original cost is reported and taxed. But there is a "rollover" if you transfer farm property to a child, grandchild or other specified relative. You can defer any gain on the property disposition until the recipient sells it at some later date.

You have seen in this chapter how special health/living/work situations can bring concerns and problems not always easily answered. Still, if one of these situations applies to you, by going to the right sources you *can* find solutions—and the way to a valuable estate plan.

The Least You Need to Know

➤ Proper planning for the child with special needs can protect him or her, as well as ensure that there will be assets for your other children.

➤ Having everything in written contracts can best protect the property rights of unmarried couples living together.

➤ Sudden wealth or financial reverses require immediate planning adjustments.

➤ Professionals and farmers have special tax penalties—and tax benefits—that are unique to them.

Chapter 15

Family Feuds: Avoiding One Over Your Estate

In This Chapter
➤ Wills can be contested
➤ Grounds are diverse
➤ Toughest challenges
➤ Making your will challenge-proof

It is the stuff of drama—challenging a will. *"Then, Lieutenant, just as Great Uncle Simon was planning to change his will ..."* or words to that effect have turned up in dialogue in motion pictures and television dramas since both appeared on the scene.

Challenging a will isn't quite that dramatic in real life. It's families squabbling, threatening, seeing lawyers, not speaking—and continuing all of this sometimes for years. Naturally you don't want to see your loved ones carrying on like that about *your* will. Here's how to prevent it.

Challenging a Will: What'll Do It

Your will *can* be contested. Any beneficiary, heir or person with an interest in the estate can challenge it. What you need to know is the "why" and the "how" of will contests, so that you can prepare a nearly lawsuit-proof last will and testament. Read on.

The person contesting the will has the burden of proof. He or she must convince the court that the will should not be admitted to probate by proving one or more of the grounds (reasons) for finding that will invalid.

Quote...Unquote

Discord gives a relish to concord.

—*Publilius Syrus, "Moral Sayings" (1st c. BC)*

If a will is successfully contested, the deceased's estate is distributed, according to provincial intestate laws, to his or her heirs. Or a contest may revive an earlier will of the deceased's.

I'll tell you first about the usual grounds for a will contest.

Plain Incompetence

The testator (that's the person who's writing his or her will) must be at least 18 years old and mentally competent. Courts look to several factors in determining mental competence. That's whether a person:

➤ knows that he or she is making a will

➤ knows the extent and value of his or her property

➤ knows the persons who would *ordinarily* be the beneficiaries of the will, and

➤ understands the disposition to the beneficiaries in his or her will

If there is a contest based on competency, expert witnesses, such as the deceased's doctor and friends and acquaintances who knew the deceased *toward the end of his life* (having last seen him five years ago won't count) will testify as to their observations.

Someone in the early stages of Alzheimer's disease who fulfills the above-mentioned requirements can have a will drawn that will stand up in court. So can a man or woman with a mental disability who, again, can satisfy those requirements. It's not the illness per se that's in question, but rather the testator's degree of understanding while suffering from it.

If you, as testator, have a history of medical problems that can affect your judgment, then that would be relevant evidence for a challenge. But quirky behaviour or cutting a child out of your will in itself is not enough to mount a successful challenge.

Undue Influence: A Toughie to Prove

Except in the most obvious of cases, this is hard for a challenger to prove. The beneficiaries who receive more than others will be suspected of unduly influencing the deceased to make a will in their favour. The usual suspects include second spouses and favoured children.

Anyone attempting to contest that will must prove:

➤ undue influence was exerted on the testator

➤ the effect of the undue influence was to overpower his or her mind and will

➤ it produced a will (or a provision of the will) that expresses the intent of the one exerting the influence, and not that of the testator, and the will (or provision) would not have been made if it weren't for that influence

What is evidence of undue influence? Well, there are a few things one can look for here:

➤ the testator was in a weakened physical or mental condition, making him or her more susceptible to undue influence or domination

➤ arranging for the will isolated the testator

➤ the person who is alleged to have exerted the undue influence had the opportunity to exercise it

➤ the disposition unduly favoured the person exerting the influence or his or her family.

Often the person contesting produces evidence that the deceased's wishes were overridden by another, usually someone trusted by the testator. This trusted person, in essence, told the deceased who was to benefit from his or her will.

The easiest cases for the courts involve a confidential relationship that is manipulated to divert the deceased's natural wishes away from his or her relatives to another person or persons. Here's an example. Lawyers, unfortunately, sometimes draft wills for clients that provide substantial devises to the lawyer or his or her family. Not only is that unethical conduct on the part of any attorney, but it also will probably result in a successful will contest by anyone who decides to take up that challenge.

Quote...Unquote

Go first class—
your heirs will.

—*Handstitching on a throw pillow*

What's harder to prove? That would be a situation involving a child or children receiving more than the others. You might not be aware that there is no law requiring a parent to treat each child equally in a will. Still, some children deserve more, such as a special needs child who will require long-term care (but it may actually be in this child's best interest to leave him *less*; see Chapter 14). Some children have more financial resources than others. Some children become alienated from their parents; others have had the burden of caring for them. There are many reasons why parents give preference to one child over another. Is that fair? In the case of the disabled child, yes, and the other children probably understand that. In the other instances, well....

If you are going to show some preference in your will, your lawyer should consider documenting your reasons for that choice. If Roberta is a doctor married to a multimillionaire and her sister Clarissa is single and a sculptor with a fairly low income, you may get away with a discrepancy in what you leave. A letter left with your lawyer may help Roberta understand why you left the bulk of your assets to Clarissa. That *could* help those who would otherwise feel short-changed to understand and accept your decision. But don't bet on it. Not dividing equally among the kids is very likely to cause resentment among them—and toward you long after you're gone.

Tip

Few wills are contested on the grounds that the deceased was forced into making one (duress) or induced to sign something that later turned out to be a will (fraud). Those illegalities do make for a good mystery plot, though. Try reading Agatha Christie's *Why Didn't They Ask Evans?*

A woman I know left half of her estate to her daughter; the other half was divided among her grandchildren. At the funeral the daughter's tears were freely flowing. But once the will was read, there was a dramatic change, and the daughter probably would have kicked the coffin if it had been there. A will contest was narrowly averted, but animosities lingered in that family for a long time.

Poor Execution

You know that your will must be signed by you, and your signature witnessed. Two independent adult witnesses are required, all signing in each other's presence.

You sign the will first, then both witnesses do, in front of each other. If you are physically unable to sign, you can request that another person do so for you in your presence and in sight of the witnesses. Your will states that another person has signed for you. You must tell your witnesses that they are signing your will, but you don't have to allow them to read it.

Slip-ups do occur, often when a person writes and executes his or her own will. Common mistakes include:

➤ no witnesses or poorly selected witnesses

➤ witnesses signing outside each other's presence

Briefs

In the Line-Forms-on-the-Right-at-Probate Department: If you're a Grateful Dead fan, you certainly remember when Jerry Garcia, the group's leader, died in August 1995. In March 1997 the final tally on his estate came in: $9 million.

Immediately after the rock musician's death there was a scurrying for parts of those assets, a battle that continues. It was also reported in March 1997 that lawyers for his third and last wife asked a judge to reverse his decision awarding a $4.6 million divorce settlement to wife No. 2. An assortment of business partners, former lovers and acquaintances also filed more than $38 million in claims against the estate.

Most will forms you can buy at stationery stores, or those that come pre-formatted on a computer disk, will have lines for witness signatures, so if you do it yourself you probably won't miss that aspect of execution.

Your two witnesses must be at least 18 years of age and otherwise competent. If there is any question about the proper execution, or your competence, then those persons will surely be called to testify in any will contest.

Witnesses, But Not Beneficiaries Too

One other point: You shouldn't have anyone who's a beneficiary (or a spouse of a beneficiary) witness your will. Laws can declare both the will and the witness's bequest in it invalid.

Here's an example. Let's say Jacob leaves one-half of his residuary probate estate to his son, Joseph, and provides the rest to his best friend Jim, who happened to be one of the witnesses. Jim would receive nothing, since he was a witness. Jacob's will could still be valid, but Jim will be left much sadder for the experience. A court could, though, establish that the gift was made without undue influence and allow it to be valid.

"Messing Up" a Will

What looks like a revoked will can also cause a court challenge. Mutilated or marked-on wills will cause a contestant to argue that the testator intended to revoke that document and the evidence is the torn will, or the one with handwritten notes on it. So be careful never to make handwritten or other changes on a will.

The "Don'ts" We Often Do

A simple will, which is all that most of us need, isn't that expensive. Save yourself worries and your family from a possible will contest: see a lawyer and shop

> **Watch Out!**
>
> Can a photocopy of a will cause a challenge because it is not an original? If the original has been lost, and a duplicate original, or a photocopy, is found, the contestant may well assert that the testator never intended to revoke his or her will. So you and your witnesses should sign only the original will. This would make the challenged will invalid.

around for the best fee. But remember, you sometimes get what you pay for.

Now that my bias has been clearly expressed, let's consider some ways you could get into trouble, legally and otherwise, with a will. And I'll tell you how to avoid such trouble.

Making Abusive Remarks

The probated will is a public document, open to anyone who cares to see it. A client wanted to vent her frustrations about her daughter, whose life, in the woman's eyes, had been less than exemplary. The phrases she proposed to put in her will were expressive and colourful, and derogatory in the extreme. She had every right to cut the daughter out of the will, but not to abuse her in public. Family disputes are tragic enough without that. I reminded her that she might reconcile with the daughter, but not get around to changing the will. In the end, she toned down her language.

Tip

If you do want to reduce a particular child's "expected" inheritance, consider giving the child some memento that he will treasure, and then indicate that other considerations resulted in that child receiving nothing else from the will. That could soften the blow a bit. It might also give the child no grounds to contest the will if you clearly indicate why his interest is not what he might have expected.

Making an Omission Without Explanation

You can choose whomever you want to receive your probate estate (remember, however, a spouse may have a right to elect against the will). If you want to delete one of your four children as a beneficiary, that is your privilege. I mentioned earlier in this chapter that a letter explaining why you have chosen to do so may be a satisfactory way to allow the child to understand your motives. The same advice applies if the child doesn't get an "equal" share and there is no special needs child involved. In any event, explaining your reasoning can head off a will contest.

Making Promises: Don't

Court decisions abound involving a deceased person who allegedly promised someone that he would be left something in the will for services rendered.

For example, Ivan promises a neighbour, Sam, that if Sam handles the upkeep of Ivan's house and yard, then Ivan will leave him something in his will. Ivan dies, and—what do you know—leaves everything to his third cousin.

Sam is incensed. Is he going to see a lawyer? Is the lawyer going to take his case? Is he going to get anything from the estate? Answers: yes, yes and maybe.

A better system for both Ivan and Sam would have been a written contract that specified Sam's duties and compensation, rather than a devise in Ivan's will. Sam can file a claim against Ivan's estate if the executor won't honour the contract.

Making Codicils That Change Beneficiaries

A codicil (a separate paper amending a will) changing an executor or a guardian probably won't overly concern anyone and hardly ever results in a will contest, unless it accidentally alters the original will in an unexpected manner. Inconsistencies can be created between the two documents. This could lead to an appearance by your executor or the estate lawyer before a judge to interpret what you intended to do.

> **Watch Out!**
>
> Never use a codicil to reduce the amount a beneficiary is to receive from your will. You are almost guaranteed a will contest from that disappointed individual. Make a new will instead.

On the next page there is a sample codicil changing executors. As you can see, it is quite a simple form. Do not consider adapting it for yourself without checking with your lawyer to make sure it meets your province's requirements.

A Joint Will? No!

Togetherness is fine, but there are some things you just gotta do on your own, you know? And making your own will is one of them. You and your spouse should have separate documents. The provisions can be reciprocal: everything to each other, then to the children. Or you can make different provisions.

Just don't have a joint will. When one of you dies, the joint will may not be changed by the surviving spouse without running the risk

SAMPLE CODICIL

THIS IS A CODICIL to the last Will and Testament of me, _____,
of the City of _____, in the County of _____, and
Province of _____, which last Will and Testament bears date
the ____ day of _____, 19___.

1. I REVOKE the appointment of _____ as an Executor and
   Trustee contained in Paragraph 2 of my said last Will and Testament and I
   appoint _____ to be an Executor and Trustee of my said last
   Will and Testament in the place and stead of the said _____.

2. In all other respects I confirm my said Will.

3. IN TESTIMONY WHEREOF I have to this Codicil to my last Will and
   Testament, written upon this single page of paper, subscribed by name
   this ___ day of October, 199__.

WITNESSES:

This is signed by the Testatrix   )
and by us, all in the presence   )
of each other.   )

)
_____
Signature of Witness

)
_____
Name

_____   )
Signature of Witness

)
_____
Name

(Note: An affidavit of execution should be used with the Codicil, just as with a Will.)

of a will contest. Those who were beneficiaries in the joint will, but are no longer in a subsequent will, may claim that the surviving spouse was legally bound to the provisions in the joint will.

Two wills really don't cost much more than one, and you can avoid that potential problem.

Making a Separate List of "Gifts"

Frequently, we have several items we'd like to leave to a particular family member or friend, but we don't want to list them in a will. You can prepare a list of that property, including the names of the people you want to receive those items. The list can be referred to in your will and stored with it for your executor's attention. It is easy to amend this list without seeing a lawyer, but since it is not included in the will, it is only persuasive and not legally binding.

It may be easier to decide which valuable items of property to give a person and put such specific gifts in the will. As to other non-valuable items, consider making gifts now, or leave a letter to your beneficiaries asking them to distribute those mementoes among your family and friends. The letter will not be legally binding, but your beneficiaries probably will honour your wishes.

Making Changes On the Will

That's right, *on*, not *in*, the will. As I have said, if you want to change your will, execute a codicil or prepare a new will. Don't scratch out cousin Calvin's name and replace it with niece Nancy's. Any changes on the will after it is executed will not be valid. You run the additional risk of the court treating substantial changes as reflecting your intent to revoke the will. A disgruntled heir may be tempted to contest the will on that basis; if he or she is successful, your estate would be distributed to the intestate heirs.

Families squabbling over an estate can be intriguing in mystery books, and funny in television sit-coms. But in real life, such feuds are not terribly attractive. You can easily avoid one by making sure your will is as challenge-proof as it can be. It's really not that difficult.

The Least You Need to Know

➤ A will can be challenged, but the burden of proof is on the challenger.

➤ To avoid a contest over your estate, take every step you can to make your will challenge-proof.

➤ Be careful: a do-it-yourself will cannot avoid all the mistakes that a disappointed beneficiary may be able to latch on to.

➤ Spouses should never execute a joint will.

PART 4
Taxes You Must Pay, and Those Maybe You Don't

Now we come to what you might not have been looking forward to reading about—taxes. You'll certainly find a variety of them here, from the provincial probate taxes to federal income taxes.

Tax matters are important to your estate, of course, because the more you can legitimately hold back from Revenue Canada, the more there will be for you and your family. So while unfortunately I do have to tell you about all these taxes, I'll also have the pleasure of helping you keep them down to a minimum, and sometimes avoid them altogether.

That's about as good as the news gets in a tax chapter, and since we're talking about your hard-earned money, you should find that darned nice to hear. Let's get on with the savings.

Chapter 16

The Wonderful World of Income Taxes

In This Chapter

➤ Taxing an estate's income

➤ Credits and other deductions

➤ Basics of computing the terminal tax return

➤ Tax return deadlines

"Isn't dying bad enough," you're probably thinking, "without being hit with a slew of taxes—in absentia, of course." I couldn't agree with you more. But for now that's the law of the land, and so here is an overview of the income taxes payable by your estate.

Quote...Unquote

...in this world nothing is certain but death and taxes.

—*Benjamin Franklin, "Letter to M. Leroy" (1789)*

Income Taxes But No Death Taxes

First you should know the good news. There is no Canadian *estate or death tax* that is levied on the transfer of property from the deceased to

Tip

You can call Revenue Canada's tax help line at 1 (800) 461-5018 (for the hearing impaired it's 1 (800) 665-0354) to talk to a real person. (Well, all right, after you listen to the recorded introduction.)

those who inherit. Instead, Revenue Canada just taxes your income from all sources when you die. Canadians have to plan to reduce or defer the "income taxes" that their estates will pay. I'll explain what those taxes are in this chapter.

The United States has estate and gift taxes, and our American counterparts must plan to deal with these levies. Unless you have assets in the United States (which is a subject beyond the scope of this book) you don't have to worry about "inheritance taxes."

All income taxes (that's provincial *and* federal, incidentally), must be paid from the estate before any distributions are made to your beneficiaries or heirs.

Capital Gains Rules at Death

Canada's income tax system has special rules that come into play when an individual dies. All capital assets are deemed to be disposed of for their current fair market value.

What's Taxed? Just About Everything

For taxation purposes, Revenue Canada deems that a sale took place at your death. This deemed sale triggers a capital gain on the increase in an asset's value since you purchased or acquired it. For example, Howard bought shares in Hydro Corp. in 1995 for $10,000, but when he died they were worth $30,000. Howard is deemed to have sold the shares immediately before his death. This means he gained $20,000, three-quarters of which ($15,000) is included in his income for his year of death—even though he never actually sold the shares.

What if Howard had wanted to leave the shares to his children? His estate would have to find the money to pay the tax liability on the taxable capital gain of $15,000. Assuming a combined federal and provincial tax rate of 50 percent, the tax on this would be $7,500. Had Howard anticipated this tax bill, could he have avoided it? Well, yes— and this is why estate tax planning is so valuable. Howard could have avoided the deemed disposition rule and deferred the tax payment. All he needed to do was to take advantage of the spousal exemption, which I'll talk about later in this chapter.

If you have real estate—stocks and jewellery, for example—you own capital property in the eyes of Revenue Canada. These capital assets (unlike cash) are considered sold for their current fair market value on your death whether or not you deal with them in your will.

This rule triggers recapture of tax depreciation, which is known as capital cost allowance (CCA), if you own depreciable property. Recapture of CCA is reported in your tax return as income. Accrued gains are taxed on your death (subject to the tax rollover rules we'll talk about in this chapter).

The government's income tax rules apply to everything. All of your property is included. Remember, your assets on death form your estate, which can be transferred by will or by designation outside of your will. Your estate includes assets—such as a jointly owned bank account— where ownership is transferred on death without a will. Probate property transfers ownership because of the provisions of your will. The only exception to the application of tax rules occurs when property is transferred to a spouse or spousal trust.

Let's use Audrey as an example. Before her death, she owned the following:

➤ her home, worth $200,000

➤ corporate stock worth $200,000, which she jointly owned with right of survivorship with her daughter, Paula

➤ RRSPs worth $300,000, with her other daughter, Diana, as the designated beneficiary

After Audrey's death, the house is in her probate estate and the stock and RRSP proceeds are transferred to her daughters. Here are the parts of her estate that are subject to income tax:

Home: worth $200,000. If this was Audrey's principal residence, the capital gain may be exempt from the tax because of the principal residence exemption. The home is considered part of her estate in the calculation of probate fees, and passes by her will.

Stocks: worth $200,000, jointly owned with Paula. Assuming all the stock was purchased by Audrey for $100,000, including all costs of acquisition, the capital gain is calculated as follows:

➤ The stocks are worth $100,000 more than what she paid for them, representing a capital gain. Three-quarters of this amount, or $75,000, is included in Audrey's terminal return as income. If an election to use the $100,000 lifetime capital gains deduction was filed with the deceased's 1994 income tax return, then the cost basis of the property will be higher than the original cost. The amount elected as the deemed proceeds of disposition will be the new deemed cost for purposes of calculating future capital gains.

➤ The stocks are jointly owned and so are not included in the value of the estate for probate.

RRSPs: worth $300,000. This amount is non-taxable to her designated beneficiary, Diana, but it has tax consequences to Audrey's estate. The RRSPs are not included in the probated estate, as the beneficiary is not the estate. Revenue Canada requires Audrey's estate to report all $300,000 as income in the terminal income tax return.

The Terminal Return for Your Estate

Your income earned or deemed earned by Revenue Canada's rules is included in a T1 tax return. This "terminal return" is filed by your executor and reports your income from your last tax return to the date of your death. There are special tax rules to consider on death—and some estate planning methods that can minimize them. But first I'll explain what gets taxed and deducted on death.

Your executor (or administrator if you have no will) is personally responsible for filing your last tax return. Executors do not personally have to pay your taxes if your estate has insufficient funds, but they must file the return, which catches all kinds of income you never thought of and may never have reported before.

The principal difference is that you may never have had to report "capital gains or losses" on your previous tax returns. Your executor will be required to report them in the terminal tax return.

Here is a partial list of the special income included on your terminal return:

➤ **RRSPs** The full amount of your RRSPs is included as income unless your beneficiary is your spouse and, therefore, the RRSP qualifies for a spousal rollover.

➤ **Registered Retirement Income Funds (RRIFs)** If you have no surviving spouse or dependent children, the fair market value of the RRIFs is brought into income in the year of your death.

➤ **Income received** Your regular taxable income actually received from employment, investment or business

➤ **Income accrued** This is income accrued to the date of death but not received. It includes interest on bonds, or rental or mortgage income, for example.

➤ **Capital property** Deemed disposed of at fair market value. Taxable capital gains will arise if the property has increased in value from its original cost. A recapture of CCA on depreciable property is also reported.

➤ **Receivables** These are rights and things that qualify for a separate return, which I'll explain later.

➤ **Annuity income** Is treated as ordinary income. There may be a capital component, which is non-taxable.

➤ **Registered Pension Plans (RPPs)** In some cases, if you receive a death benefit under a plan and have no spouse or designated beneficiary, the death benefit is taxable.

➤ **Partnership and proprietorship income** The income to the date of your death is reported in the year of death. Special rules apply if death occurs after the close of the fiscal year but before the end of the calendar year in which the fiscal year closed. In this case, a separate tax return may be filed if the taxpayer's legal representative elects to do so.

Tax Deductions and Credits Allowed

➤ **Non-refundable tax credits** No matter when you die, your estate can claim full non-refundable personal tax credits for the year of death. This means credits for basic personal, age, or dependent spouse are claimed in full and not pro-rated to the date of death.

➤ **Medical expenses** These can be pooled for a 24-month period up to the date of death, unlike the usual 12-month period.

➤ **Charitable donation credits** These are claimed as non-refundable tax credits for the year of donation except in the year of death and the preceding year; the limit is 100 percent of net income. Chapter 18 explains charitable giving in greater detail.

➤ **Net capital losses** Unlike other years, these can be deducted from other income and not just offset against taxable capital gains in the year of death.

➤ **RRSP contributions** When made prior to death, RRSP contributions are deductible in the year of death. When a taxpayer dies during that year, if the executor is the taxpayer's spouse he or she may contribute to a spousal RRSP within 60 days of the calendar year end and obtain a deduction in the calculation of net income in the terminal return.

The Taxable Estate

I'll illustrate all of this using Anita's estate. She was married to Tom, and they had two adult children. According to their prenuptial agreement, Tom waived any right to her probate estate, so her will leaves her stocks and bonds to her church and a vacation property to her children. (See Chapter 3 for more on prenuptial agreements.) Anita owned the following assets at her date of death:

Property	Ownership	Fair Market Value
house	Anita	$200,000
household goods	with husband	20,000
savings/chequing	with husband	20,000
stocks and bonds	Anita	200,000
vacation property	Anita	100,000
pension	(husband survivor)	200,000
RRSPs	(husband beneficiary)	100,000
life insurance	(children beneficiary)	200,000
	total value of the property	$1,040,000

For income tax purposes, the deemed disposition rules for capital property apply. The fair market value of the stocks, bonds and vacation property is $300,000. The total gain on these items is $200,000, of which 75 percent is included in Anita's income as a taxable capital gain. Assuming there is no other income, her executors would have to pay income tax on $150,000 with the terminal return.

Your Estate's Final Tax Bill

Your final tax bill will include some special items that you wouldn't normally find on your income tax return. Some of these items are explained below.

Principal Residence Exemptions

Anita had designated her home, as opposed to her vacation property, as her principal residence. Normally, the more valuable home receives this designation. Since 1981, Revenue Canada rules have permitted only one qualifying principal residence to be completely exempt from taxation. No capital gain is reported on an actual or deemed disposition at death on properties that qualify under the principal residence rule.

Taxpayers are only allowed one "principal residence" designation per family. If there were two properties that could qualify prior to 1982, it may be advantageous to analyze the numbers to determine the best one to select. The designation is made when you file a tax return in the year when the property is actually or deemed disposed.

Pension

Any amount received out of a superannuation or pension fund is included in the income of the recipient. Therefore, the beneficiary of the plan is subject to tax on receipt. Such amounts may be eligible for rollover to an RRSP.

RRSPs

Anita and Tom were both residents of Canada at the time of Anita's death—the condition necessary to qualify for the spousal rollover to an RRSP of which Tom was the annuitant. As such, there would be no deemed receipt of the RRSP benefits under the plan, which would be required for the proceeds to be included in income for the year of Anita's death.

Life Insurance Proceeds

The policy is payable to the children as beneficiaries, and is not a factor in calculating probate fees. There are generally no tax consequences on

Tip

Revenue Canada has a number of publications and interpretation bulletins on tax topics, which can be obtained from the nearest District Taxation office. Some material is available on Revenue Canada's Web site at <http://www.revcan.ca>.

life insurance to either the deceased, the estate or the beneficiaries of the policy.

Charitable Credits

As you have seen, Anita left her stocks and bonds to her church, which is, of course, a charity. That entitles Anita's estate to a charitable credit. Gifts made through a will, or through life arrangements that are paid by an estate, qualify for this credit.

The charitable donation of the $200,000 in stocks gives Anita a tax credit that eliminates her taxable capital gain of 37.5 percent of the capital gain. New rules introduced in the February 1997 federal budget allow taxpayers to give publicly listed securities to charities and receive favourable tax treatment until the end of 2001.

Tax Return Deadlines

The tax department doesn't just sit around and wait for its money without charging interest. Executors, administrators and your estate legal representatives must comply with the tax filing requirements, even if your will is challenged in the courts.

The executor must file the terminal tax return by the usual deadline, or six months after your death, whichever is later. If a taxpayer dies after October 31, the terminal tax return is due within 6 months of the date of death. If death occurs prior to November, the terminal tax return is due by April 30 of the following year. If the taxpayer dies prior to filing a tax return for the preceding calendar year (i.e. prior to April 30), the legal representatives have 6 months to file that tax return.

Executor's Tax Liability

Revenue Canada holds your executor personally liable to deal with your tax issues at death. Accordingly, it is prudent for executors to obtain a final clearance certificate from Revenue Canada prior to distributing estate assets.

The Least You Need to Know

➤ Canadians are taxed on income received or accrued to the date of death. There is no inheritance tax on the value of the property transferred.

➤ To calculate income at death, Revenue Canada has special rules. For taxation purposes, you are deemed to have disposed of all capital property at fair market value.

➤ Thanks to the spousal rollover provisions, an exemption to the deemed disposition rules will apply if you leave assets to your spouse or a spousal trust.

➤ Your executor is personally liable to ensure your income taxes are paid before distributing your estate's assets.

Watch Out!

Obviously, it's wise to turn to the tax lawyer or accountant who is part of your estate planning team before attempting to work around these issues. (No doubt you've been consulting the appropriate professional member of that team through major steps you've been taking with your estate plan anyway, haven't you?)

Chapter 17

Gifts and Income Taxes

In This Chapter

➤ How gifts are taxed

➤ Where you're tax free

➤ Ways around the tax

➤ Gifts to minors

A gift is a thoughtful, sometimes simple, gesture. It can be part of your estate plan.

Revenue Canada may see it differently, though, and can slap you or your estate with quite a tax. You might have done things differently if you had known the tax and estate ramifications of your generosity. Let's see how you can make someone else happy, while keeping a smile on your own face.

The government has rules to deal with the tax consequences of gifts and "non-arm's-length" transfers of property. I'll explain some exceptions, but basically the rules are considered "anti-avoidance rules."(You'll read more about this in Chapter 20.)

You will always pay the tax on any accrued gain when you transfer

property—unless you know the exceptions to the rules. We'll cover some of
them in this chapter.

How to Present a Gift

Legally, there are certain elements of
giving that make a gift a gift, as far as
your estate plan and Revenue Canada
are concerned.

Instead of my simply spelling them
out, let's imagine this scenario, which
contains those necessary elements. I'll
explain them later.

Aunt Agatha has promised you her antique oak chest—certainly a
handsome piece of furniture—when she dies. You aunt means well, but
there are several "ifs" that could be impediments to your receiving that
chest. You will receive that gift

➤ if she owns the chest when she dies

➤ if she has a will specifically devising the chest to you

➤ if her estate has enough assets to pay its debts (the chest might
have to be sold to pay outstanding bills)

In this instance I would suggest you follow my advice and have
Aunt Agatha make a gift of that chest to you now. Here, briefly, is why.

To have a valid gift three things are required:

1. the donor (in this case your aunt) has to have the intent at that
moment to make the gift

2. the donee (you) has to accept the gift

3. the gift property has to be transferred from the donor to the donee
irrevocably

Okay, now let's continue. You've explained the situation to Aunt
Agatha and she's agreed to go along with this script.

Scene: The room in Aunt Agatha's house where the oak chest is situated.

Prop: Video camera, held by a third party.

Words, Words, Words

A *bailee* is one who temporarily possesses, but does not own, a property. An example might be a parking garage near your office that has a copy of the key to your car. (This isn't a commonly used expression—as you have probably surmised since you no doubt have never heard it. Most people haven't.)

Aunt Agatha: Joanie, I give you my oak chest *[points to chest as camera goes from aunt to chest]*.

You: Aunt Agatha McCleary, thank you so very much for this lovely oak chest. I accept your gift.

[camera shows you patting the chest as Aunt Agatha moves—or appears to move—it toward you]

But Aunt Agatha, this chest looks so right in this house. Please keep it for me as bailee until later.

Aunt Agatha: I will keep it for you as bailee.

End of script.

What you now have is a gift that has been presented to you. When Aunt Agatha dies, you'll send a copy of the videotape to the executor of her estate to prove the oak chest is yours.

That's one way to handle a gift. As you have seen, it fulfills the three elements of gift giving, and there can be no mistaking the intentions of the donor, or the one accepting the gift. It's neat and clean.

We don't always have our videotape recorders handy, of course. In this chapter we'll discuss some other giving styles and their benefits and tax consequences.

The Tax Consequences of Gifts

In Canada there are no gift taxes, as there are in the United States. But there are income tax rules that apply to gifts. They protect the federal income tax system by ensuring that you cannot avoid paying any tax by making a gift of your entire estate.

Canadians do not have estate taxes to worry about. Revenue Canada is, however, interested in your gifts because any transfer of property generally is a disposition of property for income tax purposes.

Let's say you're feeling very generous. Life has been good, so you want to spread the wealth (yours) around a little. Your spouse deserves something special, so you give her 100 shares of Huge Consolidated Inc. (value $20,000). Junior and your little princess have matured more quickly than you'd expected, so you give each of them 50 shares of good old Consolidated for the holidays, with each gift worth $10,000. Shucks, it's just a little something.

When tax time comes around you ask your accountant if those gifts are deductible on your tax return.

Your accountant smiles. Deductible? In your dreams. You must report the capital gain and file an income tax return by April 30, which she will, of course, be happy to prepare for you at her usual fee. Your gift to your wife calls for no tax because of the tax-deferred rollovers to a spouse. You must qualify for the rollover and you can elect that it not apply. But the stock to your kids? You must pay tax on each of the gifts to the children even though they are minors. Any capital gains or losses are triggered by the transfer of the stock. Revenue Canada deems

Quote...Unquote

To give and then not feel that one has given is the very best of all ways of giving.

—*Max Beerbohm, "Hosts and Guests" (1920)*

Quote...Unquote

What with your friend you nobly share /At least a rescue from your heir

—*Horace, "Odes" (c. 23–15 BC)*

the gift was transferred at the fair market value of the stock. If you purchased the shares for $4.00 a share, the deemed sale price of $10.00 results in $6.00 a share of profit, or capital gains. This amount is taxable at the usual capital gains rate of 75 percent.

The income attribution rules we discussed in Chapter 9, on Trusts, also apply when your children are under 18. What if the gift to the kids had been $10,000 worth of bonds instead of stock? The bonds earn $1,000 in interest income annually. The income on the bonds would be attributed back to you, and you would have to report it and pay the tax on the interest.

Capital gains on transferred property realized by the child under the age of 18 do not attribute back to the transferor. Therefore, the child would pay the tax on the future capital gain when the property is sold and the gain is reported.

When You Aren't Taxed

Not every gift is subject to income tax. Most of us give presents to family and friends. Gifts to a spouse (more about that coming up) or a charity can be made free of any tax. Transfers can also be usually made on a tax-deferred basis to a spousal RRSP. You can also give a family farm property to your children as a gift.

There is no tax levied on joint savings accounts, joint share brokerage accounts and joint Canada Savings Bonds, which are not considered gifts and are not subject to the tax when they're established. The problems that can arise relate to the income attribution rules. The income and capital gains are taxable to the person contributing the money regardless of the registration on the account.

So, if Mom opens a savings account with Trustworthy Bank, and puts her daughter, Ming, on the account as joint owner with right of survivorship, there is no taxable transfer or gift to her daughter unless Ming withdraws funds for herself. If she does, Mom has made a gift.

Tax-Deferred Gifts to a Spouse

Outright gifts between husband and wife are technically subject to the income tax deemed-disposition rules, but the spousal rollover rule makes the transfer of property a non-taxable event. At the time of the transfer, therefore, spouses can shower each other with presents without any immediate tax concerns. The capital gains tax is deferred until the property is actually disposed to a third party. When this occurs, the capital gain attributes to the transferor unless the transferor is deceased at the time of disposition.

However—and isn't there always a however?—if a spouse is given only a life estate interest in a property (meaning that it is hers only for her lifetime; see Chapter 2), or an irrevocable trust is created in which she is the life income beneficiary (see Chapter 9), then the tax law is a bit more complicated. The gift to a qualifying inter vivos spousal trust requires that three conditions be met:

➤ The trustee and transferor are residents of Canada.

➤ The spouse is the only person entitled to all of the income from the trust before death.

> ➤ No other person, during the spouse's lifetime, may have any bene-
> fit from the income or capital of the trust.

A qualifying spousal trust allows a spouse to transfer capital property
without there being a taxable disposition; but the usual income attribution rules still apply. Remember, you can also elect out of the spousal
rollover and the spouse making the gift would pay the capital gains taxes
at the time of transfer or take advantage of any capital losses.

A Variety of Gifts

Gifts may include:

> ➤ outright transfer of property
>
> ➤ below-market interest rate loans or forgiven loans
>
> ➤ transfers to an irrevocable trust
>
> ➤ creation of co-ownerships in property or a remainder interest in
> property

Let's consider these situations in more detail.

Outright Transfer—What's That?

It means that the person getting the gift has all legal rights to it,
whether it's cash or property. There are no restrictions on ownership.

Let's say you want to either give your child corporate shares worth
$20,000, or $20,000 in cash. That is an outright gift, or transfer, and the
gift of shares, which is a disposition of capital property, would be subject to income tax. And what about the cash gift?

> ➤ First, the shares: Whether the child is an adult or a minor does not
> affect the income tax consequences for you. You would report the
> taxable capital gain on your tax return based on the fair market
> value when you transferred it. Future gains on the asset would,
> however, be taxed in the hands of the child. Stock and cash divi-
> dends from the stock would be treated differently. If your child is
> under the age of 18 all income would, under the attribution rules,
> be attributed to you and taxed in your hands.
>
> ➤ Now the cash gift: Whether or not your child is under the age of
> 18, the gift of cash has no capital gains consequences to you, the

Words, Words, Words

To *forgive* a loan, or interest on a loan, is to grant the one borrowing that money relief from payment of the debt. Any agreement like this should be in writing, of course, and dated.

transferor. However, the income attribution rules still apply on any income earned from the gift if the child is under 18.

Below-Market-Rate Loans

There are attribution rules to attack income splitting (when you try to shift income from a person in a higher tax bracket to someone in a lower one) but in some cases you can find unsavoury surprises to the rules. If you lend your adult child money interest-free, or below Revenue Canada's prescribed interest rate, then the amount of interest you *should have received* if the loan had the appropriate interest is treated as an interest income payable by you, and not your adult child. The attribution rules apply and you would be responsible for the tax on this income.

For example, let's say the loan was in the amount of $50,000, and had no interest attached. Assuming Revenue Canada's prescribed interest rate to be 10 percent, then the first year's forgiven interest would be $5,000, which you would include as income for tax purposes. Therefore, you are better off to make a gift rather than a loan.

Prescribed-Rate Loans

If you made the same $50,000 loan to your adult child but charged and collected interest at Revenue Canada's prescribed rate in effect at the time of the loan, these attribution rules would not apply. An interest-bearing loan to a spouse is a good idea when the profit from the loan amount exceeds the interest charged. This allows the net return (profit less interest) to be shifted to the child or spouse. The parent making the loan only pays tax on the interest income.

Loans to minor children may be structured to minimize taxes. Interest rates might be low enough to allow a family member who has loaned $100,000 to a child generate capital gains income, which may not be taxable to the lender.

Let's say you want to lend your child money to help him or her buy a home. The loan is $100,000, and you charge no interest. The attribution rules would not apply, as no income is being earned. You could avoid the income tax unless the main reason for the loan is to achieve income-splitting and thereby reduce taxes.

Trusts and Gifts

A gift to a spousal trust can allow the settlor of the trust to provide income or benefits from the trust during the spouse's lifetime. On the death of the spouse, the unused portion of the capital of the spousal trust could pass to the children.

The transfer of property to the spousal trust created by a will (testamentary trust) or by a living trust (inter vivos) can be done on a tax-deferred basis. However, income earned by the living trust during the settlor's lifetime is subject to income attribution.

Watch Out!

Be careful when lending large sums of money to a child and, if the child is married, his or her spouse. Be sure that you both know whether that money is a gift or a loan that you expect to be repaid. When intentions are not spelled out clearly, serious misunderstandings—and sometimes family rifts—can arise over the years.

Co-ownership: Togetherness and Taxes

Maria owns her home. She executes a new deed to the place with her son Yuri as tenant-in-common for one-half of the property. Maria has made a gift to Yuri that is not subject to income tax because it is her principal residence, and the capital gain is exempt from tax. Yuri, however, has received a gift valued at one-half of the fair market value of the home at the time of the gift. If it is not his principal residence, he will have capital gains to deal with when he disposes of his 50 percent interest.

Maria could have made Yuri a joint tenant with right of survivorship, or she could have deeded the property to him and kept a life estate (you read about that in Chapter 2.

Yuri's spouse and creditors may be entitled to make claims against the property regardless of how Yuri takes title. Maria should consider these risks and obtain legal advice before giving away any part of her property.

Briefs

There are gifts, and then there are *gifts*. There was a merchant named Guyot, who lived and died in Marseilles, France. He amassed a large fortune by very hard work and saving most of this money. His neighbours jeered at him, considering him a miser, and avaricious. Local children threw stones at him.

Eventually, M. Guyot died, and in his will was found the following: "Having observed from my infancy that the poor of Marseilles are badly supplied with water, which they can only purchase at a high price, I have cheerfully laboured the whole of my life to procure for them this great blessing, and I direct that the whole of my property be laid out in building an aqueduct for their use."

GIFT GIVING FROM REVENUE CANADA'S PERSPECTIVE

Here are some situations where you might be handed a present, perhaps a quite handsome one. What are the tax implications? It won't matter to you, because the donor is responsible for paying income tax. But these examples will give you some idea of how *you* will be taxed when you feel the urge to give someone close to you a little something.

Gift	Donor's Tax Situation
On your birthday Aunt Maude gives you her diamond earrings and brooch, valued at $4,500	"Listed personal property" if transfer exceeds $1,000. Taxable as a disposition of capital property
Your Dad gives you $15,000 cash toward the down payment on a condo	No tax due on cash gifts
Your godfather gives you his $12,000 stamp collection	Subject to capital gains as "listed personal property" if profit made on disposition
Your spouse gives you an automobile for your birthday	No tax due—an outright $20,000 transfer, spousal rollover
Your significant other gives you a $20,000 automobile for your birthday	Common-law spouses qualify for the spousal rollovers

"Non-Arm's-Length" Dealings

Attribution rules attack income splitting, but the rules for children apply only if they are "related" and not dealing "at arm's length." Usually children, grandchildren, a spouse's children and a brother and sister are included. But in these cases, if the gift is made for fair market consideration or interest is charged on loans at the prescribed rates of interest, income attribution will not apply.

The Least You Need to Know

➤ The income tax rules apply to gifts of capital property

➤ Gifts of cash may be made to anyone free of income tax but income attribution rules may apply.

➤ A loan given interest-free or at a reduced rate may be subject to tax because the interest *not* paid is considered a gift to the loan recipient.

➤ A gift of appreciating property will reduce the capital gains paid by your estate, but may generate immediate income tax obligations for the donor.

Speech bubbles: "WANNA GO FOR COFFEE?" "SURE."
(TAX)

Chapter 18

How Charitable Donations Can Save You Money

In This Chapter

➤ The basic rules of giving

➤ Many varieties of gifts

➤ Life insurance and tax implications

➤ Gifts after retirement

If you are generous to family and friends, and can afford it, you are probably also generous to your favourite charities.

Can you save money while giving to a worthwhile cause? Yes indeed. Planning allows you to arrange charitable contributions in a way that will maximize your personal objectives with appropriate tax incentives. Read on.

Tax Savings and Philanthropy

Canadians have always been a generous people. Our religious institutions, universities, local charitable organizations and community groups, among others, have all prospered with our gifts.

Here are some of the benefits of planned giving:

➤ fulfilling your charitable goals

➤ providing non-refundable tax credits calculated with reference to the value of the charitable gift

➤ avoiding the capital gains tax when giving appreciated property

➤ retaining income rights to the property donated to the charity

➤ increasing lifetime income by converting low-yielding assets

➤ supplementing retirement income

➤ obtaining professional asset management

Clearly, charitable donations should be considered part of your estate planning. The following pages point out several different methods to make them fulfill your goals, from outright gifts of cash or property to charitable trusts.

Tip

Not all charities qualify for income tax deductions. Public charities such as churches, educational institutions, hospitals and the Crown *do*. To see which others qualify for such deductions, check with the charity to make sure it has a charitable number. This means it is registered with the Ministry of National Revenue and can provide you with valid tax receipts for your donation.

Which Assets to Give

Just what you choose to give to charity has important tax implications. After all, doing good does not preclude doing well for oneself.

Charitable gifts can be made of cash, stocks, life insurance, art work, real estate or residual interests in your estate. Each different type of gift has special features and tax incentives and consequences.

The Basic Tax Rules: Tax Credits

Canadians are encouraged to make charitable gifts by the income tax system, which gives credit on such gifts. Tax credits are used to reduce your overall taxes. If the gift is made during one's lifetime, it will reduce your income tax bill for the year of the gift. The annual general donation claim limit was increased in 1997 from 50 percent to 75 percent of a taxpayer's net income. The rules allow you to carry unused non-refundable tax credits forward for five years.

On the first $200 of annual donations the federal non-refundable tax credit is 17 percent, or $34. If you make gifts in excess of $200, you will receive a credit of approximately 50 cents for each dollar donated. This means that if Sally is in the top bracket (taxable income in excess of $59,180), a gift after the first $200 will fully offset the income tax levied on a dollar for dollar basis. What if you wish to make a gift of capital property such as art work? Read on about the tax credits you'll get.

Gifts of Property: Two Different Examples

New rules introduced in the 1997 federal budget make it attractive to donate capital property. Publicly listed securities like shares or mutual funds receive special treatment. The gift must be made directly to the charity instead of first selling the property and then donating the cash.

A gift of capital property requires a valuation of the property because the donation receipt is based on the property's fair market value. A valuation report from an expert may be required for larger donations to minimize disputes with Revenue Canada.

Willie wants to make a large gift of capital property to a registered charity (not a private foundation) after February 18, 1997. Willie has the option of donating the property or selling the property and donating the cash.

This first example assumes he sells the property for $70,000. His expenses were $10,000. Assume that Willie has employment income of $75,000 in 1997.

The sale results in a $60,000 capital gain. Willie must include 75 percent, or $45,000 of this amount, in income. His net and taxable income includes $75,000 from employment and a taxable capital gain of $45,000, for a total of $120,000.

The charity issues Willie a receipt for the charitable donation of $70,000, the amount of cash donated. His maximum annual income limitation for the donation is calculated as follows:

1997 Limits: (a) 75 percent of net income of $120,000 or $90,000 plus

               (b) 25 percent of the net taxable capital gain or $0

Total Charitable Donation Limit = $90,000

Willie can claim the entire $70,000 amount as a charitable donation on his 1997 return. This credit is worth about $39,000, assuming a 50 percent tax rate.

Publicly Listed Securities Get Special Consideration

The federal budget proposals introduce, for a period of five years from February 18, 1997, to December 31, 2001, further tax incentives for charitable gifts of appreciated publicly listed securities (that is, stocks, bonds and mutual fund shares).

This second example assumes Willie gives a gift of publicly listed shares to the charity rather than cash. The taxable capital gain generally reported 75 percent of the capital gain, but the new rules reduce this rate to 37.5 percent of the capital gain. The net and taxable income will now be $97,500—as opposed to the $120,000 in our previous example.

Based on these proposed rules, 100 percent of the taxable capital gain is included in the calculation of the credit. Again, the full charitable donation of $70,000 can be used.

The advantage in donating appreciated capital property is that Willie's overall tax liability will be significantly less than if he were to sell his investment and donate the cash. Based on the second example and using 1997 tax rates, giving the publicly listed securities would save Willie approximately $9,000.

Now that's a favourable situation, and so donating appreciated capital property should be considered prior to the year 2002.

This is also an estate-planning area where you will certainly want professional help. In this case, of course, that will be the tax adviser who is a member of your estate planning team.

> **Quote...Unquote**
>
> Posthumous charities are the very essence of selfishness when bequeathed by those who, when alive, would part with nothing.
>
> —*Charles Caleb Colton*
> *"Lacon" (1825)*

What Happens in the Year of Death

Charitable donations made in the year of death are deemed to have been made in the prior year. The non-refundable tax credits for charitable

Tip

Do you like a particular charity, but are not certain you want to give them a sizable sum? If you have the time, do some volunteer work for that group first, to make certain you agree with its policies and programs and how it spends its money.

donations not claimed in the terminal return can be claimed in the preceding year.

Unlike donations made while you are alive, charitable gifts made in your will are treated differently. In the year of your death the donation is reported on your final return, and not the estate's tax return. The charitable donation limit is 100 percent of the deceased's net income. If there is insufficient income, the credit can be claimed on the year preceding death.

Getting Your Donations in Order

Timing is everything, even here. A charitable donation saves you more in taxes when your tax rate is at its highest.

Alternating years when you make charitable donations could also save you money in taxes—you can choose to save receipts and claim the credit in the next five years.

That's what Art and Susan did. They regularly give $4,000 a year to their synagogue. In 1996 they gave nothing to the synagogue, but in January 1997, they gave $4,000, and then an additional $4,000 later in the year.

Revenue Canada allows Art and Susan to combine their receipts and claim them on the tax return for the spouse in the higher tax bracket.

Lots More Ways to Donate

The tax law provides for a myriad of ways to make charitable gifts. Here are some:

➤ outright gifts

➤ charitable annuity

➤ charitable remainder trusts

➤ charitable remainder in residence or farm

➤ life insurance gifts

The first way to make a charitable contribution has been amply illustrated in previous pages. Most of us simply give our money to a charity, but perhaps we should consider some of the alternatives.

The Charitable Annuity

Maureen decides to give some cash she has to a favoured charity. In turn, the charity agrees to pay her an *annuity* or *fixed annual payment* for her life. Using Revenue Canada tables based on her age, Maureen can compute how much of the value of the gifted property will be returned to her in the form of the annuity and how much of its value the charity will keep. A portion of the interest income earned by the annuity is not taxable because part of it is a return of Maureen's capital. Her gift will also generate a donation receipt.

> **Tip**
>
> Keep in mind that a charitable receipt is only available for the net value of property transferred to the qualified charity. If the donor retains some interest in the property, the amount of the deduction will be reduced by the value retained by the donor or given to another non-charity, such as a relative.

Charitable Remainder Trusts

The tax deduction for a *charitable remainder trust* operates on the same basic principles as the charitable annuity.

Charitable remainder trusts have a non-charity as an income beneficiary, with the remainder (the principal) going to a charity when the income interest terminates.

The person creating the trust (the grantor) often will be the income beneficiary. Frequently the spouse is included as a joint/survivor income beneficiary. There is no tax for the gift to the spouse because of the spousal rollover. However, if anyone other than a spouse is an income beneficiary, then it is a gift with tax consequences to consider.

The value of the gift of the residual interest in the trust depends on the fair market value of the property and your life

> **Quote...Unquote**
>
> A small gift is better than a great promise.
>
> —*German proverb*

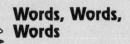

Words, Words, Words

To *endow* a hospital, university or similar public or charitable facility is to make a grant of money providing for the continuing support or maintenance of that institution.

expectancy. You should receive the normal tax credits and the income from the asset but the charity gets a vested interest in the property before you leave it in your will.

Life Insurance Gifts

You can make a charity a beneficiary under an existing policy. Let's say you have a $100,000 whole life policy with a paid-up value of $6,000. If the policy has a cash surrender value, this amount ($6,000), along with future premiums, is your donated amount. The charity gets the death benefits and you avoid probate costs on the gift.

You, however, can get a tax donation receipt for the face value of the policy ($100,000) if it is paid to your estate under your will—provided you then in your will instruct your executor to pay the proceeds ($100,000) to your favoured charity. Your estate would then get a tax receipt for the donation. You must remember that just naming a charity as the beneficiary on a life insurance policy will not give your estate any tax benefit. The gift must come from your estate.

Another way to obtain tax relief on your present income is by purchasing a new life insurance policy. The charity, if it accepts the policy, will issue a tax receipt for the annual premiums on a new policy or an existing whole life policy—legal ownership of which is transferred to the charity.

Other Charitable Gifts

The list goes on. Tax law permits you to deed your personal residence or farm to a charity, while you retain a life estate in that property and receive a non-refundable tax credit for the actuarial value of the charity's remainder interest. The personal residence doesn't have to be the home in which you are currently residing.

Tony, for example, has a principal residence and a vacation property. He may deed either or both homes to a charity while retaining a life estate, so he can use the residence and receive a non-refundable tax credit.

Retirement and Beyond

Most of us buy life insurance to protect our families while the children are growing up. After that, the life insurance becomes more expensive and less important, particularly if our estate will be ample for the rest of our lives.

Quote...Unquote

Lend before witnesses, but give without them.

—*Anonymous*

If you like, you can change the primary or contingent beneficiary of the policy and name a qualified charity.

If the charity is the primary beneficiary, you can receive a charitable deduction for the premiums you pay. Upon your death, the charity will receive the proceeds. So for a relatively modest payment in premiums, you can leave a substantial amount of money to charity. (The charity must be the owner of the policy for you to receive the non-refundable tax credit for the premiums.)

Perhaps you can't spare anything now to give to a charity, but after your death your estate could part with some money. You can leave a specified amount or a percentage of your probate estate to one or several charities. Consider allowing your executor to make gifts of publicly listed securities in your will.

The Least You Need to Know

➤ Gifts to charities may qualify for an immediate non-refundable income tax credit.

➤ Charitable gifts of capital property are usually valued at their fair market value at the time of the gift.

➤ Gifts of publicly listed securities receive special treatment under 1997 proposed federal budget changes. They are now more tax effective than other types of gifts.

➤ Life insurance policies and devises in a will allow the donor to make a substantial gift at little or no expense.

Probate Fees: When and How You Can Be Hit

Too often we focus on the big picture (federal income taxes) and forget about the little one (provincial taxes). In estate planning it's important to consider all taxes as obstacles to building wealth. That goes for real estate taxes, sales taxes and a number of others.

Inheriting? The Province Has Its Hand Out

There's good news and bad news. Every province has some form of probate fees. The good news is, those rates are considerably lower than the income tax rate.

First, a few definitions so we'll all know what we're talking about here.

Probate fees are administrative charges levied by the courts in each province. When a provincial estate court grants probate of a will, or administration of an estate without a will, it charges a "probate fee."

Most people would not mince words. Whether it's an administrative charge or a disguised tax doesn't matter. What counts is that the government takes it off the top from your estate. Minimizing probate fees is a legitimate way of keeping more of your estate for your beneficiaries.

> **Tip**
>
> Who pays the probate fee? Well, technically it is the beneficiary whose interest is reduced by the amount paid for the court filing fees.

Provincial "Probate Fees"

The words "probate fees" have become associated with the duo of "death and taxes." Popular wisdom and bad advice have prompted many to adopt an avoidance mentality to probate. Any tax you can (legitimately) avoid paying to the government is considered a victory, however small.

Probate fees are calculated as a percentage of the value of property passing under the court's supervision, whether you have a will or not. Technically, probate only relates to an estate where there is a will. But the fees are collected when estate papers are filed with the court handling estate matters in each province.

Fees are levied on a percentage of the value of the estate as shown on a "true inventory" filed with the court by an estate's representative. These fees are collected whenever the court is involved in the administration of an estate whether the person died with a will or intestate (without a will).

Let's see how we can plan to reduce or to save probate fees. But first, let's see how they are calculated.

Probate Rates: Malcolm's Situation

Ontario currently collects the highest probate fees of any province. The charge is $250 on the first $50,000 of asset value and a rate of $15 per $1,000 thereafter on declared assets passing through the estate.

Fees are only charged on assets passing by reason of the will, if there is one, and administration if there is no will. No deduction is made for estate debts except for mortgages or encumbrances on real property. Life insurance and other assets with designated beneficiaries not flowing through the estate are excluded from the calculation. Real estate holdings in other jurisdictions are also excluded from probate.

Here's an example to show you how the probate fees can add up and how they are calculated.

Malcolm lives in Ontario. He has a life insurance policy for $200,000 and RRSPs of $200,000 that are payable to his estate when he dies. He also recently purchased a personal residence for $400,000 with a mortgage of $100,000. The home contains his collection of antiques, worth $50,000, and he recently borrowed $10,000 from the bank to purchase a number of new pieces. The value of Malcolm's estate for probate purposes is based on the inclusion/exclusion rules.

Here's how to calculate probate fees after you decide what is included and what is excluded from the probate calculations.

➤ **Life insurance policy** As this is payable to the estate, it must be dealt with by the will. It is **included** ($200,000).

➤ **RRSPs** These are payable to the estate on Malcolm's death after income taxes are deducted. But income tax liability is not a deduction when calculating probate fees. The entire amount is valued as of the date of death, and is **included** ($200,000).

➤ **Personal residence** We have seen that a personal residence is exempt for income tax purposes. Not so for probate. This asset passes by the will, and the home's value as of the date of Malcolm's death is **included**. His executor obtained a current house appraisal showing $500,000. The mortgage was only $50,000, so the net for probate is $500,000 less the $50,000 mortgage, or $450,000.

➤ **Antiques** These are part of the estate even if they are specifically given as gifts to individuals under Malcolm's will. The beneficiaries of the antiques do not pay the

Quote...Unquote

Taxes, after all, are the dues we pay for the privileges of membership in an organized society.

—*Franklin D. Roosevelt, in a speech, Worcester, MA, October 21, 1936* fees. The appraised value as of death for the antiques is **included** ($50,000).

➤ **Personal loan** This is not deducted because, unlike the mortgage on the home, it is unsecured against real estate.

Using the inclusion and exclusion tests you can calculate the probate fees as follows:

Life insurance proceeds	$200,000
Total value of RRSPs	$200,000
Personal residence less encumbrances	$450,000
Antiques	$ 50,000
TOTAL value for probate	$900,000

The next step is to apply the probate rate against the estate's value:

$250 on the first $50,000	$250
$15 per thousand on remaining $850,000	$12,750
TOTAL PROBATE FEE	$13,000

Excluding Assets From Probate

How can you structure your affairs to minimize probate fees? We discussed them briefly in Chapter 10, All About Probate. But for most people, the costs of setting up and maintaining a trust are too much.

Simple strategies can also work, and we'll now look at:

➤ designated assets

➤ jointly owned assets

Designated Assets

This class of property is transferred outside of your will or probate estate. By operation of law or under a contractual arrangement, for example, property can be paid directly to a loved one without passing through your estate. Life insurance proceeds are paid because you designate a beneficiary in the policy and not because it forms any part of your estate for probate purposes. Designating a beneficiary on assets so that they are not paid into your estate will save you probate costs on those particular assets.

Joint Assets

A jointly owned stock portfolio or bank account is transferred to the surviving joint owner because of how the ownership is recorded— "jointly with right of survivorship." Real estate can also be registered as a joint asset, and this allows the property to go to the survivor without probate fees.

Other Probate-Saving Techniques

If Tom dies in a car accident and leaves his entire estate to his spouse, Linda, for example, his executor would pay probate fees on the assets to be transferred by his will to Linda. What happens if Linda dies ten days after Tom because of injuries sustained in the same car accident? Tom's entire estate would be charged double probate fees. This happens once as Tom's assets pass through probate court into Linda's hands as his beneficiary. Then as his estate is passed and probated through his spouse's estate his wife's estate will pay fees on his assets.

This potential problem of double probate costs can be avoided by having a 30-day survivorship period inserted in your will. The thirty-day period is a condition that your spouse must survive you by that length of time to be entitled to inherit your estate.

This survivorship period is an arbitrary number frequently used and 20 or 45 days could be used instead. There is no magical power with the number 30. The survivorship condition does work other wonders though.

Tom intended his estate to go to charity should his spouse not survive. If Linda did not have an identical residual beneficiary in her will, then a startling result can take place. Linda's will could, for example, direct that her residue go to her children from her first marriage. This would leave Tom's charity out in the cold without a gift, because Tom's will did not have a thirty-day survivorship condition.

Gift Away Your Assets

You may feel better giving away some of the assets you don't need while you are alive. This way you can watch your beneficiaries enjoy your gift.

You can also avoid probate on the particular property that you would not otherwise transfer except through your will. Remember your gifting options from Chapter 18 and that making a gift can create capital gains consequences as well.

The principal method of avoiding provincial probate fees is to keep assets out of your estate unless it is necessary to manage them through your executor or to claim a tax advantage such as a charitable tax credit.

Quote...Unquote

The state is never so efficient as when it wants money.

—*Anthony Burgess, "You've Had Your Time" (1990)*

For most people, their home or real estate holdings represent one of their largest investments. Just holding real estate jointly with a spouse, for instance, can save money. That is, if your marriage is secure.

Malcolm Revisited

Malcolm has reviewed his estate plan after estimating the probate fees that would be paid from his estate, and he has taken the following steps:

➤ **Life insurance** Redesignated to go directly to a beneficiary. No longer are the proceeds part of the estate for probate.

➤ **RRSPs** His wife was named a designated beneficiary on all his plans. Now these proceeds will go on a tax-deferred basis to his spouse and avoid probate as well.

➤ **Personal residence** A new deed was prepared, making the property jointly owned with his spouse—excluding the home from probate costs.

➤ **Antiques** As Malcolm and his spouse downsize and sell their large residence for a smaller condominium, they have agreed to give the larger pieces to family as gifts—this will avoid fees as well.

➤ **Personal loan** Malcolm has decided to register a collateral line of credit mortgage on his home rather than continue taking out personal loans to build his antique collection. The mortgage will qualify as a deduction against the value of the home should he survive his spouse and become the sole owner.

Dangerous Manoeuvres for Reducing Probate Costs

As it happened, Malcolm's wife predeceased him. He came into my office after his wife's funeral. As the sole owner of his home, he wanted to avoid probate fees.

He was considering placing his son on the title to his home. Malcolm figured that this would exclude the home from probate.

Malcolm also wanted his daughter, Darlene, to be the joint owner of his bank account, worth over $200,000.

I had to advise Malcolm of the risks and pointed out a few problems that could arise.

➤ **Creditors** Children can have creditors. A child's creditor or bankruptcy could result in a seizure of the child's portion of assets held with a parent.

➤ **Family law** A child's spouse may acquire property rights under a province's family law just by the child's taking title to an asset with a parent.

➤ **Child misconduct** Never forget that an adult child—because of a falling out, problem with substance abuse or just greed—may exercise their right to sever a joint tenancy, or sell and liquidate a jointly held asset.

➤ **Tax consequences** Except for your principal residence exemption, the transfer of capital property can generate tax. Transfer costs for real estate assets can be higher than probate fees.

Quote...Unquote

His money was twice tainted: 'tain't yours and 'tain't mine.

—*Mark Twain*

Advising Malcolm

Most adults want to retain control of their finances and property for as long as possible. The transfer of property to a child on joint account is a direct loss of control. Adverse tax consequences and the other potential problems I have mentioned may cause you to have second thoughts.

You should check your probate-saving techniques with your lawyer before taking any steps that may be irreversible.

You can see how important it is to give careful thought to saving your estate from unnecessary probate fees. All of those taxes, small and not-so-small, can eat away at your estate.

The Least You Need to Know

➤ All provinces (except Quebec) charge "probate fees" on assets administered through your will—or estate administration, if you have no will.

➤ Probate fee planning should be coordinated with your income tax planning.

➤ Jointly owned and designated property usually does not pass through probate. The assets are transferred to co-owners or beneficiaries by law or contract.

➤ Consider the potential for problems, tax or otherwise, if you transfer assets or hold them jointly—even with your children.

OOOOH... Whisper Whisper

Chapter 20

Income Taxes and Tax-Saving Tips

In This Chapter

➤ Tax planning

➤ Divorce and taxes

➤ Dandy business deductions

➤ Estate tax savings

I'll tell you this: You're probably paying too much income tax. And I'll tell you something else: Revenue Canada isn't about to set you straight.

Naturally the more money you keep from the government over the years, the larger your estate will be. What follows are some income tax savings that build wealth. So use these tax strategies to your—and your family's—advantage.

Be careful when reading this book. The law is constantly changing—especially the tax laws. Decisions are made daily by the court system that can change the law overnight. Professional tax advisers must be consulted. This book cannot be a substitute for professional advice, especially when you consider the next topic, the federal government's anti-avoidance rules.

General Anti-Avoidance Rules, or GAAR

Tax planning to defer or minimize income taxes is a legitimate activity recognized by the government. But some creative individuals may try to avoid taxes in ways the federal government never intended.

Sometimes these techniques are classified as tax avoidance or loopholes that are exploited until Revenue Canada cracks down on the procedures.

GAAR provides general rules for anti-avoidance for all transactions. This allows Revenue Canada to re-assess and ignore legal transactions if they are considered to be an abuse or misuse of the Income Tax Act. All tax planning takes place with this understanding: The transaction must be for a legitimate purpose other than to seize a tax benefit. To this end, Revenue Canada has published the types of transactions it considers acceptable and unacceptable under the GAAR rules. To date, the courts have seen a minimal number of cases concerning GAAR, even though the law has been on the books since 1987.

Divorce and Taxes

Canada has "no-fault" divorce laws, so the primary issues in most contested cases are child custody, support and property division. Tax planning is important. Included in the custody issue is the question of who gets the "equivalent to spouse" exemption. The parent awarded custody who receives support is entitled to claim the equivalent to spouse exemption as a non-refundable tax credit.

Property settlements between spouses usually do not result in any tax to either party at the time of the divorce settlement. But who gets to keep which assets may have significant tax implications in future years. For example, the higher bracket taxpayer might want to transfer family assets that have significantly appreciated, and will soon be sold, to the other person.

Take Cliff and his soon-to-be-ex-wife. They purchased stock several years ago for $10,000 that is now worth $60,000. It's estimated that Cliff's tax bracket after the divorce will be 28 percent; hers, 15 percent. If he receives the stock and sells it, he will pay $13,000 in taxes, while if she receives the same property and sells it, she will pay $7,500 in taxes.

Also, spousal support may be negotiable. Then support payments are usually taxable income to the recipient and a deduction from gross income to the payer. The deduction may be more valuable to the higher bracket ex-spouse than the income tax paid would be to the recipient.

Try if at all possible when negotiating property settlement and spousal support to consider tax advantages that will benefit both parties.

Canada's new tax system for child support payments applies to all new orders or agreements after April 30, 1997. Child support payments under varied or new agreements and court order will no longer be included as income in the recipient's hands. The paying spouse will not be entitled to claim a "support deduction" from income. Child support after this date will be based primarily on the Federal Child Support Guidelines.

Taxpayers' 10 Biggest Mistakes

Do you know that there are some taxpayers who don't take into account all allowable deductions when filing taxes? They're literally giving a gift to Revenue Canada! Take a look at this list, and check the common mistakes made by those who file. Do you recognize yourself anywhere here? Some of these errors result in additional paperwork for the taxpayer that, in the long run, might not really be worth the bother. But others, as I said, can cost him or her sizable amounts of money.

Here is a list of some of the biggest mistakes people make in paying taxes:

1. Not using the proper Revenue Canada forms (tables, schedules, etc.)

2. Not keeping accurate or proper records (receipts, auto mileage, etc.)

3. Not doing mathematical calculations correctly

4. Having too much money withheld from each paycheque, so that the government is holding your money interest-free. (Some people, on the other hand, view such extra withholding as a form of forced savings, and they look forward to the refund cheque.) Your employer is responsible for withholding income tax, but if you can obtain Revenue Canada's permission, source deductions can be reduced if certain criteria are met

5. Not keeping up with tax news if you're preparing your own return—what you don't know can cost you

6. Not seeking professional help when stumped. You may be missing out on legitimate deductions

7. Not being forthcoming with answers to a tax preparer

8. Not properly reporting interest on tax refunds from the previous year's income tax refund

9. Not deducting employee-related expenses—such as professional fees and memberships

10. Not including payment with a return if tax is owed, thereby attracting non-deductible interest charges.

Dandy Business Deductions

If you work for yourself or own a business, you had better hire a good tax accountant or study the books carefully because there are a number of excellent deductions out there. Revenue Canada's published guides, which are available at no cost (and on the Internet) are very helpful.

The Income Tax Act is obviously too complex to discuss every possible deduction, so I'll highlight just a few here:

➤ Consider a business vehicle as a means of private transportation. The company gets to depreciate the car, and you get to drive it, perhaps including a few personal kilometres. However, there is a personal tax cost based on the personal kilometres driven. Therefore, you may want to use your own vehicle and charge the business for its use. The rules for automobiles are very complex but the Revenue Canada guides provide the details.

➤ Think about attending a business conference. They're usually held in warm, scenic locales, making the mixture of business and

Quote...Unquote

The ceiling on taxation of capital gains reflects the national belief that speculation is a more worthwhile way to make a living than work.

—*Calvin Trillin "Uncivil Liberties" (1982)*

Quote...Unquote

It is necessary to work, if not from inclination, at least from despair. Everything considered, work is less boring than amusing oneself.

—*Charles Baudelaire, "Mon coeur mis a nu" (1887)*

Quote...Unquote

In America, it is sport that is the opiate of the masses.

—*Russell Baker, "Observer," The New York Times (1967)*

Quote...Unquote

The income tax has made more liars out of the American people than golf has. Even when you make a tax form out on the level, you don't know when it's through if you are a crook or a martyr.

—*Will Rogers*

pleasure a quite attractive "twofer." The airfare is a business deduction if the primary purpose of the travel is business.

➤ Take advantage of your right to depreciate capital expenditures, which spreads the deduction over several years.

➤ Take care, though, if you have a business that has been losing money. Beware of Revenue Canada's rules about having a reasonable expectation of profit.

Ally, for example, is an accountant with a strong love of horses and a devotion to the racetrack. She buys a horse, hires a trainer and rents a stable, all of which costs money—and quite a bit of it, too. This is an intriguing but not inexpensive enterprise.

Ally's horse wins some and loses some, but every year the operation shows a loss.

Ally can bet on an audit. Revenue Canada has a clear philosophy on this: No deductions for any activity that gives the taxpayer any enjoyment whatsoever.

Well, that's not quite true. There *is* a presumption that an activity is not a hobby if it has shown a profit in at least three of any five consecutive years (maybe two of seven if it's horse racing and you are a betting person).

The tax rules state that for any item to be deductible it must be an outlay or expense to earn income. Secondly, it must be reasonable under the circumstances. To determine if there was a reasonable expectation of profit, Revenue Canada looks at several factors, one of which is whether or not the activity is conducted in a business-like manner. Therefore you should spend sufficient time running your interest like a business and hire experts if you lack expertise in certain aspects of the operation. If you are strictly a dabbler, interested in recreation, then forget about deducting losses.

The Home Office

Revenue Canada is concerned about all of us who have offices in our homes, because we can deduct expenses related to the office. In this day and age, both employees and self-employed individuals may be able to deduct home office expenses. The rules are strict to ensure there are no abuses. To qualify for home office deductions for a business, for example, you must use the home as your principal place of business or exclusively on a regular and continuous basis for meeting clients or customers.

Lois, for example, is a law professor during the day, and at night practises law out of a room in her house, where she meets clients.

➤ Lois deducts—and you can too—a portion of the cost of utilities for the whole house, depreciates the room, and allocates some of the property tax and mortgage interest to the office. It's not a good idea to claim Capital Cost Allowance (CCA) on the portion of the house used for business purposes, because the principal residence exemption would be lost on that portion of the house and capital gains tax could arise.

➤ Self-employed individuals may also deduct any related expenses for an office in the residence. Are you putting a new roof on your house? A percentage of that bill can be deducted as an office expense if the cost of the roof is not considered to be capital in nature.

➤ No, decorating doesn't count as a deductible expense for your home, but it does for your home office. Don't forget not only the obvious deductions but also claiming CCA on capital expenditures, such as office furnishings and computer equipment.

➤ Remember if you are operating a business from your home, if you don't show a profit, your deductions for that enterprise may be questioned.

Estate Tax Savings

Reducing or avoiding taxes on death means more money passing to your loved ones, rather than to the government's tax coffers.

Avoiding taxes on death is simple: die poor. Or die and leave everything outright to your spouse, a charity or a combination of both—not always viable solutions. I offered many suggestions for tax savings in

Chapters 16 through 19. Here are some special strategies taking a broader view of the subject.

➤ Give it away. Not all at once, but each year. Very often children need money when they are rearing your grandchildren. You can accommodate their needs better now than after your death.

➤ Establish an income trust for you and your spouse, with the remainder going to a charity. You get income to live on, a current charitable credit, and the rest goes to the charity on the death of the surviving spouse.

➤ Create a qualified spousal trust for your spouse, which would impose no income taxes at your death and provide income for the spouse; the remainder could go to your children.

➤ Buy life insurance to pay your tax bill on death. If your spouse doesn't need the money and your children are all grown, you can give them a substantial legacy at very little expense to you.

Savings by Your Executor

The executor administers the probate estate, which means he or she has certain power over the property and timing of its distribution that can have beneficial tax implications.

There are several ways an executor can do this:

Briefs

Could you use a smile about now, with all the talk of your own mortality? An insurance office was naturally surprised when an elderly gentleman of 97 stopped in and asked to take out a life insurance policy. His application was turned down. The oldster stood up, shook his head at the agent who had given him the rejection, sighed and said "You folks are making a big mistake. If you look at your statistics you'll find that mighty few men die after they're 97."

➤ By reducing estate taxes by making appropriate tax elections or claiming deductions. For example, an executor can contribute to a spousal RRSP following the taxpayer's death

➤ By reducing income taxes to the estate and its beneficiaries by timing income distributions

➤ By filing additional income tax returns. Depending on your sources of income, the following returns can be filed: "Rights and Things" income (for income earned but not yet collected), proprietorship or partnership income where the deceased dies after the fiscal year end but before the end of the calendar year, or income from a testamentary trust. These tax returns, if filed, allow your executor to use full non-refundable tax credits since each is treated as a separate individual.

Let me explain some of these tax-saving strategies to you.

> **Words, Words, Words**
>
> *Fiduciary* means trust. In the context here it means the estate has earned income and has to file a tax return.
>
> The executor therefore needs to be aware of income tax rules that apply to estate distributions when the estate has taxable income.

Timing Income Distribution

Every estate that has any property-generating income (e.g. stocks, savings accounts, rentals), will have to file income tax returns for the income earned

➤ during the deceased's life (individual's terminal return T1), and

➤ during estate administration (estate's trust tax return T3).

Since there are at least two income tax returns to be filed (deceased's last return and a trust return for the estate), the selection of the trust's first year provides flexibility.

> **Quote...Unquote**
>
> If Patrick Henry thought that taxation without representation was bad, he should see how bad it is with representation.
>
> —*The Old Farmer's Almanac*

The Least You Need to Know

➤ Before filing, scrutinize your income tax return for more tax deductions; there are likely to be some.

➤ Time your income and deductible expenses to take advantage of different tax rates in different years.

➤ A will can maximize income tax savings.

➤ A good executor will seek professional advice about ways to save taxes on your estate.

Chapter 21

Keeping Your Wealth Within the Family

In This Chapter

➤ Giving to the next generation

➤ Selling to the family

➤ Gifts to youngsters

➤ The family business

Let's assume that you want a family member, or perhaps the whole clan, to inherit from your estate.

That can be done—to everyone's benefit. Here are some suggestions, a few you have read about briefly in other chapters, plus some new strategies. All are designed to keep your assets in the bosom of your family. Match them up one against the other to see which would work best for you. Just as important as keeping wealth in the family, of course, is how to make that transfer at the least cost to you (or them). I'll tell you how right now.

Quote...Unquote

An ounce of blood is worth more than a pound of friendship.

—*Spanish proverb*

Charity Begins at Home

Probate and taxes take time and toll, so our goal is to minimize both.

The transfer laws are fairly simple and you've read about them earlier in these pages. For example, making a gift requires only that the donor intends to make that gift, the donee accepts, and a physical transfer occurs. Likewise, upon death the will distributes probate assets to the named beneficiaries, or the living trust continues to provide principal and interest for its beneficiaries.

The rub in all of this, of course, is taxes. Let's see what we can do about that.

The Next Generation

Most couples with children quite naturally want to pass on their assets to those kids, either now or through their estate. There are a number of ways to do this:

➤ outright gifts

➤ trusts with income splitting and remainder interests

➤ rearranging business assets

➤ purchasing life insurance, annuities, or other easily transferable assets

➤ creating joint interests

➤ gifting property but retaining a life interest in it for the donor

➤ below-market-rate loans or gift loans (the latter might be a loan to a child that is then forgiven)

➤ employing children in the family business

➤ wills

All of these things require planning and thorough consideration of the tax consequences. You can read about some of them in earlier chapters of this book and can, of course, discuss them with your tax adviser.

Certainly transfers to your spouse are considered within the scope of this chapter, because they are most easily made, have few tax consequences, and are likely to result in your property ultimately going to the children after your spouse's death. (Of course that assumption may not be true if the spouse is not the parent of your children.)

Giving Something—and Keeping It

Perhaps you'd like to make a gift—but only sort of. How about a partial transfer of property to someone else?

Bonnie owns a condominium. She wants to keep ownership and use it during her lifetime, then wants the title to go to her daughter. Bonnie could deed the condo to her daughter and retain a life interest that would accomplish her goal. (There's more about life estates in Chapter 2.)

A retained interest in property that is a principal residence is exempt from income tax. Bonnie's daughter's interest is subject to capital gains if the property appreciates and she does not live there. She also cannot claim the exemption during her period of ownership unless the property qualifies as her principal residence.

Trust Them

You can establish a trust for yourself (and your spouse), reserving the right to the income and withdrawing the principal, with the remainder going to your child upon your (and your spouse's) death.

Ken created a living trust for himself and his spouse, deposited assets in the trust, and lived off the income. Upon the death of Ken's wife, and then Ken, the assets went to his adult children outright.

Income from revocable trusts is taxed to the grantor, or settlor, who established the trust. There are no tax consequences to the children because they receive nothing until the parent's death. But the children will not have to pay probate fees when their parent dies and they get the trust's assets.

If you create an *irrevocable* living trust, then there is a gift to

> **Tip**
>
> All transfers during your life require you to determine how much less money you can afford to live on. You don't want to give away too much; one day you may need some of that money for your own purposes.

beneficiaries of the trust. If the trust qualifies as "spousal," the tax rollover would avoid capital gains on the transfer to the trust.

Family Trusts

The term "family trust" refers to a trust created for the benefit of family members. No specific legal definition exists for this type of trust. It is used to achieve legal income splitting and to carry out an estate freeze. A trust holds the trust property for a settlor's and his or her spouse's lifetime with the remainder of the capital going to their children. The trustees, during the settlor's lifetime, can sprinkle income usually in a fixed or discretionary manner. "Spousal Trusts" would dictate that only the spouse of a settlor would receive trust income or capital to qualify for the "spousal rollover" and the tax deferral of capital gains.

Dina transferred $400,000 into a family trust for the life of her four children, which will then pass the remainder on to her grandchildren.

A cash transfer to an irrevocable trust, with the settlor retaining no rights, will have no capital gains to worry about at the time of the transfer. Income earned in the trust will be taxed to the trust and its beneficiaries if the children are all adults.

Watch Out

Be sure you talk over with your children any gifts or investing you want to make for your grandkids now rather than later. What you have in mind might conflict with your children's ideas and plans.

Estate Freezes

An estate freeze can avoid the operation of the deemed disposition rules on death that catch and tax all accrued gains. To save taxes that might otherwise arise, an "estate freeze" can be used to transfer the future capital appreciation from one generation to the next.

Estate freezes require complex tax advice and should only be considered after proper tax planning with a professional has taken place. The concept, as we will explain in more detail, is basically that an individual "freezes" the value of his capital today so that the future growth will accrue to the next generation and not be taxed on the individual's death.

If you expect an asset to appreciate, as in the case of your business, you can freeze its value. You can then, on a "tax-free" basis, exchange your assets—shares, for instance—for a different type of asset or shares with no growth potential. Your children acquire the assets with the potential to appreciate through a trust or holding corporation. The future growth after the freeze will accrue to the shares owned by the children.

Considering Co-ownership

You might want to own property, such as bank accounts or stock, with another person. When you create jointly owned property that transfers an undivided interest at the time it is created the survivor receives the entire interest at the other's death.

In case that isn't completely clear to you, I'll give you an example. Grant adds his adult son to his savings account as joint owner with right of survivorship. Grant also owns a house, and executes a deed in which his daughter is joint owner with right of survivorship.

> **Quote...Unquote**
>
> If wisdom were offered to me with the proviso that I should keep it shut up and refrain from declaring it, I should refuse. There's no delight in owning anything unshared.
>
> —*Seneca, "Letters to Lucilius"* *(1st c.)*

No tax liability arises in creating a joint ownership in a savings account (withdrawal by the non-depositor is a gift). A gift is considered complete only upon withdrawal from the bank account. But the creation of a joint ownership in other property is an immediate disposition of an interest. All this means is that Grant owes no tax for the savings account with his son when it's established, or on the property he now owns jointly with his daughter if the property qualifies as his principal residence.

Grant's daughter owns the house just like her father, and she will potentially have capital gains consequences unless the property qualifies as her principal residence.

Life Insurance

You might want to purchase life insurance, particularly term, and name a child as beneficiary. That could provide a substantial benefit to the child at little expense to you, and may be appropriate when you don't need the coverage to protect your family in the event of your untimely death.

Life insurance usually attracts no tax consequences to the beneficiary. The benefit is a tax-free payment passing directly to the child.

Words, Words, Words

Merriam Webster's Collegiate Dictionary says to *document* is "to provide with factual or substantial support for statements made or a hypotheses proposed." An example of that would be a promissory note.

Loans Within the Family

They aren't that unusual (naturally we're not talking about the can-you-let-me-have-twenty-until-payday variety), and can be an excellent means of shifting wealth to a child.

Casey lends his son $100,000 at zero percent percent interest per year, with installment payments of $10,000 each year. There is a promissory note evidencing the debt and a mortgage on the home his son purchased with the funds. While Casey never indicated any plan to do so at the time of making the loan, he has for several years completely forgiven those annual $10,000 debt payments.

Income tax applies to below-market-interest loans to the extent of Revenue Canada's prescribed rate because the borrower doesn't pay the same interest he would on a commercial loan. Thus, he is, in effect, "given" the interest by the lender. The federal income tax treats this situation as if the lender has received the interest.

Don't forget to document this loan, and enforce its provisions the way you would any other. Revenue Canada is not particularly happy with this type of arrangement, so you'll want to cover yourself.

Your Family as Buyers

Selling an asset to a family member keeps it in the family. You can structure the sale on an installment basis but ensure that all transactions are at fair market value since the anti-avoidance rules can come into play otherwise.

Alex sold some land to his son for $100,000, being its fair market value, payable in ten equal installments, with a 10 percent per annum interest rate. The property had cost him $10,000 when he purchased it. He also sold another parcel to his daughter for $50,000 (it was worth $100,000 at the time of this sale). That property originally cost Alex $10,000 as well.

The capital gains to be reported by Alex are the same in both instances (that is, $90,000), of which 75 percent is taxable. However, since the sale to his daughter was below fair market value, double taxation arises. Alex is deemed to have disposed of the property at fair market value and her cost basis is equal to her actual cost. This is punitive.

Alex's installment receipts and interest will result in taxable income each year. If he were to give the property to his daughter as a gift there would be no adverse tax consequences. Her cost would equal his deemed proceeds of disposition which would equal the fair market value of the transferred property.

Tip

You might want to consider selling appreciating property to a family member, since the appreciation occurring after the sale will not be included in the seller's estate. Only the proceeds from the sale when the property had a lesser value will.

Gifts to Minors

Outright presents to minor children are all right for birthdays and holidays, but only when they come in gift-wrapped packages or are relatively small amounts of cash.

For any sizable amount, consider one of the following:

➤ a children's trust bank account

➤ trust stock account (stocks, bonds)

➤ a minor's trust

➤ a living trust

You don't want your children to waste your hard-earned cash, so it's important to keep their hands off the money while they are still young.

Nan establishes a trust account at her local bank or trust company for her daughter and deposits $10,000 in the account each year. She purchases stock for her son for the same amount, and names a trustee. Her choice of trustee for both is her brother, Bob.

Trust accounts and property are in held in trust until the donee reaches the age of majority as indicated by provincial requirements. Income is taxed to the donor or settlor because of the attribution rules.

Nan can, however, operate a bank or stock trust account and invest her children's Child Tax Benefit. Revenue Canada considers the

investment income earned from this specific source will be taxed at the lower child's rate, since the funds belong to the child.

An alternative to trust accounts that have basically the same income, gift, and estate tax advantages is a *minor's trust*.

Ben creates such a trust for his daughter, age 2. The trustee is the Trustworthy Trustco. The trust will distribute all income and principal to the daughter when she becomes 18; if she dies before then, all the trust property will be in her estate. (A minor's trust can also be extended beyond age 18.)

The gift of shares to a properly designed minor's trust may qualify for tax savings for the family. The trust assets are not subject to the donor's income tax on death if he or she maintains no control over the trust. Although the income (including dividends and interest) is taxed to Ben because of the income attribution rules, these do not cover capital gains and appreciating assets can be placed in the trust—unlike cash, which could simply be placed into a trust bank account.

If there are capital gains, they may exceed the income attributed to the gift of the principal. When realized, the capital gains would also be taxed in the child's hands—presumably at a lower rate of tax.

If a long-term trust is considered necessary because of a child's disability, you might want to refer to Chapter 14, which discusses that particular situation.

Splitting It With Your Spouse

A transfer to a spouse or qualifying spousal trust is the major exception to the deemed disposition rule. So capital gains can be avoided as long as your spouse or spousal trust receives the property. No tax is triggered until your spouse dies or sells the asset.

An election can be filed so that the rollover would not apply. This would permit capital losses to be applied against capital gains on the transferor spouse's return or the estate's return if the transfer was to a testamentary spousal trust.

Your Business for Your Benefit

Say you own a business, whether it is a sole proprietorship, a partnership or a corporation. If you control the business, you may want to pass it on to your children. You want to leave behind your little niche of capitalism to those who can most appreciate it—your family.

Transferring Company Shares

Jay owns all the outstanding shares in House Calls, Inc., a repair service. He could give 40 percent of the shares to his two children and still control the corporation. Or he could restructure the capital and create voting and non-voting common shares, retaining all or a majority of the voting shares so that he stays in control of the business.

Gifts of shares are subject to the deemed disposition rules at fair market value. Periodically giving shares to your children as it becomes clearer that they will be responsible can significantly reduce your estate and income taxes provided there is significant capital appreciation subsequent to the transfer.

Buy-Sell Agreements

Another way to transfer your family business to a member or members of your family is through a buy–sell agreement. In such an agreement family members would purchase your interest in the business at your retirement or upon your demise. This would provide cash during retirement

Watch Out!

Be realistic in determining whether your children are interested in owning your business, or are indeed capable of running it. Also be prepared to compensate those who *don't* want the business, especially in ways that will not interfere with those who do.

Often the parent/owner wants to retain control while gradually transferring ownership to the next generation. Usually that is easier to structure with a corporation than with a partnership.

Watch Out!

Corporation shares restructuring may have adverse income tax effects. Consult a tax expert before making any move.

Tip

Children/ shareholders could purchase life insurance on the life of the parent/shareholder and use that money to fund an estate share buyout upon the death of that parent.

Quote...Unquote

Nothing is more admirable than the fortitude with which millionaires tolerate the disadvantages of their wealth.

—*Rex Stout*

years or for your estate survivors and would keep the business within the family.

Employing Your Kids

Wealth can also be transferred through the employment of your children. Many family businesses have done this. Children, even when still in their teens, can earn spending money from the business. Giving their kids jobs there allows parents to share the wealth (and responsibilities). And reasonable wages are deductible business expenses provided services are genuinely provided. The result is that income that would otherwise be subject to tax in the parents' hands at a higher marginal rate is taxed in the children's hands.

Estate Freezes

Estate freezes, which you read about earlier in this chapter, can be used to transfer appreciating business assets to the next generation, who will benefit from the appreciation.

Words, Words, Words

A *tontine* is a sort of annuity gimmick. It's named after Lorenzo Tonti, an Italian banker who died in the mid-18th century. Basically, it's a joint financial arrangement whereby the participants contribute usually equal amounts of money to a prize that is awarded entirely to the participant who outlives all the others.

The Least You Need to Know

➤ Income splitting with family members is desirable, but the attribution rules must be considered. Don't forget the general anti-avoidance rules as well.

➤ Gift loans can shift income and assets to children.

➤ A parent can purchase a life insurance policy and give it to a child, providing significant death benefits at little expense.

➤ Family businesses can be restructured to form an orderly transfer to the next generation—and defer their taxes to some extent.

PART V
Retirement, Elder Issues and the Broad Planning Picture

Time marches on. Perhaps you're just a handful of years from retirement. Or maybe that time in your life is so far into the future it seems almost science fiction: retire in 2030? Will there actually be a 2030? Will there still be a life passage known as retirement then?

You'd better count on it. And count it into your estate plan.

As you will see in the coming chapters, there is some good news ahead for retirees in the form of help with some bills. But there are some shaky happenings, too, with familiar, dependable programs that appear to be in trouble. The bottom line for all of us seems to be: Save, get organized and don't count exclusively on government aid in your retirement years.

Here's a closer look at what may be going on in your life as you approach—and then pass—65.

Chapter 22

Bring It On: Retirement

In This Chapter
- ➤ Collecting pension benefits
- ➤ Who else is eligible for your benefits
- ➤ RRSPs and RRIFs: What everyone needs
- ➤ Snowbirds and U.S. taxes

We huff and we puff—figuratively speaking—through much of our working lives. And then when we hit 65, government programs kick in to give us a hand with expenses. Thank goodness for the Canada Pension Plan (CPP) and Old Age Security! They'll still be around, won't they, when *we* retire? And the coverage will be at least adequate, won't it?

Hmmmm. There's some good and some iffy news ahead.

What You Can Expect at Retirement

If you're employed, you pay into the Canada Pension Plan a percentage of your wages and your employer contributes as well. The percentage has varied over the years.

Tip

To have your pension questions answered, call the government at Human Resources Development Canada at 1-800-277-9914.

Of course you are not thrilled about all of this, but the silver lining is that you might get some of that money back when you reach age 65.

Collecting Your Pension

Don't just sit there thinking the government will deliver your monthly cheque once you turn 65 years old. You'll have to apply for the Canada Pension Plan and Old Age Security benefits.

Get an application form from the federal Health and Welfare office. You'll have to prove your entitlement with birth certificates and the like. Its best to send the application forms in at least a few months before you turn 65.

Death Benefits Under the CPP

As well as being protected with a fully-indexed pension, the Canada Pension Plan has surviving spouse benefits. If a partner dies, you are entitled to a percentage of his or her pension if you meet the test for benefits eligibility.

A lump-sum death benefit is also paid by the Canada Pension Plan when a pensioner dies. Most funeral directors can supply the forms for your spouse or estate administrator to fill out to claim this entitlement.

The death benefit is calculated from a formula equal to six months of retirement benefits. The proposed maximum benefit as of 1998 is $2,500.

The Senior's Benefit

Ottawa wants to replace the Old Age Benefits and its Guaranteed Income Supplement (for those with very little income in retirement) with a new Senior's Benefit.

If you hit 65 after January 1 in the year 2001, you will be part of a new income-tested Senior's Benefit with a tax credit system. You and your spouse's joint income will determine if you'll qualify for a payment.

Details of the changes are not yet clear, but one thing we know is that the new benefit will not be taxable as the current payments are.

Anyone over 65 as of December 31, 1997, is not affected by the proposed changes for future government pensions on retirement.

Tip

The National Council of Welfare in Ottawa has a free guide to the proposed Senior's Benefit, which you can obtain by calling (613) 957-2961 or faxing (613) 957-0680.

RRSPs: What Everyone Needs

Everyone should have some form of deferred income plans. If you have no registered pension plan like those we mentioned in Chapter 5, you need, as a minimum, an RRSP account. RRSP stands for Registered Retirement Savings Plan. You don't have to be retired to have an RRSP account. Children with taxable income can open RRSPs.

RRSPs allow you to get a tax deduction for the amount you are allowed to contribute annually to your plan.

The money, while invested in your RRSP account in term deposits—such as shares or mutual funds—grows and compounds on a tax-free basis while it is sheltered in the RRSP. Once you withdraw money from the plan you will pay tax on it.

RRSPs can be set up easily through banks, brokers, agents and trust companies. You just fill out a form and put in your money—but it pays to do some research first. Consult with the financial planner you selected for your estate planning team.

Registered Retirement Income Funds (RRIFs)

The rules say you must convert your RRSP to some form of income in the year you reach 69. For most people, an RRIF is the best choice.

You can keep the same investments in your RRIF as you had in your RRSP. You can continue to buy and sell investments, however, you must draw a minimum amount of money each year that will be taxed as income.

Watch Out

Tax planning in Canada requires constant review of Revenue Canada's ever-changing rules. It is beyond the scope of this book to provide specific counsel for Canadian tax matters—let alone U.S. estate taxes. Competent professional advice is what you need to deal with tax issues if you plan to purchase a retirement property in the United States.

Designate a Beneficiary

A spouse or financially dependent child should be the designated beneficiary of your RRIF. If you die, your spouse gets the funds in the RRIF tax-free. You want to avoid having it paid to your estate, which would have to report it as income and pay tax on it in your final return.

Snowbirds and U.S. Taxes

Canadian snowbirds may be surprised by their potential U.S. tax exposure on death.

United States taxes can apply to Canadians even though they are not U.S. citizens. The tax can arise on U.S. investments on the death of the owner. For most individuals, this would be U.S. real estate and U.S. securities. The U.S. could also levy estate tax on an individual they consider to be a U.S. resident.

If you are planning to purchase a U.S. vacation property, then there are steps you can take to hold your investments.

Let me make these points to consider with your professional adviser:

➤ A Canadian corporation can be a way to hold U.S. assets, including real estate. The corporation does not die when you do and estate taxes may not apply. You need to know the U.S. government's and Revenue Canada's positions on this as well.

➤ Holding assets jointly with a spouse may entitle you to defer estate taxes.

➤ A properly crafted irrevocable Canadian trust may be worth considering.

➤ If there is a tax liability, consider carrying life insurance to cover it.

The final point I need to make is for those who have any real estate situated in another country. You will need a lawyer in that jurisdiction to prepare a will to deal with it and to advise you of the potential taxes.

Canadians planning to purchase U.S. retirement homes should be aware of the local state, gift and estate taxes that will govern their property after death. That's what planning is all about.

The Least You Need to Know

> ➤ The Canada Pension Plan provides survivorship and death benefits.

> ➤ When you reach 69 you must convert your RRSPs to draw income, for which you will be taxed.

> ➤ If you convert your RRSPs to an RRIF, make sure you designate a spouse as your beneficiary to obtain a spousal rollover.

> ➤ If you own real estate in the United States, you will need a will prepared in the state where the property is located. Consult with your U.S. attorney to ensure you will not be subject to American estate and gift taxes.

Chapter 23

Who's In Charge? Arranging for Others to Take Over If You Can't

How do you know you're *really* getting older? The kid serving you at the fast food place automatically gives you a senior citizen's discount!

It happens to all of us (aging, not the discount, although that, too, may be a commonly shared sign that the years are piling up). Estate planning now calls for a few more steps to bring you peace of mind—and the continuing preservation of your assets. There's some paperwork still to be done, some of which may be unfamiliar to you.

Guardianship, and Why You Wouldn't Want It

Adults do not like to be dependent on anyone else, much less on their children, if they have them. Unfortunately, as some of us get older, we don't function as well physically or mentally as we once did. That's life, and there isn't a lot we can do about it. But we *can* plan for the possibility that at some time we might not be able to manage for ourselves.

When an individual becomes incompetent and cannot manage his or her affairs, then provincial law requires that a guardian be appointed. Most jurisdictions call for evidence that an individual, because of a mental disability, can no longer cope alone.

Quote...Unquote

Old people are dangerous. They have no fear of the future.

—*George Bernard Shaw*

Here is how that basic process works:

1. Usually a close family member applies in court to be appointed the guardian.

2. If a guardian is appointed, then he or she (or it, since a financial institution could serve in some instances) must inventory all the incompetent person's assets and file that list with the court.

3. The guardian can also be responsible for the care of the incompetent individual, and must account to the court for all income and expenses. A guardian bond is usually needed.

4. Upon the incompetent person's death, the guardianship is closed and the remaining assets are released to the deceased's executor.

A guardianship situation is not only intrusive, it can also be expensive. Legal fees for all court filings, guardian's bond and guardian's fees could add up to several thousand dollars over the life of the incompetent person.

Quote...Unquote

No one is so old not to think he can live one more year.

—*Cicero*

In addition, the individual you may want to serve as guardian might not be the one the court appoints. Second marriages in particular have the potential for guardianship battles between the second spouse and the children of the first marriage. This is the stuff that front-page news is made of, particularly if there's a prominent person involved.

Not all guardianships can be avoided, but you should nonetheless determine whether having one will be in your best interests.

Here are two alternatives that are better:

➤ a revocable living trust (you've read about trusts often in this book, particularly in Chapter 9)

➤ a continuing power of attorney for property, which I'll talk about next

In any event, plan ahead for this possibility; don't let a guardianship occur by default.

Tip

You might occasionally need a *limited or special power of attorney*. It's been given that name because it's usually in force for just one transaction, such as executing a real estate deed when the seller is not available for the closing. Your lawyer can tell you more about filling out these one-time documents.

Power of Attorney for Property

A power of attorney for property authorizes an agent to act on behalf of the grantor of the power (you). My wife has my continuing power of attorney, and she can execute legal and financial documents for me. That could be especially important if I am not available or not competent to handle my property.

A continuing power of attorney remains valid even if the grantor becomes incapacitated. It terminates when revoked by the grantor, while competent, or when the grantor dies.

Within the past few years, many provinces have enacted new laws relating to powers of attorney, which would be effective even if you are incapacitated. This might mean that a power of attorney executed several years ago may not contain the durable or continuing authority provision and it should be re-executed. Nowadays you should look for the words *"durable,"* or *"continuing"* or that the document mentions that it continues to be valid in the event the donor becomes incapacitated.

The power of attorney must specifically deal with incapacity of the grantor. If the grantor becomes incompetent without the reference in the document, then a guardianship would be required.

The power of attorney for property usually lists the various powers granted to the agent. They generally are quite broad and all-encompassing. Here is a sample power of attorney so that you can see what I mean.

POWER OF ATTORNEY FOR PROPERTY

1. I, (name of principal), hereby appoint (name of chosen agent) to serve as my Attorney to exercise the powers set forth below. If (name of chosen agent) is unable or unwilling to serve, then I appoint (name of second-choice agent) as my Attorney.

2. (Use only for a standby power of attorney, in conjunction with Alternate Clause 4. Use only after consultation with a lawyer) THIS POWER OF ATTORNEY SHALL BE-COME EFFECTIVE ONLY UPON MY INCAPACITY. I HAVE NOT AUTHORIZED MY ATTORNEY TO UNDERTAKE ANY ACTS UNLESS THE EVENTS DESCRIBED IN CLAUSE 4 HAVE TAKEN PLACE.

3. I authorize my said Attorney to take all actions and perform all acts in my name concerning my affairs as my Attorney may deem advisable or necessary in his (her) absolute discretion. I give to my Attorney full power to act in the management and disposition of my property the authority that I might exercise were I present, including, but not by way of limitation, any or all of the following:

    a. To manage my affairs, handle my investments, arrange for the investment and disposition of funds, exercise all rights with respect to my investments, establish, use, and terminate brokerage accounts, collect amounts owed or payable to me, endorse cheques or other instruments drawn to my order and cash them or deposit them to any account in my name, make withdrawals from any account in my name, open bank accounts in my name, enter my safe deposit box and add to or remove from there any or all contents;

    b. To exercise all rights to securities and bonds, including the right to buy, sell, transfer, encumber, pledge, and vote and to establish, use, and terminate brokerage accounts;

    c. To buy, sell, transfer, lease, subdivide, alter boundaries, mortgage, encumber, pledge, manage, improve, and maintain real property, including the power to erect, repair, or demolish buildings;

    d. To buy, sell, transfer, lease, mortgage, encumber, pledge, manage, improve, maintain, repair, or alter personal property;

    e. To pay claims and debts, borrow money, and create security interests for the repayment;

    f. To disclaim any interest in property, renounce fiduciary positions, claim an elective share of the estate of my deceased spouse, make gifts, create trusts, and make additional gifts to trusts;

    g. To exercise all rights of mine under insurance and annuity policies, including the right to change beneficiaries, to borrow, to assign, to change owners, and to surrender the policies;

h. To expend and to distribute income or principal for the benefit of my spouse and dependents;

i. To file tax returns;

j. To engage and dismiss agents;

k. To pay my bills and to pay for all things necessary for my physical care, protection, and well-being and for that of my property;

l. To designate another person or persons, including a financial institution, to serve as my attorney in the place of (name of agent).

4. This Power of Attorney shall not be affected by my disability or incapacity.

Alternate Clause 4 (for a standby power of attorney). This Power of Attorney shall become effective only upon my incapacity. My incapacity shall be deemed to exist if I have been declared mentally incompetent upon a notarized affidavit signed by licensed physician confirming that I am mentally incapable of managing my financial affairs. This Power shall become effective on the date of the said notarized affidavit signed by a licensed physician.

IN WITNESS WHEREOF, I have signed this Power of Attorney for property on this _____ day of _____, 19___.

_____
(name of principal)

_____

_____

Witnesses

PROVINCE OF _____

COUNTY OF _____

This person appeared before me, (name of principal), who signed and acknowledged the foregoing Power of Attorney to be his (her) free act and deed, on this _____ day of_____, 19____.

_____
Notary Public

My commission expires on: _____

A word to the wise: Don't use this form for yourself without first learning if it is acceptable in your province. A standby power of attorney may not be appropriate in most cases.

As you can see, you certainly need to have complete confidence in a particular relative or friend before giving him or her authority under a continuing power of attorney. Since the powers are extensive and there is really no court supervision, the possibility of abuse always exists.

Quote...Unquote

Love all, trust a few.

—*Shakespeare, All's Well That Ends Well (1602)*

The law requires that an agent act faithfully on behalf of the grantor. If there is a violation of that standard, which is known as the *fiduciary duty*, then the court, upon request, may remove the agent and, if funds are misused, require an accounting.

Laws vary about the way you can revoke a power of attorney. Two witnesses to the revocation document may be required. Usually you just notify the agent in writing and request that he or she return the original document. You may also wish to notify any third parties that have been dealing with your attorney of the revocation.

If you are an agent under someone's power of attorney, then you might be required to show your document for any transaction you sign for the grantor. Always keep the original. Give those who request the document a copy. Sign any document on behalf of the grantor by clearly indicating that you are acting as *attorney* for the grantor.

Words, Words, Words

A *proxy* is the agency, function or office of a deputy who acts as a substitute for another. A proxy might also be a document giving such authority, such as a power of attorney authorizing a specified person to vote corporate stock. Or, in the context of this chapter, the power of attorney to make business and/or health care decisions for a specified person.

An agent under a durable power of attorney can generally not make medical decisions for the grantor. The trend is towards different rules and attorney forms for property and personal care. It is probably better to execute separate documents. Health care powers of attorney are also known as health care proxies or powers of attorney for personal or health care.

A Living Will and a Health Care Power of Attorney

Provincial laws recognize the right of competent adults to consent to, or refuse to consent to, medical treatment. Likewise, the law permits a competent adult to delegate his or her medical decisions to another person.

The *living will* is not a will. It is a written form directing that the declarant's life not be artificially prolonged if he or she is in a terminal condition or persistent vegetative state. It gives guidance as to how you wish to be treated.

The *health care power of attorney* (or *proxy*) provides that an agent named by the grantor is authorized to make health care decisions when the grantor is not capable of doing so. This document designates a person you trust to make personal or health care choices.

If you have no close relatives, then it's especially important for you to designate someone to make medical decisions for you. Doctors might otherwise have limited options.

Having a living will is not enough to protect you. You'll still need a health care power of attorney. If you want artificial life support measures terminated if you find yourself in that situation at some point in your life, then make sure that your health care power of attorney acknowledges your wish. (First, of course, you must inform your agent fully about all your options, and your wishes, in this area.)

Discuss all of these issues with your family, of course. They need to know how you feel about the subject. And you just might find that opening such a conversation leads to an interesting and informative talk about one another's wishes.

There's just one note here: A living will can sometimes be ignored by hospitals, nursing homes, rehabilitation facilities, etc. This is because some personnel are reluctant to take such drastic wishes into account. It's far better to have a health care power of attorney to go along with the living will (or instead of it)—it cannot be ignored.

On the next pages are samples of a living will and a health care power of attorney. Again, there will be differences in these forms in each jurisdiction. Some jurisdictions have a pre-scribed form, so be certain you use one applicable to where you are. You can see a lawyer, or ask around at community and local hospitals, many of which keep these forms on file for use by patients and others.

By the way—a not unimportant point—your witnesses to these documents (or their spouses or partners) should never be members of your family, or anyone who has a financial obligation for your support or who would inherit from you. Each province specifies who can witness powers of attorney with rules and qualifications for witnesses. That makes sense, of course. Execute several copies and record where all are stored in case they are ever revoked. Consider if you wish to have multiple powers of attorney, each for a limited purpose. You could allow one attorney to just handle your investments.

Where should you keep the original? Ask your lawyer. Often, providing your physician with a copy for your medical records file will ensure that your wishes will be followed.

Tip

A lawyer will probably draw up a will, a power of attorney for property and a health care power of attorney for you at a "package rate" for the documents.

Watch Out!

If you have executed a living will or power of attorney in a province where you previously lived, the form may not be valid in your new province. Check out the local laws on this subject.

I have a health care power of attorney, as does my wife. We have named each other as the attorney, and named our oldest child as the alternate agent. If I am in a coma, or otherwise incompetent, I want to know that people I trust will make the right decision. Usually the authorities will ask next-of-kin for consent to medical treatment anyway, but this makes my wishes quite clear.

Many people also have living wills because they personally believe that there is no quality of life when it is sustained by artificial means. This is an important and very personal decision. Of course, your decision might be quite different.

You can change your mind after you have executed either document; simply destroy or revoke the document and retrieve any copies.

LIVING WILL DECLARATION

Declaration made this _____ day of _____, 199_ I, _____
_____, being at least sixteen (16) years of age and of
sound mind, willfully and voluntarily make known my desires that my dying shall not
be artificially prolonged under the circumstances set forth below, and I declare:

If at any time my attending physician certifies in writing that: (1) I have an incurable
injury, disease, or illness; (2) my death will occur within a short time; and (3) the use
of life prolonging procedures would serve only to artificially prolong the dying
process, I direct that such procedures be withheld or withdrawn, and that I be
permitted to die naturally with only the performance or provision of any medical
procedure or medication necessary to provide me with comfort care or to alleviate
pain, and, if I have so indicated below, the provision of artificially supplied nutrition
and hydration. (Indicate your choice of a, b or c by initialling or making your mark
before signing this declaration):

a) I wish to receive artificially supplied nutrition and hydration, even if the effort to
   sustain life is futile or excessively burdensome to me;
b) I do not wish to receive artificially supplied nutrition and hydration, if the effort to
   sustain life is futile or excessively burdensome to me; or
c) I intentionally make no decision concerning artificially supplied nutrition and
   hydration, leaving the decision to my health care representative appointed under
   my attorney for heath care.

In the absence of my ability to give directions regarding the use of life prolonging
procedures, it is my intention that this declaration be honoured by my family and
physician as the final expression of my legal right to refuse medical or surgical treatment and accept the consequences of the refusal.

I understand the full import of this declaration.

_____   signed _____

City, County, Province of residence   printed _____

The declarant has been personally known to me, and I believe him/her to be of sound
mind. I did not sign the declarant's signature above for or at the direction of the
declarant. I am not a parent, spouse, or child of the declarant. I am not entitled to any
part of the declarant's estate or directly financially responsible for the declarant's
medical care. I am competent and at least eighteen (18) years of age.

Witness _____ Date: _____

Witness _____ Date: _____

POWER OF ATTORNEY FOR HEALTH CARE

I, _____, name _____ as my representative to act for me in matters affecting my health, in particular to:

(1) Consent to or refuse health care for me.

(2) Employ or contract with servants, companions, or health care providers for me.

(3) Admit or release me from a hospital or health care facility.

(4) Have access to records, including medical records, concerning my condition.

(5) Make anatomical gifts on my behalf.

(6) Make personal care decisions regarding my medical treatment, shelter, nutrition, clothing, hygiene or safety.

(7) Make plans for the disposition of my body.

I authorize my representative to make decisions in my best interest concerning the withdrawal or withholding of health care. If at any time, based on my previously expressed preferences and diagnosis and prognosis, my representative is satisfied that certain health care is not or would not be beneficial, or that such health care is or would be excessively burdensome, then the representative may express my will that such health care be withheld or withdrawn and may consent on my behalf that any or all health care be discontinued or not instituted even if death is the result.

My representative must try to discuss this decision with me. However, if I am incompetent, my representative may make such a decision for me, after consultation with my physician or physicians and other relevant health care providers. To the extent appropriate, my representative may also discuss this decision with my family and others, to the extent they are available.

Date: _____   signed _____

                                        printed _____

_____ has been personally known to me, and I believe him/her to be of legal age and capable of making decisions regarding his/her health care.

I am competent and at least 18 years of age (16 in Ontario).

Witness _____   Date: _____

Witness _____   Date: _____

Watch Out

Don't forget: If you are part of a seriously committed unmarried couple, it's especially important to execute the documents I've mentioned in this chapter. Without them your partner has no right to make legal decisions for you and may be limited as your spokesperson on health.

Words, Words, Words

Powers of attorney for property and health care and living wills taken together are known as *advance directives.* You'll see that expression often in reading about elder health issues.

Becoming an Organ Donor

Anatomical gifts is not an easy subject to write about. Frankly, I have never resisted the idea of giving up any of my body parts. A good friend of mine is a lung transplant surgeon, and he saves lives every day he has organs to transplant. I believe that if I can give another person life or a better quality of life then I have a moral reason to do so.

An *anatomical gift* is a donation of a body part, which may include organs, tissue, eyes, bones, arteries, blood and other portions of the human body.

Provincial laws permit the donor to make an anatomical gift in a number of ways, including mention in a will. However, because time is usually vital, most gifts are made through a donor card or other document the donor always carries with him or her. Many jurisdictions provide for an anatomical gift on the driver's licence.

In addition, the law may allow the next of kin to make a donation from the deceased's body even if that individual does not carry an organ donor card. You might not want to count on that, though. In times of grief your relatives may not be comfortable with such a decision—or might not want to go ahead with the donation, if they feel as strongly in their anti-organ donation views as you do in your pro-donation stance.

Make things easier for everyone: Tell your family about your decision, and carry an organ donor card with you at all times, probably in your wallet.

Here is an example of an organ donation form. Make sure it's witnessed if your province requires it. You can fill it out and use it, but you might find it easier to call your local hospitals, many of which supply small organ donor cards that easily fit into a wallet.

ORGAN DONOR DECLARATION

This is to inform you that I want to be an organ and tissue donor if the occasion ever arises. Please see that my wishes are carried out by informing the attending medical personnel that I am a donor. My desires are indicated below:

In the hopes that I may help others, I hereby make this gift for the purpose of transplant, medical study, or education, to take effect upon my death. I donate:

(   ) Any needed organs/tissues

(   ) Only the following organs/tissues

_____

Specify the organ(s)/tissue(s):

_____

_____

Limitations or special wishes, if any:

_____

I wish this to be a legal document under the laws of the province, signed by the donor and the following two witnesses in the presence of each other.

_____

Donor's signature

_____   _____
Donor's date of birth   City and Province

_____   _____
Witness   Witness

_____   _____
Next of Kin   Telephone

Last Words, Last Rites and Other Finalities

Throughout this book I've discussed estate planning techniques and documents, but have said very little about organizing them (although I did suggest you keep them in a safe place). Now is the time to talk about organization.

Your will, advance directives, trust documents and life insurance policies should be stored in a safe, central location. Tell your executor where they are. You should have photocopies made and placed elsewhere.

Important legal papers should be kept together in a safe location. These would include deeds to real estate or certificates of title to cars, a marriage licence, divorce, military discharge papers, and other documents important for your executor or next-of-kin.

You might want to make a master list of all vital documents and indicate where they are located and who has copies of them. Give your spouse, children and executor a copy of that list. Too often assets you know about are overlooked, so keep a current Estate Planning Information Sheet (see Chapter 2) with your important documents.

Burial Wishes

If you have any strong feelings in this area, talk them over with your family. In fact, you might want to make a few plans now. For example, do you have a cemetery plot? Or mausoleum space, if that's what you prefer? If you do not, and you have a spouse or children, this might be the time to bite the bullet and look into purchasing a final resting place for you and some or all of your family.

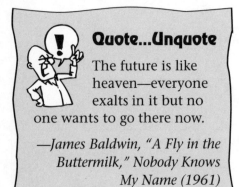

Quote...Unquote

The future is like heaven—everyone exalts in it but no one wants to go there now.

—*James Baldwin, "A Fly in the Buttermilk," Nobody Knows My Name (1961)*

If cremation interests you more, express that wish clearly to your loved ones. You may want to put it in writing and, since this is not as widely understood a concept as in-ground burial, attach some information about a local service you have called, or any other material your family is likely to find helpful when the time comes. It is not necessary to put your wishes in your will. You should know that in Canada they are not legally binding on your executors. As I've said before, perhaps no one will consult that document until it is too late.

Write down your funeral wishes and make sure your next-of-kin know them. You might want to investigate pre-arranged funeral services. You can investigate casket and coffin styles and prices, and maybe even write your funeral service, selecting the music as well. All of that will direct your nearest and dearest toward the funeral you want without your having to spend money beforehand.

> **Quote...Unquote**
>
> Life does not cease to be funny when people die any more than it ceases to be serious when people laugh.
>
> —*George Bernard Shaw, The Doctor's Dilemma (1913)*

Your death will be traumatic enough for your family without their having to search not only for your funeral wishes, but also your estate planning documents. Make sure everything is easy for them to find, and clearly understandable once they have done so.

The Least You Need to Know

> ➤ A power of attorney for property is one way to avoid a guardianship. The person you yourself designate makes decisions for you when you can no longer do so. The power of attorney document should specify it is valid in the event of your incapacity.

> ➤ A living will is not a will. It may be used to terminate artificial life support. It gives directions for your medical care. Check to make sure it is recognized in your province.

> ➤ A power of attorney for health care designates someone to make health care decisions for you when you cannot. Depending on provincial laws, this type of a document may be enforced more easily than a living will.

> ➤ It's important to organize all of your estate planning documents, including your funeral wishes, and tell someone where they can be found.

Chapter 24

Life's Big and Little Surprises

In This Chapter

➤ Helping your folks manage

➤ Getting married?

➤ Getting divorced?

➤ Updating your assets list

The title of this chapter says it all. It seems there's no such thing as sitting back and taking it easy. Just when we do, bingo, Dad becomes ill and it looks as if he's not going to be able to live on his own anymore. Or bingo—but good news this time—it looks as if we're getting married, or getting married again. Or divorced. There are any number of things going on in our lives to cause a flurry of happiness or concern.

All of those major happenings can affect your estate plan, of course. Still, you *can* keep on track, no matter what's going on in your life now, and no matter what changes lie ahead.

Looking Out for Aging Parents

Of course *you're* aging too—and so am I—but you know what I mean here. If you are 27 and your parents are in their fifties, this next section probably won't concern you, unless one of your folks has serious health concerns. But if your parents are in their 60s, 70s, or beyond, then by all means continue reading. You might have some grave problems and worries, not only about their health, but also about their, and perhaps your, finances.

We often have difficulty admitting our parents are getting older—no, getting *old*—and a role reversal may be at hand. Many of us are living longer and enjoying life's bounty in our senior years, but there may come a time when aging brings a certain dependency. We must prepare for that contingency.

Here are some suggestions for handling specific issues with elderly, perhaps ailing, parents or other relatives you are close to and for whom you feel some responsibility. I'll use Mom as an example in the next few pages, although you can, of course, substitute your father or grandfather or Aunt Lois if you wish.

Before I go any further, let me state the obvious: If your mother is competent, then of course she has the right to make her own decisions, even if they do not agree with yours. The suggestions that follow apply if she needs some help with those decisions, with learning what options she has, or if she cannot make decisions at all.

Managing Property

Avoiding guardianship should be one of your goals because of its expense and complications. A power of attorney for property that

Briefs

No matter what our age, we must beware of stereotyping the 65-plus crowd and consigning them to a rocker. In the spring of 1997 a team of Los Angeles doctors announced that five months earlier a 63-year-old woman in their care had delivered a healthy baby girl, making her the oldest woman in the world to give birth. While the event brought a news and feature article flurry, one fact was buried in most of the stories: The woman was staying at home to take care of the baby—and was being helped by her mother, who is in her eighties!

continues even if your mother is no longer competent to manage her affairs should be obtained. The power of attorney for health care should be prepared at the same time. It is too late to prepare powers of attorney if your mother becomes incapacitated.

Another option in this area besides a power of attorney is a trust. You may want to ask your mother to consider a revocable living trust, if she has significant assets but cannot manage them. You've read about trusts in previous chapters, particularly Chapter 9, and know that creating a trust is an expense not everyone can justify. In addition to managing her property, the trustee can pay her bills, a task that a child, who is often hundreds of kilometres away, cannot easily perform.

Living Arrangements

There are several choices your parent can make (or you can help make with or for her), some of which may not have occurred to you.

➤ **Adapting her present residence.**

She might continue with present living arrangement. If that's a house, it could be made more adaptable and safer for an elderly resident. Maybe you or she can find a housemate to share the rooms and expenses. A local senior citizen's agency might be able to help with making a match.

➤ **Senior citizens' housing.**

If she needs smaller quarters and is on a limited income, look into non-profit senior citizens' housing, which exists in almost any community. There are income ceilings, of course, and the nicest buildings and complexes can have quite a lengthy waiting list. You might enter Mom's name quickly—it can always be withdrawn if things change.

➤ **Reverse mortgage.**

You may want to look into a reverse mortgage, to provide Mom with some monthly income. If she owns her home and is 70 or older, she might be able to draw on the equity in that place in the form of a monthly cheque, or a line of credit that's ready and waiting if she needs it. The lender adds interest, closing costs and any other charges at the end of the loan, so Mom won't have to pay those fees at the beginning. These loans, including all charges, are payable when the homeowner moves or dies.

Reverse mortgages are complex financial tools that are not for everyone. The terms of a reverse mortgage should be reviewed independently of the institution that is offering the reverse mortgage. Get your own lawyer to explain how the mortgage works and if it can be cancelled in case you change your mind. Your options to get out may be severely limited once you get into these mortgages.

➤ **Assisted living.**

A housing option that is growing furiously these days is the assisted-living facility, which will offer Mom some help with day-to-day living—meals, for example—but no serious medical supervision. A senior's service agency in your area can recommend one near you.

➤ **Continuing care communities.**

CCRC is a set of initials you'll come across if you're looking for a specific type of care. It stands for continuing care retirement communities. These are high-rise buildings or sprawling complexes that buyers often move through in phases. The first is independent living, where you buy a patio home, condominium or cottage, or you might rent an apartment.

Stage two is assisted living, where there is some help with meals and other services. Stage three is a nursing home, which provides skilled nursing care.

Each community is different, with its own rules and fees. You are not making an investment in real estate. Instead, you are arranging for care that can require up-front fees.

Life Insurance

At this stage of your mother's life you'll want to review her life insurance policy to determine if coverage is necessary. If a parent is terminally ill insurance companies may permit a partial pre-death distribution of the proceeds.

Estate Planning

Your mom's estate plan—her investments, will, etc.—may need revising. Remember, though, it is *her* plan. If she is competent, by all means talk

Watch Out

Unless you are an only child, your parents should not use your lawyer. If a disproportionate distribution of your folks' assets is being considered, your siblings might later claim that you unduly influenced Mom and Dad through your lawyer.

Tip

You might want to contact a lawyer dealing with pension benefits, health care issues, elder abuse and the like. Elder law is a relatively new area of concentration for lawyers that is still not available everywhere. To see if there is an eldercare or estate planning lawyer near you, call your provincial law society.

with her about powers of attorney. If she is not able to make decisions for herself, talk with her lawyer.

How a Community Can Help

Don't forget to contact the local community information service in your mother's area. There are many senior's services that can help her, at little or no cost. For example, Meals on Wheels can deliver a nutritious meal to her home five days a week at a cost of a couple of dollars per meal.

These agencies can also refer you to civic, educational and religious groups that do various volunteer chores for the elderly, such as driving them to doctors' appointments and visiting with them in their homes for an hour or two when there is a special need. Adult day care may cost money, but some religious institutions and social service agencies do it for free. Ask!

As you can see, there is all kinds of assistance out there for a child looking after an aging parent—and incidentally, there is more than one "kid" in his 60s caring for a parent in his or her 90s! Here is a worksheet that can help you get a handle on where help can be found for your relative, and whether he, she, or you, or a local agency is likely to help financially.

Long-Distance Caregiving

It's one thing if you can pop in on Mom every few days, or even every couple of weeks. But what can you do when you're too far away for frequent visits? If you can, arrange for someone in your mother's community to be a *secondary* caregiver, someone who will check on her periodically, in person and by phone, look over the mail, see that Mom has food in the refrigerator, and so forth. Yes,

HOME CARE ASSISTANCE WORKSHEET

This worksheet is designed to help identify needs and ways to pay for them for both the caregiver and the care receiver. A senior often is able to remain independent in his or her own home with a little help from friends, neighbours, family, and outside resources. Caregivers, whether living close by or far away, can often arrange services for loved ones and themselves.

Service	Program	Cost	Payment Source
Examples:			
Caregiver respite:	Adult Day Care	$40 a day	Aunt Jane once a month
Meals			
Daily	Neighbour Jones (Dinner nightly)	$50 a week	Mom's income
Weekly	Meals on Wheels (Lunch Mon-Fri)	Per meal	Local agency
Special occasion	Sunday dinner	$10	Me
Caregiver respite			
Daily			
Weekly			
Vacations			
Care receiver			
Socialization			
Home health care			
Transportation			
Shopping			
Doctor visits			
Pharmacy			
Yardwork/Maintenance			
Housework, light			
Housework, heavy			
Bill paying			
Telephone reassurance			
Home safety			
Home security			
Other			

Source: *Florida Care Giver*, PO Box 380108, Jacksonville, FL 32205

you will probably have to pay for the service, but your peace of mind will be worth the money that goes with having him or her keep in touch with Mom, and then you.

When There's a Marriage or Divorce

I'm talking about you now, not your parent (although, of course, he or she could remarry or divorce too).

Obviously, a marriage or divorce will require some changes in what you thought was a firm, unalterable estate plan.

Tying the Knot

With the nuptial tie comes the new spouse's rights in your estate, making your old will invalid. A husband or wife can elect against a deceased spouse's will, and may be entitled to a share of property and support. Some provinces may limit the amount the electing spouse can receive, depending on how long the couple had lived together.

Prenuptial agreements can limit a spouse's right to elect against the estate, as well as what he or she may receive if there is a divorce.

A prenup should be considered when people remarry after the deaths of their spouses and want to keep what they bring to the new marriage in each of their separate families after death.

Family property laws give the new spouses certain vested property rights in assets obtained after marriage. In addition, many couples create joint ownership with right of survivorship. Proper estate planning must consider these spousal co-ownership rights.

If there's marriage on your horizon, you'd be wise to review the sections of this book that deal with issues relating to a new marriage—from styles of property ownership, to a will or trust, to the above-mentioned prenup (which can also be drawn up *after* the wedding).

> ### Quote...Unquote
>
> Grow old along with me!
> The best is yet to be,
> The last of life, for which the first was made:
> Our times are in His hand
> Who saith "A whole I planned,
> Youth shows but half; Trust God; see all
> nor be afraid!"
>
> —*Robert Browning (1864)*

Splitting Up

Frankly, the best estate planning suggestion I can give you if you're going to divorce is to hire a good divorce lawyer. Not a nasty one, just a good one who will ensure that you will be fairly treated. While both of you may go into the divorce with all intentions of splitting marital assets equally, the reality might be quite different.

First, there's the property division, with significant tax consequences. Then spousal support, which is income to one and a tax deduction to the other spouse.

Pension plans would be divided, and that would affect the income expectations of both ex-spouses when they retire.

If You Become Disabled

Few of us are prepared to be seriously put out of commission. Disabilities due to illness or accident can range from temporary to permanent, from partial to full. A disability may have a substantial financial impact on you and your family by reducing income and assets and by requiring additional expenses for the disabled person. If the disability is severe, he or she may not be capable of managing his or her affairs or assets.

If a disability does occur, you or your family should:

➤ assemble all estate planning documents and consult a lawyer about their effect, and any changes that are necessary

Watch Out!

If you are about to enter into marriage or divorce at this time, take a good look at all of your estate planning documents, not just your will (divorce usually invalidates any provision in the will for an ex-spouse), such as an insurance policy, pension plan and the like. Sometimes we never seem to get around to that paperwork.

Watch Out!

Think ahead—think insurance. If you're on someone else's payroll, your employer may have a disability insurance policy for you, but if you're self-employed, you don't have such coverage and you may want to consider purchasing it. You're likely to find Canada Pension disability payments insufficient to maintain your family the way you would like.

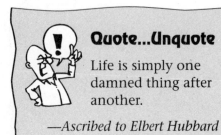

➤ contact your employer or disability insurance carrier to file a claim

➤ file for benefits with the Canada Pension Plan

➤ review any business agreements, such as a partnership agreement, that may have disability provisions

➤ consult a lawyer about your employment rights

Tick-Tock: Checking Your Estate Plan

A retired military officer come in for a new will. He was asked when he executed the last one. Just before he was shipped overseas, he responded—in 1944. Since then he had married and had had several children; he had retired from the service and then from another job.

That's 40 years—it was 1984—more than a bit too long between wills!

We need to remind ourselves that our will and estate plan are not cast in stone. They need to be regularly reviewed, and revised when necessary.

Most experts suggest that we should review an estate plan at least every two to three years and more than that when there are significant changes in finances or family.

Tip

You might make it a practice to revise your *assets list* when you do your income taxes. (You can use the Estate Planning Information Sheet in Chapter 2.) Much of the information that you need is readily at hand then.

You ought to pull out your estate documents when any of the following events occur:

➤ you move to another province

➤ your assets or liabilities change substantially

➤ laws change

➤ your family changes (remarriage, divorce, children become self-supporting adults, grandchildren are born, etc.)

➤ you want to change beneficiaries in your will, life insurance policy, trust and/or retirement plan

The Least You Need to Know

➤ If an elderly parent requires your assistance, there are lots of private and public sources of assistance.

➤ Marriage immediately gives a spouse certain rights to your estate and cancels an old will.

➤ Disability insurance paid for by your employer, or by you, should be part of your estate plan.

➤ Review your will and overall estate plan at least every three years. If you have experienced any important changes in assets or beneficiaries, an annual review may be better.

Tip

If you are going to make substantial changes to your will, such as revising beneficiaries, it's better to execute a new will rather than add a codicil to the present one. That may lessen the possibility of a beneficiary whose devise is reduced or eliminated from one day contesting the will.

Chapter 25

Stage by Stage: Estate Planning Throughout Your Life

> **In This Chapter**
> ➤ Looking ahead if you're single
> ➤ Strategies for single parents
> ➤ Planning with minor children
> ➤ Retired, and still planning

Now, with 24 chapters of information and advice under your belt, you should have a good idea of what you've got in the way of assets, how they are likely to grow and how you want your estate plan to proceed.

To sum up and review things in this final chapter what I'm going to do is... well, I hate to say put you in a category—we're all different, after all—but nevertheless I'm going to put you in a StatsCan-like category of people: married/single, with children/without, that type of thing. Such simple categorization should help you find yourself quickly and see what you need to do to ensure an estate that's in fine order now, and likely to remain so in the future, thanks to your continued diligence.

Broadly Speaking

There are some points I've made in past chapters that apply to all of us, and some that do not. For example, we all need a will, but not everyone needs a trust. A power of attorney for property is appropriate for most of us. Life insurance is an excellent idea for those with a young family, but a close-to-retirement policyholder might want to re-think some coverage.

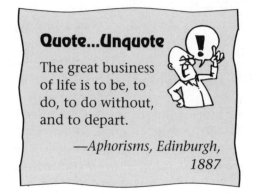

Quote...Unquote

The great business of life is to be, to do, to do without, and to depart.

—*Aphorisms, Edinburgh, 1887*

Take a look at this worksheet to see what still needs to be done to complete your estate plan which will, of course, differ from those of Harry down the street and your coworker Linda.

Now let's get on with some tips for what you might be doing planning-wise at various stages of your life, based on how things are with you right now.

Single, With No Kids

Many assume that the life of a single person is free of responsibilities. If you are single you know that that is frequently not the case. You may have an elderly parent to care for or other family responsibilities. You might put in long hours at work. Perhaps you are the driving force behind a successful, but demanding, local volunteer effort.

Your estate planning needs are clearly different in many respects from those folks who have children.

At a minimum you should have a will. The provincial intestate law provides that your heirs could be your parents and your siblings, if any of them survive you. If you have no immediate family, your nieces, nephews and cousins may inherit. Probably not all of them are deserving of your estate, so a will allows you to specify whom you want the inheritors to be.

You need not wait for your retirement years to benefit from using powers of attorney for property and health care. You may need someone to manage your affairs when you no longer can and have no children to rely on. Also, put as much money into your retirement plans as

ESTATE DOCUMENT CHECKLIST

You've read, you've pondered. But have you taken any action yet on the suggestions in this book? Here is a checklist of what you might need to do to complete your own estate plan. Not every item will apply to you, of course. Or at least not just now. (The most important paper is, of course, a will.)

In the third column, under "Comments," you can jot down what you need to complete a particular course of action. For example, under "Guardianship for minor children" your comment could be "Talk to Nancy and Tom." Under "Trust," it might be "N/A" for "not applicable."

	Accomplished		
Estate Plan Ingredient	Yes	No	Comments
1) Estate Planning Information Sheet	_____	_____	_____
2) Will	_____	_____	_____
3) Trust	_____	_____	_____
4) Life insurance policy(ies)	_____	_____	_____
5) Company pension plan	_____	_____	_____
6) RRSPs	_____	_____	_____
7) Prenuptial agreement	_____	_____	_____
8) Guardianship for minor children	_____	_____	_____
9) Trust for children	_____	_____	_____
10) Power of attorney for property	_____	_____	_____
11) Living will	_____	_____	_____
12) Power of attorney for health	_____	_____	_____
13) Organ donor card	_____	_____	_____

possible because living on just the Canada Pension Plan benefits may mean some significant changes in your lifestyle at retirement.

A Few Words for the Single Parent

Single parents have to do double duty during the child-rearing years, not an easy task in the best of times. Often they must be father and mother and... no, make that *triple* duty. There's also work, and perhaps more than one job at that.

> **Quote...Unquote**
>
> As wise women and men in every culture tell us: The art of living is not controlling what happens to us, but using what happens to us.
>
> —*Gloria Steinem, "Revolution From Within" (1992)*

Hectic days and nights might not give you time to think much about estate planning; after all, you've got more pressing demands, right? Wrong. You may be the only source of support for those growing children, and your untimely death would leave a significant emotional and financial void. You can ensure with good planning that at least the financial void will be minimized. Here are my suggestions:

➤ Get as much term life insurance coverage as possible; this is an inexpensive means of leaving a substantial estate for the children.

➤ Put as much as you can into your RRSPs at work, so you won't have to depend only on the Canada Pension Plan when you retire.

➤ Make a will, and provide for a trust and a guardianship for minor children. If you are divorced, your ex-spouse may be entitled to custody of the children if you die; if you do not think that that is appropriate, contact a lawyer to determine what you can do to avoid it.

➤ Execute powers of attorney and make your agent someone you trust implicitly; you may want to make them effective only if and when you become incapacitated.

> **Tip**
>
> After a divorce, make sure that your life insurance policies and retirement plans are changed; more than one person has benefited from his or her ex's procrastination.

➤ Finally, if you are divorced and your ex-spouse is behind in child support, see a lawyer about enforcing your children's rights in that regard.

If you are a single mother and your child's father is not in the picture (you are widowed, the child has been adopted by you as a single person, etc.), then of course there is no possibility of child support. You must pay particular attention to your estate plan, especially guardianship for your child.

Tip

With no children, your life insurance needs will be modest if your spouse is working and can be self-sufficient. However, if children are planned, then purchase a policy that allows higher coverage when the kids begin arriving.

Married With No Children

Wills for each spouse are important here. If children are likely in the future; there should be a clause in each spouse's will making any afterborn or adopted children the secondary beneficiaries of that will. The will should also have a third beneficiary to take the probate estate if both spouses die simultaneously and there are no children.

Mature spouses need to arrange for someone to arrange their affairs when they don't want to or cannot do so. They need the "powers" that can help: power of attorney for property and health care, and perhaps a living will.

Deciding who benefits after both spouses' deaths may be difficult. If this applies to you, then no doubt you are close to some relatives and particular friends. You might want them to inherit. Or you might prefer that part of your estate to go to charity. A charitable remainder trust (where you receive income during your lives, then the charity is entitled to the balance after death) could be a viable choice for part of your estate (see Chapter 18).

Married With Children

Children are with us at all ages, which makes your estate planning needs vary from one age, or stage, to another. The family with youngsters has different concerns than the family with adult children. Here is a checklist for both.

First, here's what both husband and wife with kids of any age will need:

➤ wills

➤ powers of attorney for property

➤ substantial life insurance coverage

➤ individual retirement plans

Both young and mature couples should discuss executing:

➤ health care powers of attorney

➤ living wills

Obviously, families are not all alike, but these documents are essential to any estate planning.

When There Are Minors

Let's look in more detail at the family with minor children—those under 18. If that's you, then I suggest a testamentary trust for those children.

Quote...Unquote

Children are a great comfort in your old age, and they help you reach it faster too.

—*Lionel Kauffman*

If you have minor children who are going to inherit at least $100,000, you could have a trust that manages their property beyond age 18 to a more mature age when they are less likely to waste that inheritance.

In addition, young parents must consider the selection of a guardian to rear those children, and to manage their funds if there is no trust.

When the Children Are Adults

How about mature parents of adult children?

Most parents, in their desire to be fair to their children, simply divide their estate equally. That is your call. But "fair" and "equal" are not necessarily the same. For example, the child with a serious disability that will limit his or her earning potential is likely to require more from

Watch Out

Even a prenuptial agreement will not be effective if you and your spouse have all your assets in joint ownership. The surviving spouse will take the property no matter what the prenup says.

you. If you do distribute your assets unequally, be sure to explain your reasoning in your will, or in a personal note to those involved.

If you've remarried you may have children from a prior marriage. Often prenuptial agreements will specify that each spouse's will distributes his or her probate estate to his or her children from a prior marriage. You don't want one family to resent the other for taking what they consider to be their share of their parent's estate.

Retired But Not Retiring

Retired folks are living longer and seem to be enjoying their retirement years more these days. Part of this is because of the considerable planning they did when they were younger—planning that's paid off in a comfortable lifestyle now.

If you are approaching retirement, you ought to sit down with your financial adviser to determine just how much money you are going to have for those years. *Exactly* how much.

Besides a will you should certainly have powers of attorney for property and health care and a living will. You truly do need these papers.

In addition, I would suggest the following:

➤ Obtain a certificate of competency if there could be any question as to your mental capacity to execute a will or other legal document, to avoid a later contest by obtaining a physician's certificate showing that you are indeed competent.

➤ Examine your estate's liquidity to pay income taxes on death.

➤ Review the contents of your safe deposit box and remove anything that you may want to give away. You might make those gifts now instead of promising the recipients the items will be left in your will.

➤ Examine your entire set-up if you own or co-own a business; you may need to let go of control, but not at a significant sacrifice to your financial well being.

➤ Consider whether making gifts to the family now makes financial and tax sense.

➤ Arrange your finances to minimize the income tax and probate fees on both your estate and that of your spouse.

➤ Make a mental note to review your estate planning at least annually. Your financial picture may change—and certainly tax and other laws change often.

How Far You've Come Since Chapter 1!

You may recall back in that first introductory chapter I asked you to fill out an estate planning checklist, which includes a number of questions you should be answering while reading this book—from how you can reduce income taxes now, to gauging your expected retirement income. I suggested you might turn down the corner of that page and refer to it again later. This would be a good time to take a look at it. The questions probably sound quite familiar now that you've read about all those topics. You might even have moved a long way past some of them by now.

See how much you have learned?

Briefs

An extremely old John Quincy Adams was feebly walking down a Boston street when an old friend stopped him. Shaking Adams's trembling hand, the friend asked "And how is John Quincy Adams today?"

"Thank you," said the former U.S. president, "John Quincy Adams is well, quite well. But the house in which he lives at present is becoming quite dilapidated. It is tottering upon its foundations. Time and the seasons have nearly destroyed it. Its roof is pretty well worn out. Its walls are much shattered, and it trembles with every wind. The old tenement is becoming almost uninhabitable, and I think John Quincy Adams will have to move out of it soon. But he himself is quite well, quite well."

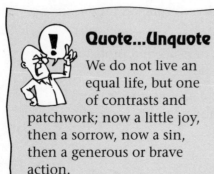

Quote...Unquote

We do not live an equal life, but one of contrasts and patchwork; now a little joy, then a sorrow, now a sin, then a generous or brave action.

—Emerson, "Journals" (1845)

And in Conclusion...

If you haven't yet completed your estate plan you're certainly quite prepared to do it now. And when you do, you'll have documents that will serve you well for the years ahead. Think of the peace of mind you'll have, just knowing that you've put things in order and have done what you can to look after your family and others close to you through a will.

Don't forget to refer to your plan often through the years, always fine-tuning the decisions you have made and projects you have undertaken. And stay in touch with your estate planning team as new family and lifestyle situations and financial possibilities crop up in your life. These professionals can really help.

Much luck and good fortune to you in the years ahead. May all the new elements that arise in your life having to do with your estate plan be beneficial, and perhaps even profitable, bringing you satisfaction and contentment.

The Least You Need to Know

➤ Everyone needs a will.

➤ A single person should have a power of attorney for property, which becomes effective if he or she becomes incapacitated.

➤ A trust might be the answer for minor children.

Words for the Wise— Key Terms You'll Want to Remember

actuarial value: Value of a property interest, or a right that you own, based on life expectancy tables; for example, a life estate is valued based on the life expectancy of that person.

administrator: Person appointed by a court to represent an estate when no will was provided or the will does not name an executor. May also be called a personal representative or estate trustee without a will.

annuity: Investment that pays a fixed amount for a specified number of years or for life.

annuity trust: One form of charitable remainder trust that pays a fixed amount regularly according to the value of a gift at the time it is set up, age of donor, and interest rates.

appreciated or appreciating asset: An asset whose value has increased or continues to increase due to a variety of factors, including inflation.

beneficiary: A person designated to receive income or assets in a will or trust. Can be a named beneficiary under a life insurance policy, pension plan or RRSP.

buy–sell agreement: Contract between partners or co-owners of a business that determines the conditions and price for a buyout by one or more of the owners at the death or retirement of a partner.

cash surrender value insurance: Life insurance that contains a savings account along with coverage for the life of the insured.

charitable trust: Gift made in trust to a recognized charity that includes income payable to the charity for a set time, with the remainder returned to the donor or another non-charity.

charitable remainder trust: Gift made in trust to a recognized charity that includes income payable to the donor during that person's lifetime. At the death of the donor, the remaining value of the gift belongs to the charity.

codicil: A written and properly witnessed legal change or amendment to a will.

creator: The person who establishes or funds a trust. Also referred to as a settlor or grantor.

condominium: Several persons owning their own apartments in a building or complex, with an undivided interest in the common areas.

cooperative: Housing style where buyers purchase shares in the corporation that owns the building. Tenant shareholders hold a proprietary lease that gives them the right to their units.

devise: A gift by will.

domicile: A person's fixed place of residence that he or she considers the permanent address.

donee: Person who receives a gift.

donor: Person who gives a gift.

estate: Total dollar value of all of one's property for estate tax purposes.

estate planning: Orderly arrangement of assets and a plan for conveying them to heirs and others in a manner calculated to minimize taxes, expenses, and delays.

executor: Person or institution named in a will to carry out its provisions and instructions. The female term is executrix. Also known as personal representative or estate trustee.

fair market value: A price agreed to by a willing buyer and a willing seller in a free negotiation.

family property: A term used to describe assets and property acquired after marriage and owned equally by marriage partners. Also called community property.

fiduciary: A person acting primarily for another's benefit in confidence, good faith, prudence, and fair dealing, such as a trustee or executor.

future interest: A property interest that gives the right to future possession or use; a remainder interest in a trust is a future interest.

grantor: The person who establishes or creates a trust. Also called a settlor.

guardian: A person who is legally responsible for managing the affairs and the care of a minor or incompetent person. A guardian is appointed by the court.

health care power of attorney: A document that gives another person (the attorney) the authority to make medical or personal care decisions for the person executing it. Also called power of attorney for personal care to authorize health and non-property decisions when one is incapacitated.

heir: A person legally entitled to receive another person's property through inheritance.

income tax: Federal and provincial tax that taxes income upon death.

inheritance tax: A tax levied on inherited property in some U.S. states. Tax rates typically depend on the relationship of the heir to the deceased. There are no inheritance taxes in Canada.

intestate: Dying without a will.

irrevocable: When applied to a trust, indicates it cannot be changed or cancelled. Contrast with revocable which can be cancelled.

joint tenancy: Owning property jointly in some form, with the right of survivorship. The last survivor inherits the property.

life estate: An interest, such as income from a trust, that continues for the life of the person holding that interest. Can also refer to real estate, where ownership is divided in half: one half is the length of the homeowner's life, the remainder is willed to the heir and becomes his or hers when the property owner dies.

living trust: A revocable or irrevocable written agreement into which a person (called the settlor or grantor) transfers assets and property along with instructions to the trustee for the management and future distribution of assets.

personal property: Movable property (tangible), such as furniture and motor vehicles, and property that represents an interest in other property (intangible), such as stock certificates and bank accounts.

personal representative: Another name for a person who is charged with managing an estate; same as executor or administrator.

power of attorney for property: A power of attorney is a legal document that gives another person full legal authority to act on one's behalf, including signing cheques and similar means of handling money. A power of attorney, when specified to continue in the event the person giving the power is incapacitated, is referred to as continuing. It can be general purpose or a restricted power to deal with financial matters.

prenuptial agreement: A contract agreed to by a couple prior to marriage that defines rights upon death or divorce. Also known as domestic or marriage contracts, which can be entered into during the marriage.

probate court: A specialized court in each province set up to handle the management of wills, estates of persons dying without a will, and other functions, such as guardianships. This court levies probate fees on the value of assets it handles.

probate estate: Property and assets of the deceased, distributed under direction of the will. The property in probate is used to calculate "probate fees" which are a percentage of the estate's value, whether or not you have a will.

qualified retirement plan: A plan that is entitled to special tax treatment upon contributions to that plan and income earned during its existence. Examples are defined benefit and defined contribution plans.

remainder interest: Property usually left in trust to another after the death of one or more who has an income interest.

separate property: Property owned only by one marriage partner that is kept segregated from the couple's family property.

spendthrift trust: Trust established for a beneficiary who lacks money management skills; to prevent the beneficiary from spending a legacy unwisely.

tenancy in common: Co-ownership of property without right of survival: each owner can leave his or her share to whomever he or she chooses. Contrast this with a joint tenancy which has a right of survivorship.

term life insurance: Pure insurance coverage only, with no savings component.

testamentary trust: A trust created by the deceased's will. Most wills include this for minors' interest.

trust: A written and formal agreement that enables a person or institution to hold property and manage it for the benefit of identified beneficiaries in accordance with instructions in the trust agreement.

trust agreement: Document setting out instructions for managing property left in a living trust, including who is to receive each portion of the trust assets.

trustee: Person or institution empowered to manage trust property according to the instructions contained in the trust agreement.

will: Basic document for transferring property to successors through probate court. Defines beneficiaries, executors and guardians for the maker of the will.

Index

More Great Canadian Complete Idiot's Guides

If you liked this *Complete Idiot's Guide*, check out these other titles!

The Complete Idiot's Guide to Making Money in the Canadian Stock Market

by Christy Heady and Stephen Nelson

The Complete Idiot's Guide to Making Money in the Canadian Stock Market helps you make sense of the complicated world of finance. You will learn the best financial strategies, feel confident about investing your money, and build your wealth with the help of this exciting new guide.

346 pages
$24.95
ISBN 0-13-779134-8

The Complete Idiot's Guide to Personal Finance

by Bruce McDougall

Follow the simple tips in this fact-filled volume to get on the road to prosperity. Comprehensive, yet written in the friendly style of the *Idiot's Guide* series, this updated version of a Canadian bestseller contains helpful information for Canadians who want to manage their money for maximum prosperity.

272 pages
$19.95
ISBN 0-13-080126-7

The Complete Idiot's Guide to Winning Everyday Legal Hassles in Canada
by Jerry Levitan

The Complete Idiot's Guide to Winning Everyday Legal Hassles in Canada answers basic legal questions so that you can feel more comfortable with contracts, know that to do when there's a dispute, and understand the legal issues that affect your life. Packed with solid information and with a forward by Edward Greenspan, this book includes tips, definitions, and warnings to help users along the way, as well as handy sample letters and legal documents that demonstrate techniques for solving a variety of problems.

_____

312 pages
$19.95
ISBN 0-13-575150-0

The Complete Idiot's Guide to Exploring Canada
by Joe Chidley

Canada is every traveller's dream — a big, beautiful country with plenty to see and do. Boasting mountain ranges, two scenic coasts and many metropolitan centers, it has something for everyone looking for adventure and enjoyment. *The Complete Idiot's Guide to Exploring Canada* is an easy to use, up-to-date travel guide that makes planning your trip a sure success.

_____

272 pages
$21.95
ISBN 0-13-080125-9